MATHS
NOW!
· · · · · · · · · ·

RED & BLUE
ORBIT

1

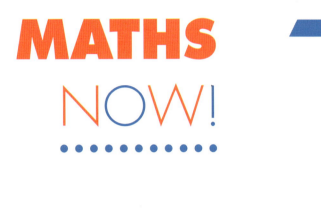

MATHS NOW!

RED & BLUE ORBIT

MATHS NOW!
National Writing Group

JOHN MURRAY

To the memory of three inspiring teachers – Sam Fisher, John Luzio and Ian Gunn.

Photo acknowledgements

Cover: Pictor International Ltd; **p.28** *left* Mary Evans Picture Library; *centre and right* Science Museum/Science & Society Picture Library; **p.187** *left to right* Mehau Kulyk/Science Photo Library; Hartmut Noeller, Peter Arnold Inc./Science Photo Library; Sinclair Stammers/Science Photo Library; John Townson/Creation; **p.274** *all* © Rijksmuseum-Stichting Amsterdam; **p.304** John Townson/Creation; **p.319** Mary Evans Picture Library

Acknowledgements

The authors and publisher would like to thank all the teachers, schools and advisers who evaluated *Maths Now!* and whose comments contributed so much to this final version.

Particular thanks go to: Mike Humphrey, Educational Development Officer for Oldham LEA Schools Development Service; John D Collins, Education Consultant and Inspector of Schools; David J McLaren, Adviser in Mathematics, South Lanarkshire Council; and to St Margaret Ward RC High School, Stoke-on-Trent; Mortimer Wilson School, Alfreton; Bishop of Hereford Bluecoat School, Hereford; Henry Beaufort Secondary School, Winchester; Frodsham High School, Warrington; Desborough Comprehensive School, Maidenhead; Hartford County High School, Northwich; Tormead Girls' School, Guildford; Belmont Comprehensive School, Durham; Watford Girls' Grammar School, Watford; Antrim High School, Antrim; Aquinas Grammar School, Belfast; Harrytown RC High School, Stockport; The John of Gaunt School, Trowbridge. And most of all, to the Headteacher, L.S.C. MacDonald, staff and pupils of Claremont High School, Harrow.

First published in 1998
by John Murray (Publishers) Ltd
50 Albemarle Street
London W1X 4BD

Layouts by Stephen Rowling, unQualified Design
Artwork by Oxford Illustrators Limited
Cover design by John Townson/Creation

Typeset in 12/14pt Times by Wearset, Boldon, Tyne and Wear.
Printed and bound by G. Canale, Italy.

A CIP catalogue record for this book is available from the British Library.

ISBN 0 7195 7095 6
Teacher's File ISBN 0 7195 7096 4

Contents

CONTENTS

CONTENTS

Introduction

Some people can read a bit of maths and see what it's about straight away – lucky them! Other people have to work at it very carefully and with patience.

That's one reason why this book has been written – to explain thoroughly a step at a time. But you must read the explanations carefully and not miss anything out. Work through all the questions and, if you still need help, ask your teacher.

Read the chapter summaries, make your own glossary (list) of mathematical words, use the index, ask your teacher for the revision exercises, supplementary exercises, mental tests and the final summary (all in the Teacher's Resource File).

But then remember! Maths teachers like explaining things – so always ask if you aren't completely sure.

Symbols

 Think carefully

 Use a calculator

 Do not use a calculator

 This is a particularly challenging question

Timeline

Note: dates represent the approximate time of principal activity or major publication, not date of birth.

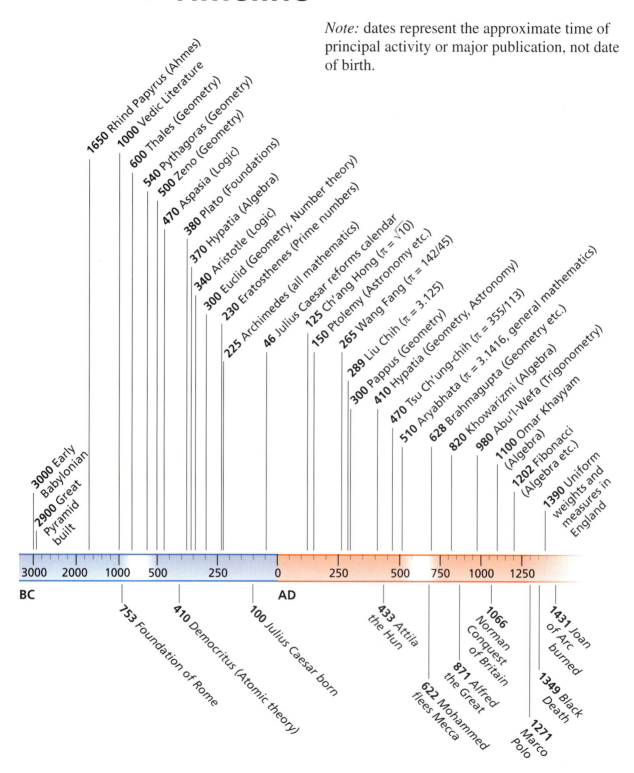

3000 Early Babylonian
2900 Great Pyramid built
1650 Rhind Papyrus (Ahmes)
1000 Vedic Literature
600 Thales (Geometry)
540 Pythagoras (Geometry)
500 Zeno (Geometry)
470 Aspasia (Logic)
380 Plato (Foundations)
370 Hypatia (Algebra)
340 Aristotle (Logic)
300 Euclid (Geometry, Number theory)
230 Eratosthenes (Prime numbers)
225 Archimedes (all mathematics)
46 Julius Caesar reforms calendar
125 Ch'ang Hong ($\pi = \sqrt{10}$)
150 Ptolemy (Astronomy etc.)
265 Wang Fang ($\pi = 142/45$)
289 Liu Chih ($\pi = 3.125$)
300 Pappus (Geometry)
410 Hypatia (Geometry, Astronomy)
470 Tsu Ch'ung-chih ($\pi = 355/113$)
510 Aryabhata ($\pi = 3.1416$, general mathematics)
628 Brahmagupta (Geometry etc.)
820 Khowarizmi (Algebra)
980 Abu'l-Wefa (Trigonometry)
1100 Omar Khayyam (Algebra)
1202 Fibonacci (Algebra etc.)
1390 Uniform weights and measures in England

| 3000 | 2000 | 1000 | 500 | 250 | 0 | 250 | 500 | 750 | 1000 | 1250 |

BC   **AD**

753 Foundation of Rome
410 Democritus (Atomic theory)
100 Julius Caesar born
433 Attila the Hun
622 Mohammed flees Mecca
871 Alfred the Great
1066 Norman Conquest of Britain
1271 Marco Polo
1349 Black Death
1431 Joan of Arc burned

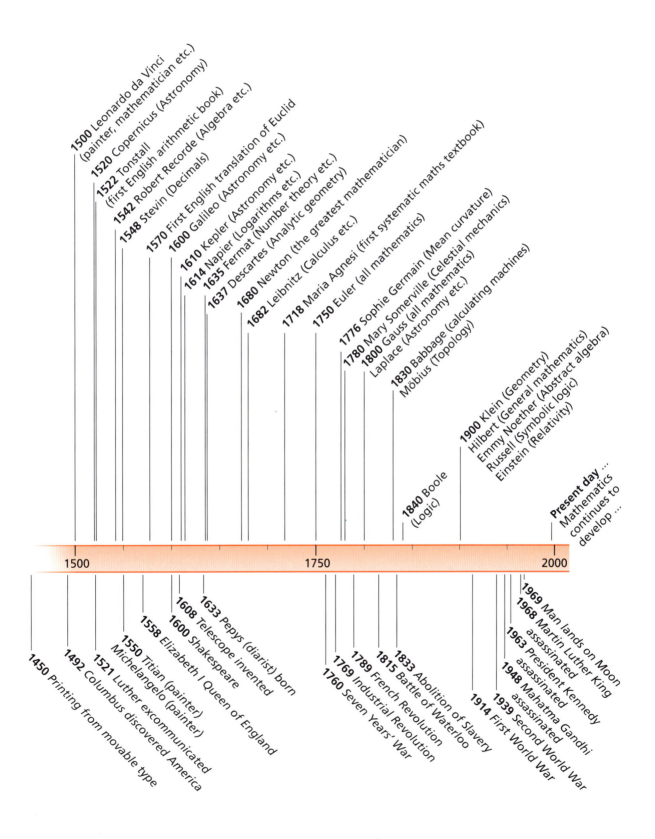

1500 Leonardo da Vinci (painter, mathematician etc.)
1520 Copernicus (Astronomy)
1522 Tonstall (first English arithmetic book)
1542 Robert Recorde (Algebra etc.)
1548 Stevin (Decimals)
1570 First English translation of Euclid
1600 Galileo (Astronomy etc.)
1610 Kepler (Astronomy etc.)
1614 Napier (Logarithms etc.)
1635 Fermat (Number theory etc.)
1637 Descartes (Analytic geometry)
1680 Newton (the greatest mathematician)
1682 Leibnitz (Calculus etc.)
1718 Maria Agnesi (first systematic maths textbook)
1750 Euler (all mathematics)
1776 Sophie Germain (Mean curvature)
1780 Mary Somerville (Celestial mechanics)
1800 Gauss (all mathematics)
Laplace (Astronomy etc.)
1830 Babbage (calculating machines)
Möbius (Topology)
1900 Klein (Geometry)
Hilbert (General mathematics)
Emmy Noether (Abstract algebra)
Russell (Symbolic logic)
Einstein (Relativity)
1840 Boole (Logic)
Present day ...
Mathematics continues to develop ...

1500
1750
2000

1450 Printing from movable type
1492 Columbus discovered America
1521 Luther excommunicated
1550 Michelangelo (painter)
1558 Titian (painter)
1600 Elizabeth I Queen of England
1608 Shakespeare
1633 Telescope invented
Pepys (diarist) born
1760 Seven Years' War
1769 Industrial Revolution
1789 French Revolution
1815 Battle of Waterloo
1833 Abolition of Slavery
1914 First World War
1939 Second World War
1948 Mahatma Gandhi assassinated
1963 President Kennedy assassinated
1968 Martin Luther King assassinated
1969 Man lands on Moon

1 : Uses of mathematics

Welcome back to mathematics!

It's probably several weeks since you did any!

Why do schools make children do mathematics? Not to be nasty to them! Although some people seem to think that!

Mathematics is everywhere, and if you follow this book and your teacher step by step, you should have no problem in learning many useful and exciting things.

Look around the room and think of the people who helped build and decorate it.

In your exercise book, make a list of some of their jobs.

Discuss this with your teacher.

Now make a list of the mathematics they would have used. See who can make the longest list!

Think about the outside of the school, make your lists longer.

How did you travel to school this morning?

Train? Think of the people who make and drive the trains. Any maths? How about the timetables?

Bus? Car? Walk? Think of the pavement. Any maths there?

Perhaps you cycled to school. Think of the wheels, the gears. Any other maths?

Think about where else maths is used. Ask the adults at home. Look around as you go home tonight.

And what about the maths you use in other school subjects? Write down a list.

For homework, write a page about the people who use maths in their work. Try to think of something unusual! Draw pictures if it helps. Perhaps you could make a poster to put up in school.

Good luck with your work.

2 Number

People who use maths in their work need to know about many different things. They use numbers and letters and shapes and charts and they need to be good at investigations.

Over the next few years you will find out about these things – some you may have heard about, some you may have done, but most of them will be completely new. And then one day you will be ready to use maths in *your* future job!

Matching

If there were 200 chairs in a hall and you asked everyone to sit down, you could tell at a glance whether there were more or fewer than 200 people in the hall. How?

If there were any chairs empty, there must be **fewer** than 200 people present. If there were people standing, there must be **more** than 200 people present.

If you put a very young child in front of some cups and saucers, the child could match up the cups with the saucers without being able to count.

In a cricket match, the umpire makes sure not to mis-count the six balls in an over by transferring a pebble from one pocket to the other for each ball played.

In these examples, none of the number names, one, two, three, four, . . . are used.

Let's start off by looking at counting.

Exercise 2.1

Describe at least three different situations where the idea of matching is used (without saying the individual number names) to decide how many people or things are present.

Compare your list with others in the class.

Counting

The idea of matching extends to the idea of counting. What you do is to match the objects you are counting to the number names said in order:

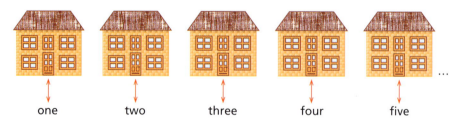

Exercise 2.2

Have you started to learn the French or German language?

Copy the drawing above but match the objects to the number names in French or German. Go up to ten.

Exercise 2.3

Do you or your friends (or pupils in other classes) know languages other than French or German? Find out the number names up to ten in these other languages. You could go to a library to find out.

Make a poster displaying your results.

Different number systems

Nobody knows when counting started. It was probably one of the first things anybody, anywhere, learnt to do. And alongside the many different languages, there have been many different ways of counting.

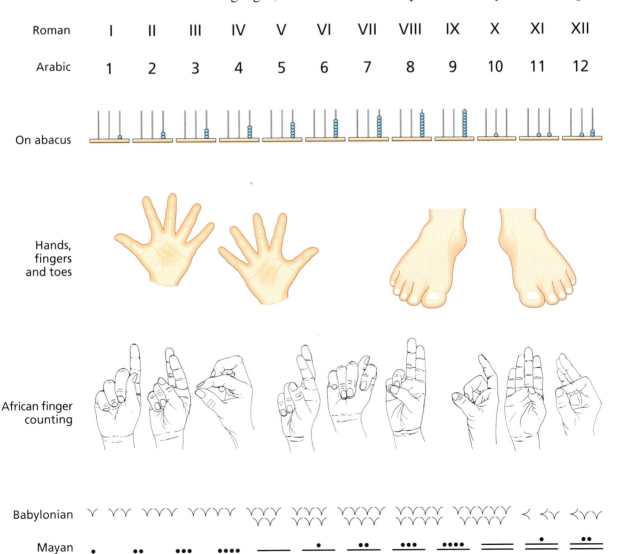

Roman	I	II	III	IV	V	VI	VII	VIII	IX	X	XI	XII
Arabic	1	2	3	4	5	6	7	8	9	10	11	12

Exercise 2.4

1 There are people who use the same word for 'five' as they do for 'hand'. Imagine you counted like this in groups of five using fingers, hands, toes, feet (so 'six' becomes 'a hand and a finger' and 'eleven' becomes 'two hands and a toe' etc.). What would the number 'two hands and three toes' be in our usual (tens) counting?

2 Still counting in fives, describe the ordinary number 'eight' in this system.

3 In the fives system, what would the number 'two hands, one foot, four toes' become in our tens system?

4 Many clocks and watches use Roman numerals. Write eleven and twelve in Roman numerals. Now draw a clock face putting in the hours using Roman numerals.

5 Read this number on an **abacus**:

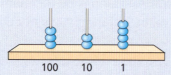

100   10   1

> An abacus is an old calculating device, traditionally used in China, Japan, Russia, Korea and Turkey.

6 Draw an abacus and record the number '503'.

7 Find out the name for the Babylonian counting system.

8 In the Mayan notation, a bar was used for 'five' and a dot for 'one'. So seven would be drawn as ____••____ . How would 'twelve' be drawn?

9 How would we represent the Mayan number ☰ ?

10 Draw the Roman numeral XVII in the Mayan notation.

Complements to ten
0 + 10   10 + 0
1 + 9   9 + 1
2 + 8   8 + 2
3 + 7   7 + 3
4 + 6   6 + 4
5 + 5

Addition

It is interesting and useful to know some of the ways that people around the world have used (and sometimes still use) for counting and calculating.

How good are you at doing these things today?

We will look at **addition** first.

Do you know the **complements to ten** – the sets of numbers which go to make up 10?

Exercise 2.5

Work with a partner. Your partner will say a number less than 10 and you will write down the complement to 10. For instance, your partner says 'seven' so you would write down '3'. Then change round.

7

3

Knowing the complements to ten is one of the keys to being good at mental arithmetic. You must also be good at the other **addition bonds**.

Exercise 2.6

Work with a partner.

The following are all **single-digit addition sums**.

Your partner places a sheet of paper so that it covers the third row of figures in the first set of sums. (These sums are available as a worksheet in Teacher's Resource File 1.)

You say the answer to the first addition sum $8 + 3$ ($= 11$).

Your partner moves the paper to the right so that you can both see that $8 + 3$ *does* equal 11. You then say the *answer* to $2 + 7$.

Your partner reveals that the answer to $2 + 7$ *is* 9.

Continue like this to the end of the line so that you say the answer to the addition sum *before* your partner moves the paper to see if you were right.

Your partner keeps a note of any you get wrong!

If you get to the bottom of the page without a mistake, you know all 81 possible addition bonds from 1 to 9!

Change over and test your partner.

8	2	5	4	1	6	3	7	9		5	1	9	3	8	6	7	2	4
3	7	6	3	8	4	5	2	5		8	5	7	7	9	2	6	6	4
11	9	11	7	9	10	8	9	14		13	6	16	10	17	8	13	8	8

6	7	2	4	9	1	8	3	5		8	4	2	5	1	3	6	7	9
8	5	2	2	4	3	2	6	2		5	7	1	4	6	9	6	7	2
14	12	4	6	13	4	10	9	7		13	11	3	9	7	12	12	14	11

9	3	6	1	5	4	7	2	8		9	7	1	4	2	6	5	3	8
9	1	1	9	7	6	4	9	1		8	8	6	5	5	3	9	8	8
18	4	7	10	12	10	11	11	9		17	15	7	9	7	9	14	11	16

8	2	7	3	1	5	4	9	6		4	7	2	6	3	1	9	5	8
4	3	1	2	2	3	1	1	5		8	9	8	7	5	7	6	5	6
12	5	8	5	3	8	5	10	11		12	16	10	13	8	8	15	10	14

6	7	1	4	3	2	5	8	9
9	3	1	9	3	4	1	7	3
15	10	2	13	6	6	6	15	12

Grouping in tens

Add: $3 + 6 + 7 + 9 + 4 + 1$.

If you can see two numbers which make 10 (complements to ten) add those first, saying in your head:

$$3 + 7, \quad 6 + 4, \quad 9 + 1; \quad \text{that's } 10 + 10 + 10 \text{ or } 30$$

Add: $7 + 4 + 2 + 5 + 3 + 6$

Say in your head: $7 + 3$, $4 + 6$ (put a dot by the numbers as they are collected so as not to get in a muddle),

$$\dot{7} + \dot{4} + 2 + 5 + \dot{3} + \dot{6}$$

and then see that $2 + 5$ is 7, so the answer is 27.

Exercise 2.7

Add these rows of numbers, noticing any pair which makes a 10 first. Try to write down only the answers.

1 $3 + 6 + 5 + 4 + 7$
2 $8 + 5 + 2 + 3 + 5$
3 $5 + 3 + 1 + 7 + 4 + 9 + 6$
4 $1 + 8 + 3 + 2 + 9 + 2 + 4 + 3$
5 $3 + 4 + 2 + 6 + 1 + 8 + 3 + 5 + 8 + 9 + 2$

If you are very good at your addition bonds, it may be quicker just to go straight through the list of numbers:

$$2 + 5 + 6 + 1 + 6 + 7 + 8 + 3 + 4 + 4$$

Say: 2, 7, 13, 14, 20, 27, 35, 38, 42, **46**, answer.

Adding nines

Notice that, to add '9' to a two-digit number, you **increase** the **tens** digit by 1 and **reduce** the **units** digit by 1

$$23 + 9 = 32; \quad 48 + 9 = 57; \quad 12 + 9 = 21; \quad 83 + 9 = 92;$$
$$31 + 9 = 40, \quad \dots$$

Exercise 2.8

Write down the answer only.

1 67 + 9	**4** 61 + 9	**7** 27 + 9	**9** 235 + 9
2 38 + 9	**5** 88 + 9	**8** 151 + 9	**10** 672 + 9
3 57 + 9	**6** 15 + 9		

Adding tens

It is very quick to add 10; just increase the tens digit by 1.

$$10 + 10 = 20; \quad 12 + 10 = 22; \quad 46 + 10 = 56; \quad 61 + 10 = 71;$$
$$728 + 10 = 738, \quad \ldots$$

Exercise 2.9

Add 10 to each number. Then start the exercise again and see if you can add 11. Write the answers only.

1 23	**4** 91	**7** 52	**9** 207
2 82	**5** 9	**8** 146	**10** 217
3 16	**6** 48		

Grand totals

```
3  5 | 8

1  4 | 5

4  9 |
```

Notice that 3 + 5 = 8, 1 + 4 = 5, 3 + 1 = 4 and 5 + 4 = 9.

Now notice that 8 + 5 = 13 and so does 4 + 9 = 13 so it's likely the other additions are correct. In fact 3 + 5 + 1 + 4 is 13. This can be called the **grand total**.

Notice how the following 3 by 3 square of numbers has been set out and where the various totals have been put.

You can see the grand total of 45 checks both ways.

5	6	7	18
8	1	3	12
4	9	2	15
17	16	12	45 / 45

Set out the numbers in the next exercise in a similar way.

Exercise 2.10

Find the grand totals.

1 2, 5, 8
   7, 4, 9
   6, 3, 5

2 3, 6, 7, 5
   4, 7, 3, 8
   9, 4, 2, 6
   5, 3, 7, 4

3 2, 5, 8, 1, 7, 9
   4, 6, 9, 3, 5, 4
   3, 7, 8, 3, 8, 7
   4, 2, 8, 7, 2, 7

4 Arrange these 30 numbers in (any suitable number of) rows and columns and so find their grand total:

3, 5, 7, 2, 9, 7, 1, 3, 6, 4, 5, 8, 7, 6, 2, 4, 7, 5, 2, 5, 8, 9, 6, 4, 1, 3, 4, 7, 4, 3

5 Arrange these 48 numbers in (any suitable number of) rows and columns and so find their grand total:

2, 6, 4, 8, 9, 6, 4, 1, 2, 5, 3, 4, 7, 8, 6, 9, 8, 7, 5, 6, 4, 3, 1, 2, 5, 6, 7, 8, 9, 5, 6, 3, 4, 2, 6, 7, 5, 3, 4, 2, 6, 7, 8, 2, 5, 1, 4, 3

Place value

The most important advance in writing down numbers was made when it was realised that you could use a zero to keep the other numbers in their right places. It seems that the Mayan civilisation was the first to use a 'zero' systematically though they drew it to look like an eye or shell.

> The Mayans, 4th–9th century AD, Central America, probably used 'zero' systematically.

Now when *we* write down a column of figures we keep all the units, tens, hundreds, etc. in places which line up, one over the other.

The best guide is to *keep all the unit figures above each other*, like this:

```
1 0 3
  3 0
3 0 0
    1
1 3 0
5 6 4
```

But, if the numbers are listed in a row, you need to be careful to add the correct figures together, keeping the places separate.

Find the total of 103, 30, 300, 1 and 130.

The units:
3 + 0 + 0
+1 + 0 = 4

Write 4 in the units place of the answer.

The tens:
0 + 3 + 0
+ 3 = 6

Write 6 in the tens place of the answer.

The hundreds:
1 + 3 + 1 = 5

Write 5 in the hundreds place of the answer.

Answer: 564

Add together the numbers 36, 104, 7, 21 and 243 without copying the numbers.

You say:

'6 + 4 + 7 + 1 + 3 = 21, write the units figure and carry the tens (so write 1 and remember 2);

3 + 0 + 2 + 4 = 9 plus 2 to carry is 11, so write 1 and remember 1;

1 + 2 = 3 plus 1 to carry is 4 so write 4.'

'Answer: 411.'

Exercise 2.11

Do these addition sums in your head, writing only the answers, by picking out the units, tens and hundreds figures. Don't forget any 'carry' figure.

1 14 + 40 + 104
2 32 + 2 + 20
3 320 + 2 + 200
4 3 + 230 + 20 + 302
5 13 + 5 + 152 + 19
6 153 + 361 + 274
7 214 + 38 + 102 + 5
8 342 + 31 + 16 + 25 + 128
9 7 + 170 + 17 + 107 + 70 + 700 + 707 + 71 + 770 + 701 + 77
10 431 + 18 + 121 + 5 + 62 + 7 + 22 + 149

Don't write them in columns on a spare piece of paper!

More on place value

A thorough understanding of the **place value** idea is essential. We shall refer to it many times!

The counting system we use today is based on ten, so it is called **decimal** or sometimes **denary**.

● *The central idea of the decimal system is that, when you move one position to the left, the value of a digit is multiplied by 10.*

You can see this when you look at an abacus.

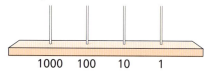

Two beads on the 'units' rod means '2',

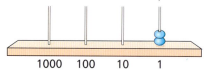

but two beads on the 'tens' rod means '20'.

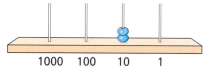

What does this represent?

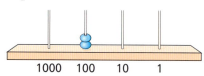

You can see how important the 'zero' is. It's the only way we can do without an abacus!

If we write:

$$1 \quad 1$$

do we mean 'eleven' or 'one hundred and one'? It's clear enough if we draw an abacus:

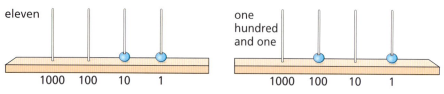

But we certainly don't want to keep on doing that! So if we mean 'eleven', we write '11' and if we mean 'one hundred and one', we write '101'.

The **zero** shows there is *no bead* in that position on the abacus.

Exercise 2.12

Write the following numbers without an abacus:
a using figures,
b using words.

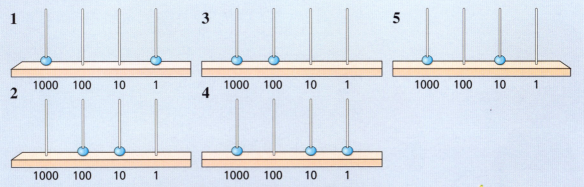

Draw an abacus representing each of the following numbers.

6 One thousand
7 One thousand, one hundred and one
8 Two hundred and three
9 Three thousand and twenty
10 Two thousand, three hundred

Even if you don't draw an abacus you could keep it in mind.

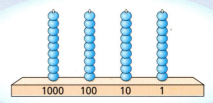

Exercise 2.13

Write these numbers using figures.

1 Four thousand and forty
2 Four hundred and forty
3 Four thousand and four
4 Four thousand and forty-four
5 Four thousand, four hundred and four
6 Four thousand, four hundred and forty
7 Fourteen thousand, four hundred and four
8 Forty thousand, four hundred
9 Fourteen thousand and four
10 Forty thousand and forty

Exercise 2.14

Put the ten numbers in the previous exercise **in order of size**, smallest first.

● *Listing numbers in order, least first, is called **ascending order**, like going **up** a staircase.*

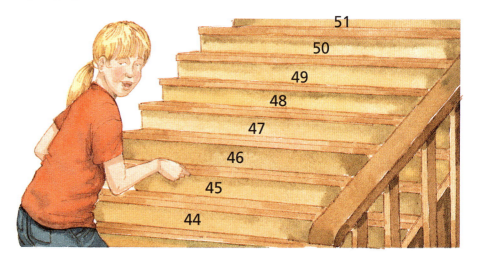

Exercise 2.15

Write each group of numbers in columns, in **descending order** (that means largest at the top) lining up the units figures, and add.

You must *not* use a calculator at first, but you *may* use a calculator to check your answers!

1 3042, 4023, 3200
2 192, 1920, 209
3 5051, 501, 5105
4 304, 34, 430, 43
5 4162, 319, 5286, 49

6 6301, 1472, 8563, 942
7 5832, 4169, 2167, 3856
8 9009, 99, 90 009, 909
9 6103, 9057, 3008, 240
10 73, 7003, 307, 37, 730

Subtraction

Subtract 48 from 701. To do this on an abacus is fairly complicated.
Start with the larger number:

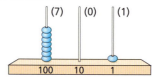

Subtract 48. But there aren't 8 beads in the units column to 'take away' so break up one of the 'hundreds' beads into ten 'tens':

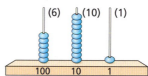

Still not enough units, so break up one of the 'tens' into ten units:

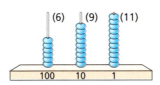

Now there are enough 'tens' and 'units' to 'take away' the 4 tens and 8 units we wanted to subtract originally:

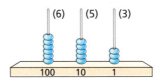

giving the answer of 653.

But of course, it would be impossible to have to do something like that every time you needed to subtract!

Your method of subtraction might look like this:

$$
\begin{array}{r}
9 \\
6\ \ \cancel{10}\ \ 10 \\
\cancel{7}\ \ \cancel{0}\ \ 1 \\
-\ \ \ \ \ \ 4\ \ 8 \\
\hline
6\ \ 5\ \ 3 \\
\end{array}
$$

which is close to the abacus method.

Exercise 2.16

Do these subtractions.

1 549 − 326
2 983 − 561
3 743 − 225

4 651 − 438
5 835 − 251
6 746 − 382

7 835 − 168
8 724 − 285

9 340 − 128
10 500 − 362

Exercise 2.17

Do these subtractions.

1 5643 − 2631
2 3728 − 3325
3 9482 − 605

4 8205 − 1234
5 4092 − 106
6 4135 − 3136

7 2019 − 628
8 4162 − 1289

9 8183 − 95
10 2001 − 978

SUMMARY

- Counting is a matching of objects to number names in order.
- There are many different ways of counting.
- Several words we use today are connected with ancient ways of calculating.
- The numbers 0 to 9 are called **digits**.
- An **abacus** is an old calculating device.
- You need to know the **complements to ten**.
- You must know the **addition bonds**.
- **Place value** is a central idea in mathematics.
- Using a **zero** simplifies the writing of numbers.

Exercise 2A

1 Write these numbers in figures:
  a eight thousand and eighty,
  b eighteen thousand, eight hundred and eight.
2 Draw an abacus representing the number 'five thousand and thirty-four'.
3 Write down the answer only to:
  a 635 + 10
  b 451 + 100 + 40 + 8
  c 7249 + 500 + 31
4 Write in a column in descending order and add:
  a 356 + 472 + 95 + 763
  b 191 + 374 + 690 + 27
5 Subtract:
  a 479 − 284
  b 712 − 557

Exercise 2B

1 Write these numbers in words:
  a 841
  b 18 401
2 Write this number in figures:

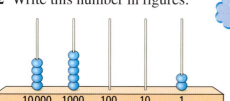

| 10000 | 1000 | 100 | 10 | 1 |

3 Write the answer only:

  a 736 + 40

  b 325 + 600 + 50 + 5

  c 6541 + 400 + 50 + 9

4 Write in a column in descending order and add:

  a 9752 + 35 + 1047 + 694

  b 2045 + 611 + 7290 + 1114

5 Subtract:

  a 1792 − 843

  b 4511 − 3912

Exercise 2C

1 Do these calculations, writing your answers firstly in Roman numerals and then in our numerals:

  a 4 + 5

  b VI − IV

  c XII + IX

2 Do these calculations, working in order from left to right:

  a 405 − 297 + 691

  b 2976 + 4089 − 3571

3 Work these, doing the part in brackets first:

  a 250 − (95 + 41)

  b 7561 + (6541 − 2719)

Exercise 2D

Investigate how the Romans wrote the numbers for a thousand, five hundred, one hundred, fifty. Use a very old maths book or an encyclopedia.

  Notice how copyright dates on cinema films are written in Roman numerals.

  Write your birthdate in Roman numerals, and the current year.

  See if you can discover how the Romans might have done the following calculations. Even they found this very difficult to do properly!

1 49 + 53

2 271 − 144

3 4101 + 227

4 949 − 651

5 274 + 385

3: Introducing geometry

A very short history of geometry

One of the subjects you probably study at the moment is geography. Do you know where the name comes from?

It comes from two words *geo* (earth) and *graphia* (writing), so that geography means 'writing about the earth'.

From this, you can probably guess the origins of the word **geometry**. It comes from *geo* and *metria* (measure). So geometry originally meant 'measuring the earth'.

> The early Egyptians (3000 years ago) used a knowledge of geometry to mark out their fields and to build the Great Pyramids. People called 'rope stretchers' knew how to set out a right-angle using a knotted rope.
>
> A Greek merchant called Thales learnt these things and took the knowledge back to Greece.

Exercise 3.1

Try this to see how the Egyptian 'rope stretchers' set out a **right-angle**. Use a strip of paper instead of a rope! Centimetre squared paper works well.

Measure and fold a strip of paper with the lengths shown in the diagram. The small shaded flap at the end is for sticking the bottom end to the top.

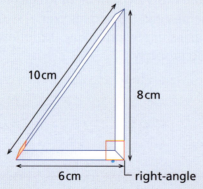

You can see from your own triangle where the right-angle is.

Later on in this course you will be able to **prove** how this always works.

Geometrical vocabulary

Many words are used to describe shapes.

word	origin	meaning
line	*linum* (Latin)	flax (a plant used to make rope)
straight	*streht* (Old English)	stretched
point	*punctum* (Latin)	to make a small hole
surface	*sur-face* (French)	on the front
solid	*solidus* (Latin)	solid
plane	*planum* (Latin – flat surface)	flat
face	*facies* (Latin – form, face)	surface of a solid
edge	*ecg* (Old English)	line where two surfaces meet
vertex	*vertex* (Latin)	point where edges meet

Look at this picture of a cube.

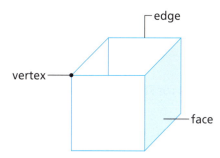

It shows examples of a **face**, an **edge** and a **vertex**.

Drawing cubes and cuboids
Cubes

Examine a real cube and count the number of faces, vertices and edges it has. It's surprising how many there are, isn't it?

Each face is a square. This gives a clue about drawing its picture. Try this on squared paper.

Draw a square of edge (about) 2 cm.

Draw another square the same size but moved down the page so that the new square starts at the centre of the first one.

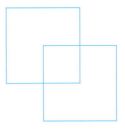

Draw the four edges you can see in the diagram.

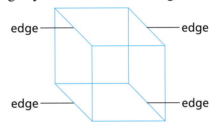

This looks as if it is made of glass. If you want to make it look more like a closed box, rub out the bits of edge which would be hidden.

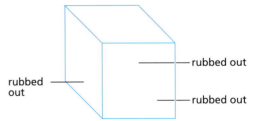

If you want to make it look like an empty box without a lid, draw in a bit of the inside edge like this:

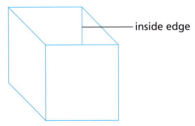

Exercise 3.2

Practise drawing cubes several times on squared paper. Draw some cubes as if you are looking from different directions. Draw at least five. Then try the same thing on plain paper.

Cuboids

A cube has all six faces in the shape of a square. If some of the faces are made into rectangles, the solid shape you get is called a cuboid.

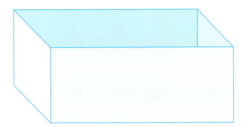

Exercise 3.3

Practise drawing different-shaped cuboids on squared paper. Again draw some from different angles. Draw at least five. Then try the same thing on plain paper.

Dimensions

Look at this drawing of a cuboid:

If you were going to make it from modelling clay, how many measurements would you need to be told?

You would need to know its

- length
- width
- and height

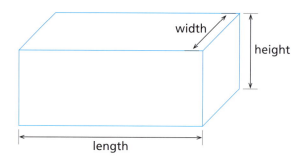

Look at this drawing of a rectangle:

If you were going to make it from cardboard, how many measurements would you need to be told?

You would need to know its

• length
• and breadth

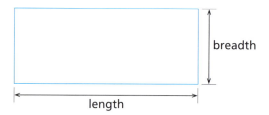

Because you would need *three* measurements for a cuboid it is called a **three-dimensional** shape, written 3D for short.

Because you would need *two* measurements for a rectangle it is called a **two-dimensional** shape, written 2D for short.

Exercise 3.4

1 From this list of objects make two new lists, one of two-dimensional things and another of three-dimensional things:
a painting, a shoe, a book, a face of a cube, a sculpture, your skin, your arm, a football, the surface of a football.
2 Look round the room and see if you can list any other three- and two-dimensional objects.
3 Would you say we live in a two-dimensional world or a three-dimensional world? (geometrically speaking)
4 Does Mickey Mouse exist in a two-dimensional or a three-dimensional world?
5 Make five sketches in your book which represent simple, solid objects.

Parallel lines

Look at the arrowed lines on this diagram of a cuboid:

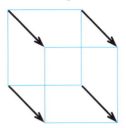

All four point in the same direction.

● *When lines point in the same direction, they are called* **parallel**.

Copy the above diagram onto squared paper.

Exercise 3.5

Make two copies of the last cuboid on squared paper but *don't* draw in the arrows.
   On your first diagram find a set of four parallel lines, different from those shown above, and put arrows on these.
   On the second diagram find a third different set of parallel lines and put arrows on these.

The fact that you can draw *three* different sets of parallel lines in a cuboid emphasises that it is a *three*-dimensional object.

Exercise 3.6

Make a list of some sets of parallel lines you can see in the classroom, and also outside the room. Compare your list with others in the class.

Exercise 3.7

Look at these attempts to spell the word which means 'lines pointing in the same direction'. Copy out the only one which is correct!

parralel	piryllol
parrallel	parallel
paralell	porallel
parrallell	pirullal
parallell	parollel

Learn to spell the word 'parallel' correctly!

Horizontal and vertical

If you put some water in a glass and slowly tilt the glass, the level of the water remains the same.

This constant level is called the **horizontal** direction.
The horizontal can be measured by an instrument called a **spirit level**.

If you hang a heavy mass by a string

Plumb-line: from Latin *plumbum* meaning 'lead'. Originally lead was always used as the heavy mass.

it hangs at right-angles to the horizontal. This is called the **vertical** direction. It can be measured using a **plumb-line**.

Some spirit levels can also be used to find the vertical.

Exercise 3.8

Make a list of people who might use a spirit level and a list of those who might use a plumb-line, and the purpose for which they are used.

Perpendiculars

Lines which are at right-angles to each other are called **perpendicular**.
So horizontal and vertical lines are perpendicular to each other.

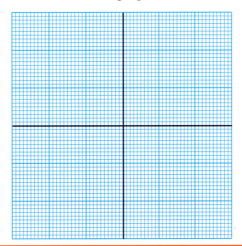

SUMMARY

- **Geometry** originally meant measuring the earth.
- Geometry is about points, lines, planes and solids.
- We live in a 3D world but often have to represent it in 2D pictures.
- In building and other construction, horizontal lines are measured with a spirit level and vertical lines are measured with a plumb-line.

Exercise 3A

There have been a large number of words in this chapter. Some you have probably come across before, others may be new to you. Mathematicians all over the world use these same words so that they can talk to one another about the subject. It is important that you too understand what they mean.

Go back through the chapter and make your own list of the words in **bold type**. Write down in your *own* words what each word means. Use illustrations if you think they help. Write descriptions which will mean something to *you* when you read them again!

Exercise 3B

To fold a pair of perpendicular lines, take a smallish piece of paper and make a fold in it:

fold line —

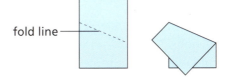

Keep the paper folded and make a second fold so that the first fold lies along itself.

You have folded a *right-angle*. Unfold the paper and notice that the two folds are perpendicular. Glue the folded paper into your exercise book so that it can still be unfolded.

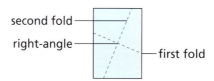

Exercise 3C

Draw this shape on squared paper making each square of edge 3 cm. Label the squares as shown. Cut out the shape and cut along the line indicated.

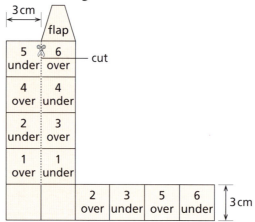

Then crease *every* line very carefully.

Starting from the two squares numbered 1, fold one under the other. Then take each pair of numbered squares in turn folding over and under as shown. Proceed slowly and you should end up by tucking the flap into the slot next to square number 1. No glue needed! Name the solid obtained.

Exercise 3D

A challenge! Using the shape from exercise 3C as a start, design a new shape which will fold into a cuboid of dimensions 3 cm by 2 cm by 2 cm. Then design a shape which will fold into a cuboid measuring 4 cm by 3 cm by 2 cm. Investigate further.

4 Multiplication and division
Various methods of multiplication

From ancient times to the present, people have found that they needed to use more and more mathematics in their work. Over the centuries many different methods for doing calculations were discovered.

Let's examine some of the methods used for multiplication.

Gelosia multiplication

One method, popular in Italy in the fifteenth century, was called **lattice** or **gelosia multiplication**.

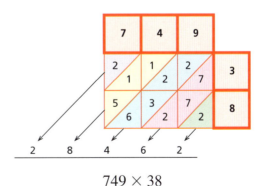

749×38

Write the products in the appropriate places.

Add the partial products as shown by the arrows, starting at the right.

Don't forget the 'carry'.

To use this method you would either need a set of multiplication tables to refer to, or know them by heart!

Napier's bones

Because so few people learnt their tables, a Scotsman, John Napier, in 1617, invented a set of rods with the tables engraved upon them. Bone would often be used as a material on which to do the engraving, so the rods became known as 'Napier's bones'. They were the first calculating aid. The way they are used is similar to gelosia multiplication.

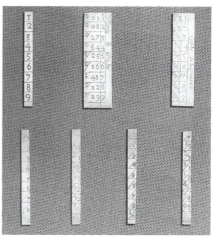

0	1	2	3	4	5	6	7	8	9
0	2	4	6	8	10	12	14	16	18
0	3	6	9	12	15	18	21	24	27
0	4	8	12	16	20	24	28	32	36
0	5	10	15	20	25	30	35	40	45
0	6	12	18	24	30	36	42	48	54
0	7	14	21	28	35	42	49	56	63
0	8	16	24	32	40	48	56	64	72
0	9	18	27	36	45	54	63	72	81

4	8	7
8	16	14
12	24	21

To multiply 487 × 3, put together the vertical strips for 4, 8 and 7.
Look at the *third* row.
Add the numbers going along the diagonals on this row to get 1461.

Exercise 4.1

Make a set of Napier's bones on fairly thick card, as follows.

Draw a grid like the diagram above, where the vertical strips represent the multiplication tables for 0 to 9. You will have to measure the grid accurately, or you could use squared paper and then stick the paper on to card.

Then cut out the vertical strips.

Try these multiplications with the strips. Check them on a calculator.

1 53×7 **2** 28×3 **3** 351×4 **4** 4092×5 **5** 1857×8

Russian multiplication

Russian multiplication was still in use for a while after the Russian Revolution of 1917.

Another method, sometimes called **Russian multiplication**, uses halving and doubling.

Successively halve the smaller number and double the larger.

Cross out any number opposite an even number in the 'halved' column and add the remaining numbers in the 'doubled' column.

Multiply 23×31 Multiply 28×21

(halve)	(double)			
23 ×	31	even numbers,	~~28 × 21~~	
11	62	so ignore	~~14 42~~	
5	124		7	84
~~2~~	~~248~~		3	168
1	496		1	336	add these numbers
	713			588

Check the two answers on your calculator.

Although this method is longer than the gelosia method, all you need to know is the two times table.

Exercise 4.2

Do these multiplications by halving and doubling.

1 20×47 **2** 35×61 **3** 15×38 **4** 43×52 **5** 36×32

Learning multiplication tables

In seventeenth-century England it must have been unusual to learn multiplication tables. A very famous man called Samuel Pepys was alive at that time. He kept a diary of everything he did and one of the entries mentions learning his tables. He was then 29 years old and a senior civil servant in the Navy Office!

This is what he writes:

'July 4th, 1662. Up by five o'clock . . . Comes Mr. Cooper, mate of the *Royal Charles*, of whom I intend to learn mathematics, . . . After an hour's being with him at arithmetic (my first attempt being to learn the multiplication-table); then we parted till tomorrow.

'July 9th, 1662. Up by four o'clock, and at my multiplication-table hard, . . .

'July 11th, 1662. Up by four o'clock, and hard at my multiplication-table, which I am now almost master of.'

Samuel Pepys must have been very hard-working! Could you learn your multiplication tables *for the first time, in a week*?

Exercise 4.3

Work with a partner.

The following are all **single-digit multiplications**.

Your partner places a sheet of paper so that it covers the third row of figures in the first set of multiplications. (These multiplications are available as a worksheet in Teacher's Resource File 1.)

Multiply these.

7	5	8	9	8	7
4	5	6	2	8	6

You say the answer to the first multiplication sum, 7 × 4 (= 28).

Your partner moves the paper to the right so that you can both see that 7 × 4 *does* equal 28.

You then say the answer to 5 × 5 (= 25).

Your partner reveals that the answer to 5 × 5 *is* 25.

Continue like this to the end of the line saying the answer to the multiplications *before* your partner moves the paper to see if you were right.

Your partner keeps a note of any you get wrong.

If you get to the bottom of the page without a mistake, you know all 36 possible **multiplication bonds** from 2 to 9.

Now change over and test your partner!

Multiply these.

7	5	8	9	8	7
4	5	6	2	8	6
28	25	48	18	64	42

3	7	9	8	4	7
3	2	5	3	2	5
9	14	45	24	8	35

3	9	5	7	6	8
2	4	3	3	6	7
6	36	15	21	36	56

4	6	7	6	8	9
4	5	7	2	4	9
16	30	49	12	32	81

9	2	9	4	8	6
8	2	6	3	2	4
72	4	54	12	16	24

5	9	8	6	9	5
2	3	5	3	7	4
10	27	40	18	63	20

Place value in multiplication

If you compare using our place-value system of multiplication with either the lattice method or doubling and halving, you will soon see what an advantage it gives us knowing about the use of zero.

Multiply 47 by 20.

1 Doubling/halving method

~~20 × 47~~
~~10   94~~
    5   188
~~2   376~~
    1   752
       ———
       940

2 Lattice method

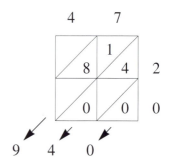

3 Place-value method

        47
      ×20
      ———
      940

We will look at the place-value method more closely.

The power of the place-value method depends on knowing that *moving a number one position to the left multiplies that number by 10.*

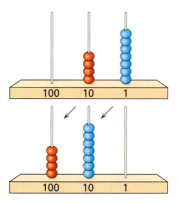

The abacus diagrams illustrate that:

- moving seven beads from the units column to the tens changes seven to seventy;
- moving four beads from the tens column to the hundreds changes forty to four hundred.

But when you write the result without the abacus you have to put in the zero to show that the units column is empty:

$$47 \times 10 = 470$$

So then to get 47×20 just multiply 470 by 2 (= 940).

And the really useful method is when you do without the abacus entirely.

If you use squared paper, it's easier to see the movement.

Work out 14×30.

$14 \times 10 = 140$ (moving the figures one place to the left)
then $140 \times 3 = 420$ (answer).

		1	4
	1	4		14×10
	4	2		14×30

Find 23×50.

$23 \times 10 = 230$ (moving the figures one place to the left)
then $230 \times 5 = 1150$ (answer).

		2	3
	2	3		23×10
1	1	5		23×50

Multiply 102 by 40.

$102 \times 10 = 1020$ (moving the figures one place to the left)
then $1020 \times 4 = 4080$ (answer).

	1	0	2

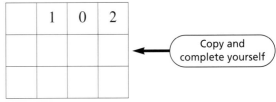

Copy and complete yourself

But we usually do the whole calculation in one step:

14	23	102
×30	×50	×40
420	1150	4080

The use of zero

It is absolutely essential that you understand how **zero** (or 'nought') is used. We have emphasised that zero is really used to show that there is an empty rod on the abacus. When we write, for example, $14 \times 10 = 140$, the zero is there to show that, after moving the 14 one position to the left on the abacus, the units rod is empty. If we always drew an abacus to record a number we wouldn't need a zero at all!

Multiplying by 10

Do not *ever* say 'to multiply by ten, add a nought'!

To multiply a number by 10, the digits in the number are moved one position to the left and the empty place is filled with a zero. This is the *only* mathematically correct way to describe multiplying by 10.

Zero is a **placeholder**: it keeps the figures in their right places. So it becomes possible to tell the difference between 11, 101, 1001, 10 001, etc.

> **Remember:**
>
> *There is absolutely no sense in which the phrase 'add a nought' can have any meaning with regard to multiplication.*

Multiply 14×32.

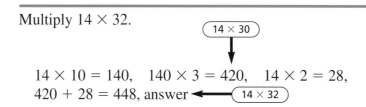

$14 \times 10 = 140$, $140 \times 3 = 420$, $14 \times 2 = 28$,
$420 + 28 = 448$, answer $\longleftarrow$ 14 × 32

....

Find 23×54.

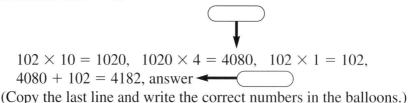

$23 \times 10 = 230$, $230 \times 5 = 1150$, $23 \times 4 = 92$,
$1150 + 92 = 1242$, answer $\longleftarrow$ 23 × 54

....

Calculate 102×41.

$102 \times 10 = 1020$, $1020 \times 4 = 4080$, $102 \times 1 = 102$,
$4080 + 102 = 4182$, answer $\longleftarrow$ ◯
(Copy the last line and write the correct numbers in the balloons.)

....

It's better to set them out like this:

14	23	102
×32	×54	×41
420	1150	4080
28	92	102
448	1242	4182

Work out 27 × 53.

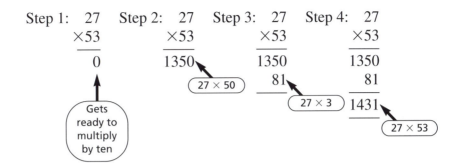

Exercise 4.4

Do these multiplications. Show the working. Set out the first three like the last example, showing the reasons for the working.

1 54 × 32

2 46 × 53

3 61 × 27

4 58 × 94

5 83 × 52

6 43 × 81

7 73 × 58

8 91 × 75

9 47 × 59

10 86 × 73

Exercise 4.5

Do these multiplications.

1 264 × 38

2 374 × 51

3 705 × 38

4 609 × 86

5 532 × 72

6 123 × 320

7 312 × 302

8 231 × 203

9 529 × 743

10 3056 × 708

Multiplication and addition

Multiplication and addition are connected. In fact, multiplication is repeated addition. By this we mean that 6 × 3 is really

$$3 + 3 + 3 + 3 + 3 + 3 \quad \text{(six lots of three)}$$

and 9 × 5 means

$$5 + 5 + 5 + 5 + 5 + 5 + 5 + 5 + 5 \quad \text{(nine lots of five)}$$

Exercise 4.6

Write these additions in a shorter way as multiplications. Don't give their value.

1 $2 + 2 + 2 + 2 + 2$

2 $7 + 7 + 7 + 7$

3 $23 + 23 + 23 + 23 + 23 + 23 + 23$

4 $8 + 8 + 8 + 8 + 8 + 8$

5 $309 + 309 + 309 + 309 + 309 + 309 + 309 + 309 + 309 + 309$

Subtraction and division

Subtraction and division are connected. The division $45 \div 9$ really means 'How many lots of 9 can be subtracted from 45?'

$$45 - 9 = 36, \quad \text{one lot}$$
$$36 - 9 = 27, \quad \text{two lots}$$
$$27 - 9 = 18, \quad \text{three lots}$$
$$18 - 9 = 9, \quad \text{four lots}$$
$$9 - 9 = 0, \quad \text{five lots}$$

So $45 \div 9 = 5$.

But it's also clear that this can be shortened by using our knowledge of the multiplication tables backwards. Since $5 \times 9 = 45$, $45 \div 9 = 5$.

Exercise 4.7

Write down the answers to these divisions.

1 $12 \div 4$ **4** $35 \div 7$ **7** $15 \div 3$ **9** $21 \div 3$

2 $32 \div 8$ **5** $42 \div 6$ **8** $72 \div 9$ **10** $81 \div 9$

3 $54 \div 9$ **6** $63 \div 9$

The reasonableness of an answer

Since $48 \div 8 = 6$, $480 \div 8 = 60$, the answer to $480 \div 8$ being ten times larger than $48 \div 8$.

What is $4800 \div 8$? It's 600.
What is $48\,000 \div 8$? It's 6000.
But what is $480 \div 80$? It's 6 again.

● *Notice, if you want to check a division, you can always reverse it by using a multiplication: 80 × 6 = 480.*

But you should also notice whether the answer is reasonable. For instance, if you gave the answer to 480 ÷ 60 as 60, this would not be of the right size!

This is why *you must not use a calculator* for exercise 4.8. Otherwise you will not get a feeling for the size of an answer.

Exercise 4.8

Write down the answers to these divisions, being very careful to make sure each one is *reasonable*.

1 210 ÷ 3	**4** 2100 ÷ 300	**7** 300 ÷ 30	**9** 540 ÷ 9
2 210 ÷ 30	**5** 70 000 ÷ 100	**8** 1500 ÷ 30	**10** 540 000 ÷ 600
3 2100 ÷ 3	**6** 72 000 ÷ 800		

Work out 216 ÷ 3.

Since 210 ÷ 3 = 70 and 6 ÷ 3 = 2, 216 ÷ 3 = 72.

Work out 608 ÷ 8.

Now 8 × 70 = 560 and 8 × 80 = 640, so the answer is between 70 and 80.

608 − 560 = 48 and 48 ÷ 8 = 6 so the answer is actually 76.

This calculation is usually set out:

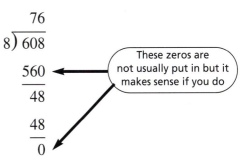

These zeros are not usually put in but it makes sense if you do

It all works out when the numbers are put in their right places!

Divide 322 by 7.

$7 \times 40 = 280$, $7 \times 50 = 350$ so the answer is between 40 and 50.
$322 - 280 = 42$, $42 \div 7 = 6$,
so answer is 46.

```
      46
  7)322
    280
   ----
     42
     42
   ----
      0
```

Calculate $924 \div 3$.

$3 \times 300 = 900$ so 24 is 'left over'. $24 \div 3 = 8$

so answer is 308.

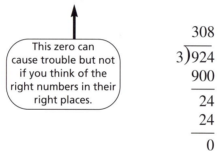

This zero can cause trouble but not if you think of the right numbers in their right places.

```
     308
  3)924
    900
   ----
     24
     24
   ----
      0
```

Find $45\,360 \div 9$.

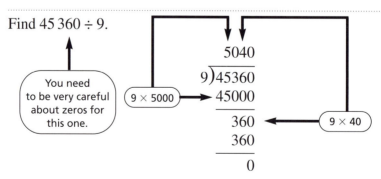

You need to be very careful about zeros for this one.

9 × 5000

9 × 40

```
       5040
  9)45360
    45000
    -----
      360
      360
    -----
        0
```

Exercise 4.9

Do these divisions.

1 $224 \div 4$	**4** $335 \div 5$	**7** $504 \div 8$	**9** $138 \div 3$
2 $342 \div 9$	**5** $3328 \div 8$	**8** $552 \div 6$	**10** $5508 \div 6$
3 $2107 \div 7$	**6** $10\,018 \div 2$		

Further division

There is no real point in distinguishing between 'long' or 'short' division. What matters is recognising how the method works.

Find $1984 \div 64$.

We could subtract 64 from 1984 until there is nothing left. This is not a practical method!

But it becomes a possible method if we subtract **multiples** of 64.

```
64)1984
    640     10 lots of 64
   ─────
   1344
    640     10 lots of 64
   ─────
    704
    640     10 lots of 64
   ─────
     64
     64     1 lot of 64
   ─────
      0     31 lots of 64
```

and this easily becomes the usual way of setting out:

```
      31
64)1984
   1920     30 × 64
   ─────
     64
     64     1 × 64
   ─────
      0    31 × 64
```

> But the problem with this method is making the first estimate of 30.

Work out $4032 \div 56$.

Since $56 \times 100 = 5600$ and this is more than 4032, the answer can't be in the hundreds so it must be in the tens;

$40 \div 5 = 8$ and this gives a start. But 56 is nearly 60 and $80 \times 60 = 4800$ which is too big.

So try $70 \times 56 = 3920$ which is less than 4032 which means the answer is between 70 and 80.

```
      72
56)4032
   3920     (70 × 56)
   ─────
    112
    112     (2 × 56)
   ─────
      0
```

Exercise 4.10

1 $1643 \div 53$	**4** $3225 \div 43$	**7** $5213 \div 13$	**9** $9888 \div 48$
2 $1296 \div 27$	**5** $2324 \div 28$	**8** $9100 \div 35$	**10** $32\,508 \div 54$
3 $5980 \div 92$	**6** $5246 \div 61$		

SUMMARY

- There are many ways to multiply numbers.
- Three methods are the 'lattice' method, 'Napier's bones' and 'doubling and halving'.
- You need to know the **multiplication bonds**.
- The key to multiplication and division is **place value**.
- To multiply by 10, the digits are moved one position to the left, and the empty place is filled with a zero.
- Zero keeps the other digits in their correct (relative) places.
- Multiplication is repeated addition.
- Division is repeated subtraction.
- Division is also the reverse of multiplication.
- You must always check that answers to calculations are of the right size.

Exercise 4A

Calculate these.

1 47×24

2 329×51

3 947×861

4 Write down the answers to these.

   a $48 \div 6$

   b $2000 \div 4$

   c $7200 \div 80$

Calculate these.

5 $498 \div 3$

6 $435 \div 5$

7 $128 \div 16$

8 $552 \div 24$

Exercise 4B

Calculate these.

1 34 × 17
2 867 × 25
3 4513 × 324
4 Write down the answers to these.
    a 54 ÷ 6
    b 24 000 ÷ 60
    c 40 000 ÷ 500

Calculate these.

5 720 ÷ 6
6 5056 ÷ 4
7 325 ÷ 13
8 1904 ÷ 34

Exercise 4C

Using:
a Napier's bones,
b doubling and halving,
calculate these.

1 31 849 × 274
2 4675 × 3166
3 24 010 × 12 009
4 45 063 × 70 971
5 6017 × 45 698

Exercise 4D

Investigate **Vedic multiplication**.

5 : Introducing algebra

Letters to represent numbers

In the maths cupboard there are some jars for keeping odd bits and pieces.

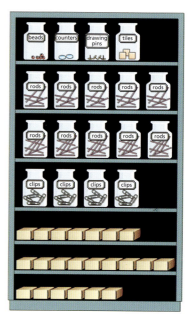

Two pupils were sent to make a list of the things on the top shelf and came back with this:

$b = 5$

$c = 2$

$d = 4$

$t = 3$

The teacher asked what it meant.

What does it mean?

It's a code. It means there is a jar containing five beads, a jar containing two counters, another containing four drawing pins and another containing three tiles.

The teacher went to the cupboard and the shelf looked like this:

That's a good code. Please continue with the rest of the cupboard.

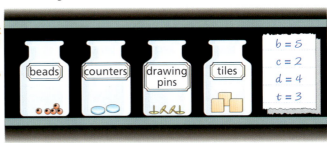

beads

counters

drawing pins

tiles

b = 5
c = 2
d = 4
t = 3

The pupils tried the next shelf. It looked like this:

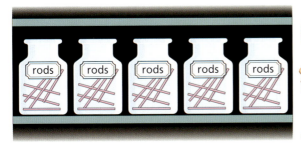

rods rods rods rods rods

There are five jars, each containing six rods. How can we code that?

rods

Since there are six rods in each jar we could put r = 6. But how could we use the code to tell people there are five jars?

Altogether there are five lots of six which is 30.

So we could say that the number of rods is 5 lots of r, where r = 6.

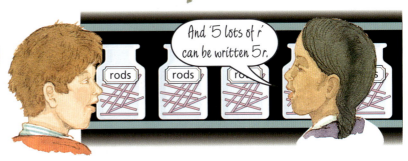

On the next shelf there are five jars but each jar contains seven rods. So that's 5 lots of r, but now r = 7.

And '5 lots of r' can be written 5r.

rods rods ro...

The number of rods is 5r where r = 7

When the teacher looked at the new bit of code, she realised that 5*r* meant five containers of rods, and *r* = 7 meant seven rods in each container. So there were 35 rods altogether. Can you see how she worked that out?

The next shelf had paper-clips in the jars:

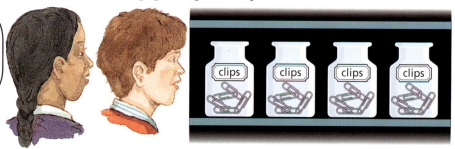

Write down what this should be in the code.

[Answer: 4*s*, where *s* = 5]

The next shelf contained seven cardboard boxes. When the pupils looked inside them, the boxes were full of pegs. Each box contained six pegs:

So the answer to a question like 'What is $7x$ if $x = 6$? would be 7×6 or 42, whether you had beads, counters, pegs or anything!

You've got it! Well done!

Evaluation by replacement

What is $9z$ if $z = 3$?

This is like having nine boxes with three things in each box. Total number of things: 27.

What is $4z$ if $z = 5$?

This would be four boxes of things with five in each box, so 20 altogether.

What is $10w$ if $w = 6$? Answer: 10×6, which is 60.

So, to summarise so far, when you are asked 'What is $7m$ if $m = 8$?', this is like being asked: *count the total number of things if you have seven boxes and in each box there are eight things.*

Exercise 5.1

1 What is $5t$ if $t = 9$? **5** What is $6t$ if $t = 5$? **9** What is $3t$, $t = 0$?
2 What is $7t$ if $t = 6$? **6** What is $10t$, $t = 2$? **10** What is $237t$, $t = 0$?
3 What is $3t$ if $t = 10$? **7** What is $10t$, $t = 1$?
4 What is $4t$ if $t = 7$? **8** What is $9t$, $t = 3$?

Did you notice that we dropped the 'if' after question 5?

Using words in maths

Maths books, maths exams and maths teachers use many different words to ask questions. Here are some of them: 'evaluate', 'calculate', 'find', 'work out', 'find the value of . . .'

They all mean 'What is . . .'; which only means: 'Work out the answer . . .'. This book uses them all, at different times, so that you get used to them and won't be puzzled when you see them on exam papers.

Exercise 5.2

1 Work out $2x$ when $x = 3$.
2 Evaluate $7x$ when $x = 9$.
3 Find $8x$ when $x = 1$.
4 Calculate the value of $11x$ when $x = 6$.
5 If $x = 5$, find the value of $5x$.
6 Find the value of $13x$, $x = 3$.
7 Give the answer to $6x$ if $x = 8$.
8 Evaluate $7x$ if $x = 7$.
9 Work out $100x$ when $x = 0$.
10 Find the value of x if $x = 2$.

Using two letters

Here is a rather different situation:

There are three jars each containing two counters, together with four jars each containing five drawing pins.

This time we want to know the *total number* of *objects* there are in the seven jars.

Count the total number of objects in the jars. (There are 26.)

How could this be calculated? There are three lots of two counters and four lots of five drawing pins. This is:

$$3 \times 2 + 4 \times 5 \text{ objects}, \quad \text{which is } 6 + 20 \text{ or } 26 \text{ objects}$$

Let's say there were five boxes each with seven counters in them, and three boxes each with four drawing pins in them. How many things (counters and drawing pins) altogether?

There would be:

$$5 \times 7 + 3 \times 4 = 35 + 12 = 47$$

And in the code this would be written:

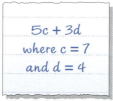

$5c + 3d$, where $c = 7$ and $d = 4$;
or $\qquad 5x + 3y$, where $x = 7$ and $y = 4$;
or $\qquad 5s + 3w$, where $s = 7$ and $w = 4$; etc.

Work out $2c + 5d$, where $c = 7$ and $d = 4$.
This would be: $2 \times 7 + 5 \times 4 = 14 + 20 = 34$.

Exercise 5.3

Let $c = 7$ and $d = 4$. Find the value of these.

1 $2c + 3d$	**4** $c + d$	**7** $2c + 2d$	**9** $c + 4d$
2 $4c + 2d$	**5** $c + 2d$	**8** $4c + d$	**10** $c - d$
3 $3c + 3d$	**6** $2c + d$		

Did you get question 10 right? The answer is $7 - 4 = 3$.

Exercise 5.4

Let $c = 5$ and $d = 3$. Find the value of these.

1 $c + d$	**4** $2c - d$	**7** $3c - 4d$	**9** $3c + 5d$
2 $c - d$	**5** $2c + 3d$	**8** $4c + 3d$	**10** $5c - 3d$
3 $2c + d$	**6** $2c - 3d$		

To summarise again:

If c is 3, when you write $5c$, it actually means 'multiply 5 by the value of c', which in this case becomes 5×3 or 15.

● *Remember that when you say 'the value of c' it is no more than a different way of saying: 'the number of things in a jar labelled c'.*

This process is called **substitution** or **replacement**, because the letter c has been *replaced* by the number 3.

What you have been doing is part of the study called **algebra**, which is a very, very important part of mathematics.

The word 'algebra', comes from the title (in Arabic) of an ancient book, written by a great Arab scholar called Mohammed Ben Muse Al-Khowarizmi (Mohammed, son of Moses, of the city of Khowarezm). He lived around AD 825 and you can still find his birthplace on an atlas. It is now called the city of Khiva (41°31′ N, 16°30′ E).

SUMMARY

- The **value** of a letter means the number of things (say, in a box) representing that letter – for instance: '$s = 5$' would mean that we have one box labelled 's' with five items in it and '$r = 3$' would mean that we have another box labelled 'r' with three things in it.
- We say 's has been **replaced** by 5' or we could say '**substitute** 3 for r'.
- Many different words can be used to ask questions. You have to get used to all of them.
- Substitution is part of the study of **algebra**.
- The word 'algebra' comes from the title of an ancient book.

Exercise 5A

If $b = 7$, find:

1 $3b$	**4** $6b$	**7** $100b$	**9** b
2 $5b$	**5** $10b$	**8** $1000b$	**10** $7b$
3 $8b$	**6** $14b$		

Exercise 5B

If $c = 4$, work out:

1 $5c$	**4** $2c$	**7** $3c$	**9** c
2 $10c$	**5** $9c$	**8** $8c$	**10** $4c$
3 $6c$	**6** $200c$		

Exercise 5C

If $b = 1$, $c = 2$, find the value of:

1 $c + b$	**4** $5c - 10b$	**7** $c + c + c + c$	**9** $298b + 43c$
2 $c - b$	**5** $10b + 5c$	**8** $4c$	**10** $2b - c$
3 $5c - 9b$	**6** $b + b + b$		

Exercise 5D

If $a = 8$, $b = 5$, $c = 3$, evaluate:

1 $a + b + c$	**4** $a - b - c$	**7** $8a + 5b + 3c$	**9** bc and $b + c$
2 $a + b - c$	**5** $a + b$	**8** ab (guess, not 85!)	**10** ca and $c + a$
3 $a - b + c$	**6** $a - c$		

6 Describing and constructing geometrical figures

One of the most difficult parts of doing geometry is to describe the diagrams. It would be so much easier if you could just say 'that line' or 'that angle'. But in order to tell someone which point or line or angle you are talking about, you have to be able to write something down, so this chapter emphasises the naming of figures.

Drawing and naming points and lines

Points

You need a sharp pencil and a ruler. Keep the pencil sharpened.

A **point** is named with a single letter. And it's always a CAPITAL letter, like this:

P •

It doesn't matter where the letter is as long as it is *near* the point:

• Q Z • T •

• F

Put your finger on the point labelled Q.
Put your finger on the point labelled T.
Put your finger on the point labelled F.

Nor does it matter which letter of the alphabet is used. Of course, if you are copying a diagram from a book or from the board, you must use the *same* letters and in the same order as the ones you are copying.

Now, in order to explain better, we have used a *big* dot in this book. But when you draw a diagram in *your own* book you should make as small and neat a dot as possible; no bigger than a normal full-stop like this. ←

Lines

A **line** has two ends and so needs two points to name it, like this:

> Always use CAPITAL LETTERS when naming lines.

This is called the line *DE*. (It could also be called the line *ED*.)

Draw two points *D* and *E* on a piece of plain paper. Put your pencil on the point *D*, bring your ruler up to the pencil, wiggle the ruler a bit until it lines up with the point *E* and draw a smooth thin line in one go without moving the ruler again. Your teacher will show you how.

What mistake has been made here?

Drawing points on lines

Draw a straight line *ST* which goes from left to right, *S* to *T*.

Now mark on this line *ST* a new point *G*.

If you haven't been told anything more about *G* then you can put it *anywhere* as long as it is *on* the line *ST*.

On the same diagram, draw a new line *GL*.

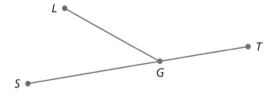

Again, we have used heavy dots to make the diagram clearer. You should draw dots that can scarcely be seen.

Now draw the line *SL*.

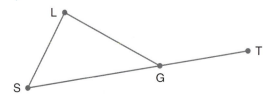

This is *wrong*:

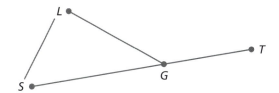

> Draw from left to
> right in
> alphabetical order.

Can you see why? Instead of joining the *points S* and *L*, the *letters* have been joined. It's true that the description doesn't make it clear that you are expected to join up the points, but that's what *is* expected so don't make that mistake yourself.

Finally, if we say *AB* (and nothing more) it's expected that you draw from left to right in alphabetical order.

Exercise 6.1

Follow these directions carefully. Don't look at the answers until you have finished.

1 Draw a line *AB*, followed by a line *BC* sloping upwards to the left, followed by *CD* sloping upwards to the left. Join *DA*.
2 Draw *XY* to cross *LM*. Label where they cross as *P*.
3 Draw *OA*, *OB* and *OC*. *B* is a bit above *A*, and *C* is a bit to the left of *B*.
4 Put a point *W* on a line *ST*.
5 Draw *GH* parallel and slightly above *EF*.
(See page 56 for Answers.)

Did you remember what parallel means?

Lines drawn in the same direction (parallel), and therefore not meeting, are usually shown by having arrows drawn on them like this:

Always draw them like this in future.

Drawing and naming triangles

A triangle is a closed, three-sided figure consisting of straight lines.

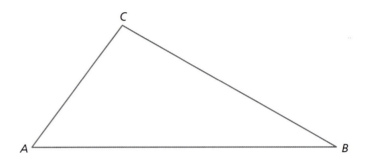

So you will need three points to describe it.

You are not usually specifically told to complete the separate sides, you are expected to know what is meant. Unless you are told something else, label the points alphabetically in an anti-clockwise direction.

Draw and label a triangle *LMN*.

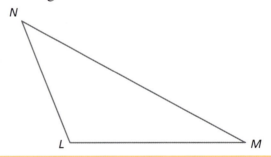

If you are not told anything special about the triangle, you can draw it any shape and size you like.

● *When drawing a triangle, be careful not to assume anything special about it unless the instructions say so; for example, don't draw one with sides equal unless instructed.*

Special triangles

- A triangle with *all three sides equal in length* is called **equilateral**.

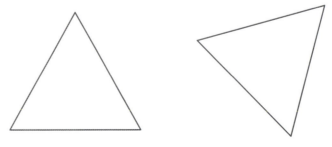

- A triangle with *only two sides equal in length* is called **isosceles**.

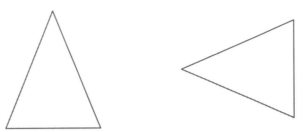

- A triangle with *no sides equal in length* is called **scalene**.

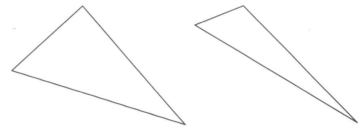

Learn the spelling of these words NOW! Say them correctly out loud!

Making precise drawings

You will need a pair of compasses and a short sharp pencil. Start about five lines below the last piece of writing in your exercise book.

Constructing an equilateral triangle

1 Draw a line.

_____

2 Mark a point *A* on the line (you could do this with the point of the compasses).

_____
A

3 Place the point of the compasses on *A*. Open out the compasses and draw a small **arc** above the line (label it point *C*).

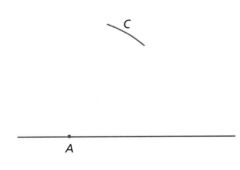

4 Keeping the compasses at the same setting, draw another small arc across the line (label it point *B*). Put a dot where the arc crosses the line at *B*.

5 Again, being very careful not to disturb the compasses, place the point of the compasses on point *B* and draw a small arc which crosses the arc already at *C*.

Note that if you haven't made a good guess about where the two arcs for *C* will cross you will need to go back and make one or both arcs longer.

6 Join *AC* and *BC*. Point *C* is *where the two arcs cross*. Remember, you don't join up to the letter!

If you have been very careful you should have an equilateral triangle *ABC*.

Practise this several times with different lengths *AB*.

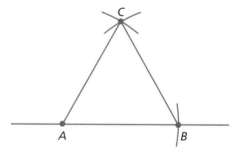

Constructing an isosceles triangle

The procedure is nearly the same as for an equilateral triangle but when you get to step 5 you open out or close down the compasses to draw the second arc for *C*.

With this procedure, side *AB* is the same length as side *AC*, but side *BC* will be different.

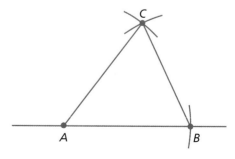

Constructing a scalene triangle

The procedure for this is very similar to the previous two constructions but you change the compasses before *each* arc, that is, for each of steps 3, 4 and 5.

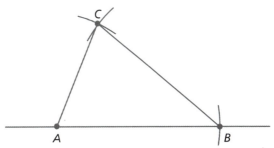

None of the previous constructions had measurements. See if you can now draw triangles with precise measurements.

It helps to make a sketch first.

Exercise 6.2

1. Construct an isosceles triangle of sides 4 cm, 4 cm and 6 cm.
2. Construct an equilateral triangle each of whose sides measures 5 cm.
3. Construct a triangle of sides 7 cm, 6 cm and 3 cm.
4. Construct a triangle with sides 6 cm, 5 cm and 3 cm.
5. Construct a triangle with sides 8 cm, 4 cm and 7 cm.
6. Read the whole of this question before you start, so that you leave enough space. Begin with a line *AB* of length 4 cm. Construct an equilateral triangle *ABC* so that *C* is above *AB*. Now construct a triangle *ABD* so that *D* is below *AB*. The four-sided figure *ADBC* is called a rhombus.
7. Construct an isosceles triangle *UVW* of sides 4 cm, 5 cm and 5 cm. Start with *UV* the 4 cm side and draw *W* above *UV*. Then construct triangle *UVX* with the same measurements so that *X* is below *UV*.
8. Construct an isosceles triangle *PQR* where *PQ* = 4 cm, *PR* = 6 cm and *QR* = 6 cm. Draw *R* above *PQ*. Then construct triangle *PQS* so that *S* is below *PQ* and *PS* = 5 cm, *QS* = 5 cm. This shape *PRQS* is called a kite.
9. Construct a triangle *ABC* where *AB* = *BC* = *CA* = 5 cm. Now construct a triangle *BCD* on side *BC* where *CD* = *BD* = 3 cm.
10. Construct an equilateral triangle *ABC* with side 6 cm. Now construct equilateral triangles on each of the sides *AB*, *BC* and *CA*. If you drew this construction on thin card and cut it out, you could fold it up to make a solid shape.
    You could join the edges with sticky tape or draw small flaps on some of the edges before you cut out the shape and use these.
    The solid shape is called a tetrahedron (because it has four faces).

Project

If everyone in the class made a tetrahedron, you could stick them all together to make an imaginative paper sculpture.

You could ask your art teacher for advice. The tetrahedra could be of different sizes and colours.

Answers

Your diagrams don't have to look *exactly* like these. Ask your teacher if you're not sure whether yours are correct.

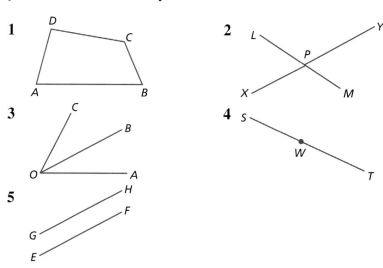

Drawing circular patterns

Exercise 6.3

These shapes can be constructed using only a ruler and a pair of compasses. Copy them onto plain paper. Make them a suitable size of your own and colour them in. You will need to look at them very closely to work out how to draw them.

Invent some shapes of your own and make a display.

1 Draw a circle. Keep the same radius and put the compass point on the circle. Draw an arc. Where this arc cuts the circle, put the compass point again. Draw arcs like this round the circle. This gives six equally spaced points. Finish the figure. Use the same idea to construct the next 'flower' pattern.

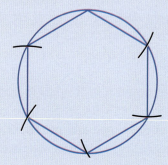

2

3 Start with two perpendicular lines 8 cm long and look carefully to see where the centres of the circles are.
Rub out the original straight lines when you have finished.

4 Start with a line 6 inches long and mark every inch. Look carefully to see where the centres of the semi-circles are and finish off by rubbing out the original line.

5 Start with the horizontal and vertical lines, making each 8 cm long. Construct the four semi-circles and two quarter-circles. Look carefully to see where the centres are.
Rub out the original lines.

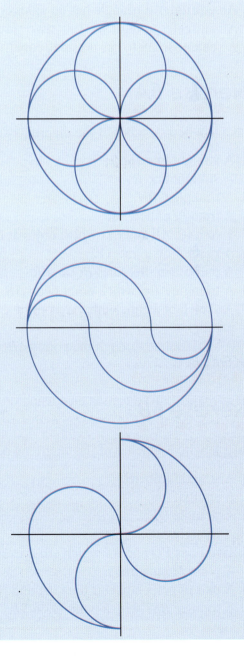

SUMMARY

■ In order to communicate geometry you have to be able to describe diagrams using letters.
■ A **point** is described by a CAPITAL letter written near the point.
■ A **line** is described using two capital letters.
■ Always draw a line in the direction of the alphabetical order of the letters.
■ Join up points, not the letters describing those points.
■ If not told otherwise, label points alphabetically, normally moving anti-clockwise.
■ Parallel lines are indicated with arrows pointing in the same direction.
■ An **equilateral** triangle has all sides equal.
■ An **isosceles** triangle has only two sides equal.
■ A **scalene** triangle has no sides equal.

Exercise 6A

Make labelled sketches of the diagrams described below.

  1 A straight line *JK*.
  2 A straight line *RV*.
  3 A triangle *GBH*.
  4 A triangle called *PAT*.
  5 Two lines *AB* and *CD* which cross at *E*.
  6 A point *P* on a line *XY*.
  7 A pair of parallel lines *PQ* and *RS*.
  8 A triangle *ABC* with a point *D* on *AB*. Join *CD*.
  9 A sketch of a cube with the front face labelled *PQRS*. Indicate that *PS* and *QR* are parallel.
 10 A straight line through the points *ABCD*; a line *AE* with *E* above *AC*; join *AC*, *BE*, *CE* and *DE*.

Exercise 6B

Make labelled sketches of the diagrams described below.

  1 A straight line *AB*.
  2 A straight line *CM*.
  3 A triangle *QPR*.
  4 A triangle called *JIM*.
  5 Two lines *PQ* and *RS* which cross at *T*.
  6 A point *M* on a line *EF*.
  7 A pair of perpendicular lines *JK* and *NP*.
  8 A triangle *RST* with a point *Q* on *ST*.

9 A sketch of a cuboid with a front face labelled *EFGH*. Indicate that *EF* and *FG* are perpendicular.

10 A straight line through the points *WXYZ*; a line *XF* with *F* above *XY*; join *WF*, *YF* and *ZF*.

Exercise 6C

Take this exercise slowly!

1 First make a labelled sketch, then construct and label the following triangles, writing next to each its special name:
  a triangle *XYZ* where *XY* = 6 cm, *YZ* = 4 cm, *ZX* = 3 cm;
  b triangle *LMN* where *LN* = 7 cm, *LM* = 5 cm, *MN* = 7 cm;
  c triangle *RST* where *RS* = 6 cm, *ST* = 6 cm, *TR* = 6 cm.
2 Draw an equilateral triangle *RMT* of side 3.5 cm.
3 Draw a triangle *TUC* where *TU* = 9 cm, *UC* = 7 cm and *CT* = 4 cm.
4 Draw an isosceles triangle *ABC* of base 3 cm and where the equal sides are of 5 cm. Write down the length of *BC*.
5 Draw a triangle *NUT* where *NU* = 6.5 cm, *UT* = 3.5 cm and *TN* = 5.5 cm.
6 Draw an isosceles triangle *EFG* with *EF* = 5 cm, *EG* = *FG* and the two equal sides measuring 7.3 cm.

   On the same diagram draw an isosceles triangle *EFH* with the two equal sides measuring 3.7 cm. Join *GH*.

   By looking back through the chapter decide whether you have drawn a rhombus, a kite or a tetrahedron.
7 Draw an isosceles triangle *RSE* where *RE* = *SE* = 8 cm and *RS* = 6 cm. Mark a point *O* on *RS* which is the middle point of *RS*. Join and measure *EO* to the nearest millimetre.
8 Draw triangle *PQR* where *PQ* = 8.3 cm, *QR* = 7.3 cm and *RP* = 5.6 cm.
9 Draw *LMN* where *LM* = 6 cm, *MN* = 10 cm and *NL* = 8 cm.
10 Draw *ABC* where *AC* = 6 cm, *AB* = 3 cm and *CB* = 3 cm.

Exercise 6D

1 Try to construct a triangle *ABC* where *AB* = 7 cm, *BC* = 2 cm and *AC* = 3 cm. What goes wrong?

2 Try to construct a triangle *DEF* where *DE* = 8 cm, *EF* = 3 cm and *DF* = 4 cm. Again, what goes wrong?

3 Try to construct triangle *PQR* where *PQ* = 7 cm, *QR* = 2 cm and *PR* = 2 cm.

4 Construct triangle *STU* where *ST* = 7 cm, *SU* = 3 cm, and *TU* = 4 cm. Still wrong!

5 Look back carefully at the lengths given in the four previous questions and try changing one length in each case so that the triangle could then be drawn.

    Can you find a general rule for the connection between the lengths of the sides of a triangle so that it could always be drawn?

7 Approximation

Imagine you were suddenly caught in the street in a violent rain-storm. The sensible thing to do would be to run to the nearest open door-way!

Say you were in a playground game and one hiding place was 6 metres away and another was 4 metres away from you. You would go to the one 4 metres away.

If you were stuck on a ledge of a cliff and it was 2 metres to climb to the top but 8 metres to climb to the bottom, you would climb to the top.

In each of these examples the sensible thing to do is to go to the nearer 'safe' place if there are two possible places.

Let's say you have a ruler which is marked only every 10 cm up to 100 cm, like this:

and you are measuring a stick, like this:

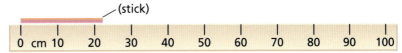

(stick)

Make sure the left-hand end of the stick is opposite the zero mark and look at the right-hand end of the stick. It's between the 20 and the 30 cm marks.

Which mark is it nearer?

How about this stick? (between lines)

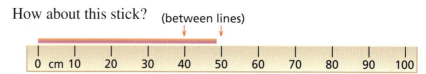

The right-hand end of the stick is between two numbers on the ruler. Which are these? Which is the nearer number?

Exercise 7.1

Look at the following sticks and rulers. In each question, say which two numbered marks are nearest to the right-hand end of the stick. Which is the nearer mark?

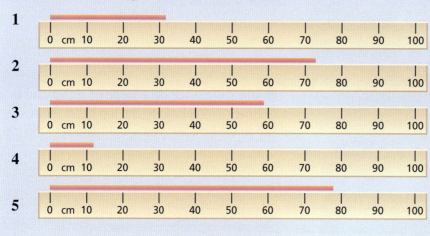

Look back at the last exercise and imagine the spaces between the 10 cm marks filled in with 1 cm marks.

33. But this is a guess!

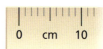

Look again at the right-hand end of the stick for question 1. Which **1 cm** mark would be nearest?

Exercise 7.2

Have a *guess* where the ends of the lines would come if the 1 cm marks were filled in for each of the rulers in exercise 7.1.

Approximating

There are many situations where you don't need an exact answer to a problem. There are also situations where you *can't* have an exact answer. Finding a *good* answer in these cases is called **approximating**.

For example, if you go into a shop and buy something for, let's say 27p, you may not have the exact money in your pocket or purse. You would give the shopkeeper the nearest larger amount you could, say 30p, and get change.

When aiming to get to school on time, it's a good idea to over-estimate the time needed for travelling!

If running a bath, it would be safer to have it too cool rather than too hot; too shallow rather than too full.

There are other situations where it's important to make things as accurate as possible. For instance, models won't work out if measurements aren't accurate; clothes won't fit if you approximate too much when choosing or making them!

There is a third group of situations where you may have to begin by measuring very carefully but as you become more experienced you don't need to measure so precisely. Even an experienced cook will measure out ingredients for a new recipe, but doesn't need to do so as the dish becomes more familiar.

Exercise 7.3

List two examples of your own:

a where there is no need to be very accurate,
b where it is not possible to be very accurate,
c where a high degree of accuracy is required,
d where things can be relaxed as the situation becomes more familiar.

Compare your answers with those of the rest of the class.

How close can you get?

You probably have realised by now that some measurements need to be more accurate than others. If you go out for a walk, it's good enough to know you are going for, let's say, 2 kilometres and if it's a few metres more or less it doesn't matter. If you are running a 100 metres race on the track for sports day, you would expect the distance to be measured as accurately as possible.

Degree of accuracy

In measuring or approximating, just how close you need to get for a particular purpose is called the **degree of accuracy** (or **degree of approximation**) and will be discussed more thoroughly in later books.

In the exercise using the ruler marked only every 10 cm (exercise 7.1) you could only give an answer of 10, 20, 30, . . . cm. If you want to be more accurate, then you would either have to guess, or use a ruler with a larger number of divisions on it.

When we measure a line, we give an answer to the nearest mark on the ruler. If the ruler is marked only every 10 cm, we are giving our answers 'accurate to the nearest 10 cm'.

● *So a measurement of 33 cm 'to the nearest 10 cm' would be given as 30 cm.*

What would 59 kg be 'to the nearest 10 kg'?

59 kg lies between 50 kg and 60 kg. But it is nearer 60 kg.
So the answer is 60 kg.

What is 12p, 'to the nearest 10p'?

12p lies between 10p and 20p, but is nearer 10p.
So the answer is 10p.

What is 37 m, 'to the nearest 10 m'?

37 m is between 30 m and 40 m but nearer 40 m.
So the answer is 40 m.

Approximating to the nearest 10

We must also be able to give approximate answers when talking about numbers on their own. To do this, just count up or down **to the nearest 10**.

What is 78, 'to the nearest 10'?

70 would be too small and 80 would be too big. But 78 is nearer 80 so '78 to the nearest 10', is 80.

Remember that a number on the ten times table is called **a multiple of 10**: 10, 20, 30, 40 . . .

In the following exercise, first write down the multiple of 10 which is *smaller* than the given number, then the multiple of 10 which is *bigger* than the given number and then the multiple of 10 which is *nearer*.

For instance, starting from the number 43, 40 is too small, 50 is too big but 40 is the nearer.

You can still think of the numbers as if they were marks on a ruler, but there is no need to draw one unless you think it will help.

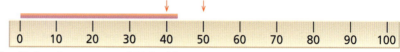

So 43 'to the nearest 10' is 40.

Exercise 7.4

Write down the two multiples of 10 between which each of the following numbers lies, and then give the nearer.

1 56	**4** 38	**7** 41	**9** 66
2 71	**5** 47	**8** 64	**10** 99
3 83	**6** 8		

Exercise 7.5

Write down the nearest two multiples of 10 between which each of the following numbers lies and give their approximation to the nearest 10.

1 41	**3** 43	**5** 46	**7** 48
2 42	**4** 44	**6** 47	**8** 49

In exercise 7.5 can you tell easily which way to go?

Since each of the numbers lies between 40 and 50, and 45 is half-way between them, you only need notice whether the number is more or less than 45. If less, go to 40; if more, go to 50.

The rule for numbers ending in 5

There is a little problem about numbers ending in 5. Since such numbers are exactly half-way between two multiples of 10, *you can't say* whether to go up or down.

Whenever this sort of thing happens, mathematicians *make a rule* which people agree to keep. It could be a disaster for people to get different answers for the same situation!

● *When a number is half-way between two multiples of 10 (that is, ends in a 5), we always put the number **up** to the higher multiple.*

So 45 approximates to 50, 35 to the nearest 10 is 40, and 25 goes to 30.

Exercise 7.6

Approximate these numbers to the nearest 10.

1 23		**4** 93		**7** 3		**9** 37
2 76		**5** 14		**8** 5		**10** 98
3 65		**6** 78				

Numbers greater than 100

Can you count in 10s after 100? It's easy: 110, 120, 130, . . . , 240, 250, . . . , 320, 330, 340 . . .

Exercise 7.7

Write down all the multiples of 10 between 321 and 467.

Now consider the number 107. It lies between 100 and 110 but is nearer 110. So 107 to the nearest 10 is 110.

Between which two multiples of 10 does 234 lie?

230 is too small and 240 is too big but 230 is nearer.
So 234 to the nearest 10 is 230.

Approximate 365 to the nearest 10.

365 lies between 360 and 370 but our rule says go to 370.

Approximate 438 to the nearest 10.

438 lies between 430 and 440 but 440 is nearer.

Exercise 7.8

Write these numbers to the nearest 10. First write down the two nearest multiples of 10 between which each number lies.

1 103		**4** 526		**7** 425		**9** 245
2 301		**5** 254		**8** 524		**10** 452
3 353		**6** 542				

Different words, same meaning

Very often in maths, the same question can be asked using different words. Finding the nearest multiple of 10 can be said in different ways. You could be asked:

'write the following numbers correct to the nearest 10'

'round these numbers to the nearest 10'

'give to the nearest multiple of 10'

'approximate to the nearest 10'

All these directions only mean the same as the exercises we are doing.

Exercise 7.9

Write the following numbers correct to the nearest 10.

| **1** 37 | **3** 64 | **5** 93 | **7** 55 | **9** 63 |
| **2** 137 | **4** 264 | **6** 893 | **8** 655 | **10** 263 |

Notice that, when approximating to the nearest 10, putting in a hundreds figure doesn't alter the tens figure answer.

Exercise 7.10

Write the following numbers, rounded to the nearest 10.

| **1** 4029 | **3** 1472 | **5** 6375 | **7** 3187 | **9** 5917 |
| **2** 9256 | **4** 1427 | **6** 7204 | **8** 4063 | **10** 9989 |

The point is that, even if we're dealing with thousands, you need only look at the tens and units figures.

● *But be careful! You must keep to the same size of number, so you still have to write down the thousands and the hundreds figures. That can sometimes be forgotten.*

Approximating to the nearest 100

It's just as easy to write figures correct **to the nearest 100** as it is to the nearest 10.

Write 234 to the nearest 100.

234 lies between 200 and 300 but is nearer 200 so the answer is 200.

Round 264 to the nearest 100.

264 lies between 200 and 300 but is nearer 300 so the answer is 300.

Again, the test is whether the number to be corrected is more or less than half-way: in the last two examples, more or less than 250. As you'd expect, *exactly* half-way goes *up*. 250 to the nearest hundred is 300.

Exercise 7.11

Write these numbers to the nearest 100.

1 437	**4** 734	**7** 450	**9** 989
2 374	**5** 745	**8** 122	**10** 998
3 743	**6** 754		

Don't get muddled by the next one. Remember to put the thousands figure each time.

Exercise 7.12

Write these numbers to the nearest 100.

1 3564 (Notice that 3564 is between 3500 and 3600.)

2 4276	**5** 6721	**8** 9349
3 3192	**6** 6725	**9** 1123
4 3129	**7** 9353	**10** 5555

You have to be careful in reading the question in the next exercise. 437 to the nearest *10* is 440 but to the nearest *100* is 400.

Exercise 7.13

1 Write 564 to the nearest 10.
2 Write 456 to the nearest 100.
3 Write 2934 to the nearest 100.
4 Write 2934 to the nearest 10.
5 Round 450 to the nearest 10.
6 Correct 666 to the nearest 100.
7 Put 67 to the nearest 100.
8 Give 178 written correct to the nearest 100.
9 Write 178 correct to the nearest 10.
10 Approximate 3787 to the nearest 10.

Exercise 7.14

Write down the letter corresponding to the correct answer to the following questions.

1 4561 to the nearest 10 is
 a 60
 b 456
 c 4560

2 4561 to the nearest 100 is
 a 4600
 b 460
 c 46

3 472 to the nearest 10 is
 a 47
 b 470
 c 70

4 472 to the nearest 100 is
 a 50
 b 500
 c 5

5 3076 to the nearest 10 is
 a 308
 b 31
 c 3080

6 3077 to the nearest 100 is
 a 3100
 b 31
 c 310

7 681 to the nearest 100 is
 a 700
 b 68
 c 70

8 681 to the nearest 10 is
 a 690
 b 68
 c 680

9 2050 to the nearest 100 is
 a 2100
 b 20
 c 200

10 2053 to the nearest 10 is
 a 200
 b 2050
 c 205

SUMMARY

■ You sometimes can't or don't need to or don't want to measure exactly.
■ Finding an answer in these circumstances is called **approximating**.
■ How close you get is called the **degree of approximation** or **degree of accuracy**.
■ We have been working in this chapter with a degree of accuracy **to the nearest 10** and also **to the nearest 100**.
■ You first decide the multiples of 10 or 100 between which your starting number lies and then see which multiple is the nearer.
■ Numbers exactly half-way between multiples go *up* to the next multiple.
■ You have to be careful to keep the answer the same size as the starting number.

Exercise 7A

Write these numbers to the nearest 10.

1 56 **2** 93 **3** 16 **4** 174 **5** 4650

Write these numbers to the nearest 100.

6 649 **7** 651 **8** 43 **9** 1055 **10** 7562

Exercise 7B

Round these numbers to the nearest 10.

1 63 **2** 46 **3** 35 **4** 325 **5** 3715

Correct these numbers to the nearest 100.

6 550 **7** 632 **8** 174 **9** 417 **10** 9845

Exercise 7C

Approximate each of these numbers, first to the nearest 10, then to the nearest 100 (two answers for each question).

1 436 **2** 656 **3** 871 **4** 5462 **5** 7603

Exercise 7D

Write each of these numbers correct to the nearest **7**.

1 15 **2** 25 **3** 38 **4** 60 **5** 1630

Measure the length of each of these lines with a ruler, correct to the nearest ten millimetres.

6

7

8

9

10

8 Splitting up units

The meaning of fractions

If you 'fracture' something you break it into pieces.

The word **fraction** comes from the same Latin word as *fracture*, meaning 'to break into parts'.

So the study of fractions is about taking a **unit** and seeing what happens when you break it up into bits.

If you look at builders making a brick wall or putting tiles on a roof or laying paving stones in the street, you often see them breaking bits off a brick or a tile or a paving stone, because the 'unit' in which the blocks are made doesn't fit exactly into the space which has to be filled.

So you start with some 'unit' – a brick, a tile, a paving stone, a recipe – and change it by taking some *part* of the original unit.

And this can be the first problem with fractions. The 'unit' might be different from one example to the next.

Breaking up the unit

Exercise 8.1

Try to think of at least three different examples of your own where a 'unit' is broken into parts for some purpose.

In each case, name or describe the unit involved.

You might have used money as an example in the last exercise.

£1 is a unit of money which can be 'broken' into many different parts. In this case the different parts are the different coins.

Exercise 8.2

List the different parts (coins) into which £1 can be changed.

Denominations

The answers to the last exercise are: 1p, 2p, 5p, 10p, 20p and 50p coins. When you break up £1 into coins like this, the different coins are called the *denominations* of £1.

Exercise 8.3

Find out the denominations of the US dollar, the Indian rupee and the German mark.

Different units

If you needed some 20p coins for the 'phone but only had £1, you would expect *five* 20p coins in exchange. Any one 20p coin is as good as another 20p coin – that is, they all have the same value. And because *five* 20p coins, each with the same value, make up £1, each 20p coin is called

one fifth of £1.

Notice that the £1 is being used as the **unit**.

How many 5p coins would you exchange for £1? Answer: twenty.

So each 5p coin is called

one twentieth of £1.   (*Here, £1 is the* **unit**.)

How many 5p coins would you exchange for 50p?   Answer: ten.

So each 5p coin is called

one tenth of 50p.   (*Here, 50p is the **unit**.*)

How many 2p coins would you exchange for 10p?   Answer: five.

So each 2p coin is called

one fifth of 10p.   (*Here, 10p is the **unit**.*)

Numbers like one fifth, one tenth and one twentieth are *fractions* because some *unit* has been broken into *parts*.

But here is another possible difficulty with fractions in mathematics.

A bricklayer will break off just the right amount to make the brick fit and not need to give it any name.

● *When we break up a unit to make fractions in mathematics, and give the parts a name, all the parts have to be **equal** to each other.*

So although this line:

has been broken into three parts, because the parts are **not equal** to each other, *no* part could be called *one third*!

But if you break the same line into three **equal** parts:

then *each* part can be called (in mathematics) *one third*.
So why is this line:

not broken into *fifths*,
but this line:

is broken into *fifths*?
The units in the last few examples were the original lines, but you can start with anything at all as the unit.

Exercise 8.4

Which of these diagrams, **a**, **b**, **c** or **d**, illustrates *one fourth*?

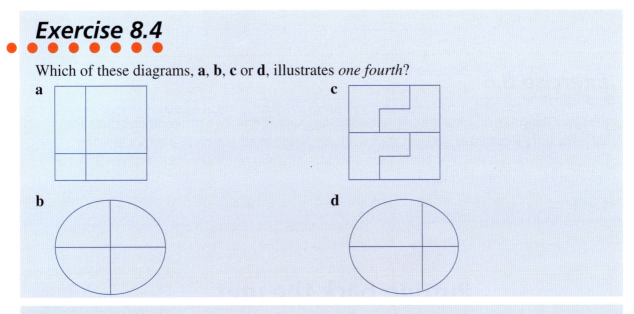

Exercise 8.5

Find four different ways of illustrating *one third*. Try to be imaginative!!

Denominator – equal parts

The *number of equal parts* into which a diagram is broken to illustrate a fraction is called its **denominator**, like splitting money into different coins.
So the denominator of one third is 3; the denominator of one seventh is 7 and denominator of one fifth is 5.

These are written:

$\frac{1}{3}$ (one third)

$\frac{1}{7}$ (one seventh)

$\frac{1}{5}$ (one fifth)

So to illustrate $\frac{1}{3}$ we could start with some unit, for example, a rectangle

and break it up into three equal parts:

$\frac{1}{3}$	$\frac{1}{3}$	$\frac{1}{3}$

To illustrate $\frac{1}{7}$ we could start with this rectangle as unit

and break it up into seven equal parts.

$\frac{1}{7}$	$\frac{1}{7}$	$\frac{1}{7}$	$\frac{1}{7}$	$\frac{1}{7}$	$\frac{1}{7}$	$\frac{1}{7}$

Exercise 8.6

Illustrate the following fractions by drawing diagrams. Draw two different diagrams for each fraction. Remember you can start with any shape at all but each diagram must be broken into equal parts. You could use squared, triangular or other paper. You could use a computer to draw interesting diagrams.

1 $\frac{1}{2}$ 2 $\frac{1}{6}$ 3 $\frac{1}{4}$ 4 $\frac{1}{5}$ 5 $\frac{1}{8}$

Putting back the unit

To draw a diagram illustrating $\frac{1}{5}$ you take some unit and break it up into five equal parts.

If all five of these parts are put together again you are back to the original unit.

one fifth shaded   five fifths shaded

So five lots of $\frac{1}{5}$ is a single unit.

Look at these diagrams illustrating $\frac{1}{10}$ and the original unit:

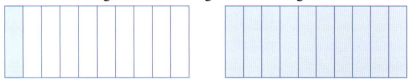

one tenth shaded   ten tenths shaded

So ten lots of $\frac{1}{10}$ is a single unit. Thus ten tenths could also be written as $\frac{10}{10}$.

This will work whatever the unit and however many parts we use. For example:

three lots of $\frac{1}{3}$ is a single unit which could also be written as $\frac{3}{3}$
or

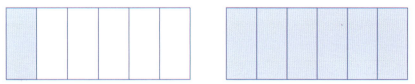

six lots of $\frac{1}{6}$ is a unit which could also be written as $\frac{6}{6}$.

A *single* unit is *one* unit, and could be *represented by the number 1*. It can be written with any denominator we would like to use.

So, for example, $1 = \frac{7}{7}$, or $1 = \frac{11}{11}$, or $1 = \frac{9}{9}$, etc. Invent three more like these.

Exercise 8.7

 1 Write the number 1 in eighths.
 2 Write the number 1 in fifths.
 3 Write the number 1 in twelfths.
 4 Write the number 1 in hundredths.
 5 Write the number 1 in twenty-thirds.
 6 Write $\frac{15}{15}$ in another way.
 7 Write $\frac{33}{33}$ in another way.
 8 How many $\frac{1}{14}$ are the same as 1?
 9 How many $\frac{1}{46}$ are the same as 1?
10 29 lots of some fraction is the same as 1. Write the fraction.

Numerator

Up till now we have been shading in the whole unit. For example, here is $\frac{13}{13}$ shaded.

But there is no need to shade all the parts. Count the number of parts shaded in the next diagram:

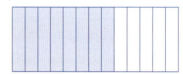

There are eight. But we haven't changed the original unit nor the number of parts. So eight out of the original thirteen have been shaded and this is written $\frac{8}{13}$.

Count the number shaded in the next diagram:

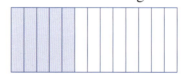

There are five so the fraction shaded would be written $\frac{5}{13}$.

Exercise 8.8

Write down the fraction shaded in each of these diagrams.

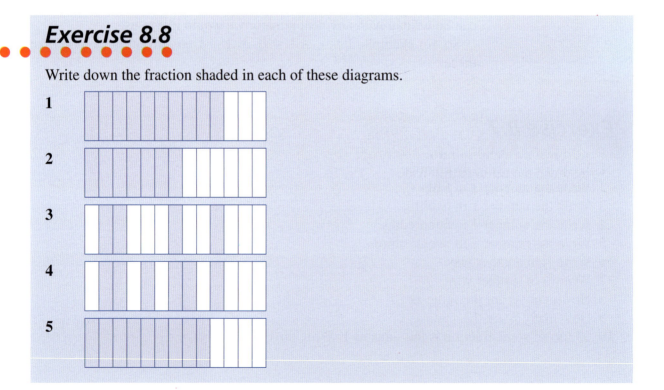

Recall that the *number of equal parts* into which the unit is broken is called the **denominator**.

The *number of those parts shaded* is called the **numerator**.
So, in question 5 of the last exercise, the numerator is 9.

In the fraction $\frac{5}{17}$, the numerator is 5 and the denominator is 17.

In the fraction $\frac{3}{5}$, the numerator is 3 and the denominator is 5.

In the fraction $\frac{17}{18}$, the numerator is 17 and the denominator is 18.

You can see that to illustrate $\frac{3}{4}$, for example, a unit is broken into four equal parts (the denominator) and three of these parts are shaded (the numerator).

To illustrate $\frac{2}{5}$, a unit is broken into five equal parts (the denominator) and two of these parts (the numerator) are shaded:

Exercise 8.9

For each of the following fraction diagrams:
a copy (trace) the shape of the **unit** used,
b write down the **denominator** described,
c write down the **numerator** shaded,
d write down the **fraction** illustrated.

1

3

2
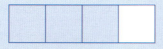

4

5

6

7

8

9

10

Exercise 8.10

Illustrate the following fractions with accurate diagrams. Remember the unit can be any shape and the denominator has to be represented by equal parts.

Draw two different diagrams for each of these fractions:

1 $\frac{3}{5}$ 2 $\frac{3}{8}$ 3 $\frac{4}{5}$ 4 $\frac{2}{3}$ 5 $\frac{5}{8}$

SUMMARY

- **Fractions** arise where some **unit** is broken into parts.
- Mathematical fractions must be broken into **equal** parts.
- The number of those equal parts is called the fraction's **denominator**.
- The number of those equal parts *used* is called the fraction's **numerator**.
- Any unit is represented as the number 1.
- The number **1** can be written as a fraction split into any number of equal parts; and then its numerator is the same as its denominator.

Exercise 8A

1 Describe the coin which is one fifth of £1.
2 Describe the coin which is one fiftieth of £1.
3 Draw a diagram to illustrate $\frac{1}{12}$.
4 Draw a diagram to illustrate $\frac{1}{10}$.
5 Write the number 1 in sixteenths.
6 How many $\frac{1}{51}$ are the same as 1?
7 Write down the fraction shaded in this diagram.

8 Write down the fraction shaded in this diagram.

9 Draw *two different* diagrams to represent $\frac{7}{12}$.

Exercise 8B

1 Describe the coin which is one tenth of 10p.
2 Describe the coin which is one twenty-fifth of 50p.
3 Draw a diagram to illustrate $\frac{1}{15}$.
4 Draw a diagram to illustrate $\frac{1}{7}$.
5 Write the number 1 in thirty-fourths.
6 How many $\frac{1}{49}$ are the same as 1?
7 Write down the fraction shaded in this diagram.

8 Write down the fraction illustrated in this diagram.

9 Draw *two different* ways of representing $\frac{5}{12}$ in a diagram.

Exercise 8C

1 If I had one half of 50p and one half of 20p how much money would I have?

2 If I had one fifth of 50p and one fifth of 20p how much money would I have?

3 Copy and complete: $2 = \frac{}{20}$.

4 Copy and complete: $\frac{}{12} = 1$.

5 Copy and complete: $1 = \frac{}{20}$.

6 Draw two diagrams next to each other which show that $\frac{1}{2}$ is less than $\frac{3}{4}$.

7 What is one half of 70p? Compare with question 1.

8 Write down the value of one fifth of 70p (compare with question 2).

9 Find two different collections of coins which give the same value as three fifths of £1.

10 Find two different collections of coins which give the same value as nine tenths of £1.

Exercise 8D

Examine these diagrams in sequence. Write down the fraction represented in each case. Continue the pattern a few steps.

   What is being demonstrated? Don't look for too long!!

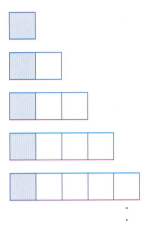

9 Finding the mathematics

Imagine you have been told to post a letter.

The letter-box is at the end of the road, 300 metres away.

You have a bike, locked safely away in a shed. The key is in a kitchen cupboard. The kitchen is rather small and just at the moment is full of aunts and uncles helping to do the cooking for your baby sister's birthday party. You know that if you go near the kitchen you will be shouted at for being in the way. One of the aunts is very bad-tempered and rather frightening.

What do you do?

You walk to the letter-box!

In other circumstances it might be worth getting the key and taking your bike. You might be feeling so tired that, even though it's going to be uncomfortable, you would risk the shouting. If the kitchen were clear you could get the key easily but it might still not be worth it. Or you could simply decide that you needed the exercise of a short walk!

Whatever you decided to do in any of these circumstances, there isn't much school **mathematics** in the situation at all in the sense of calculating or measuring.

Imagine a quite different situation. You are sent on an errand to the corner shop to buy some groceries. Here there is much, though simple, maths involved. You need to work out how much money to take; work out whether the bill is correct; see that the change is right:

That's what this chapter is about. In a particular problem or situation, is there maths involved and if so how do you go about sorting things out?

If you were a professional computer programmer and you were asked to consider writing a new system for a client, the first question you would ask is:

'Is using a computer for this job the right thing to do at all?'

If you needed to multiply a number by ten, it's just silly to do it on a calculator. You could have written down the answer long before you had found your calculator and switched it on.

Exercise 9.1

Examine the following situations and for each one state:
a whether there is mathematics involved,
b the sort of maths which might help solve the problem,
c any materials or apparatus you think might help,
d how you might set about solving the problem.

There may not be a 'correct' answer at all!

Situation 1. You are sorting your football card collection to put them in your album. Is it better to put them in one at a time or would it save time to organise them first into the separate teams?

Situation 2. It is your first morning doing your paper round. Unfortunately the newsagent has been unable to sort them for you. How would you go about it?

Situation 3. You decide to tidy your book collection. Think of ways you could do this.

Situation 4. Draw rectangles on centimetre squared paper and count the number of centimetre squares through which the diagonal passes.

Situation 5. You are having a birthday party and must decide whom to invite.

Situation 6. You have never really learnt your multiplication tables properly. You decide now is the time to get on top of the problem. How do you go about it?

Situation 7. How could you make a schedule for the coming week for yourself regarding television and radio? Don't forget your homework!

Situation 8. Count the number of all the possible different-sized squares on a chess-board.

Situation 9. You are working for a music exam which is three weeks away. Is it best to do half-an-hour's practice each day before school or when you get home in the afternoon or wait until the weekend and do an hour or two on each of Saturday and Sunday?

Situation 10. You decide to improve your table-tennis. How should you go about this?

10 Products, powers and factors

Products

Multiply 3 by 5.
The answer of course is 15.
Multiply 7 by 4.
The answer is 28.

We could have asked these questions without using the word 'multiply'. To do this we need the word **product**. Write it in your exercise book. It's used like this:

Find the product of 3 and 5. Answer: 15.
Find the product of 7 and 4. Answer: 28.

So, to find the product of two numbers, just multiply them together.

The product of 9 and 6 is $9 \times 6 = 54$.

Exercise 10.1

Write down the following.

1 The product of 7 and 3.
2 The product of 4 and 6.
3 The product of 8 and 5.
4 The product of 9 and 7.
5 The product of 3 and 3.
6 The product of 2 and 0.
7 The product of 6 and 10.
8 The product of 4 and 1.
9 The product of 8 and 8.
10 The product of 10 and 10.

Check your answers now.

Continued products

Find the product of 3, 5 and 2.
To do this, you multiply the three numbers together.
$3 \times 5 = 15$ then $15 \times 2 = 30$.
So $3 \times 5 \times 2 = 30$.

Find the product of 6, 5 and 7.

Answer: $6 \times 5 \times 7 = 30 \times 7 = 210$.

This multiplication could be called a **continued product**.

Find the continued product of 23, 15, 3, and 12.

Answer: $23 \times 15 \times 3 \times 12 = 12\,420$ (by calculator).

Does the order of multiplication affect the answer?

Exercise 10.2

Find the following continued products.

1 $8 \times 4 \times 5$	**4** $5 \times 13 \times 7$	**7** $2 \times 3 \times 4 \times 5$	**9** $9 \times 6 \times 14 \times 3$
2 $6 \times 3 \times 7$	**5** $6 \times 6 \times 9$	**8** $15 \times 4 \times 19 \times 31$	**10** $12 \times 12 \times 12 \times 12$
3 $3 \times 2 \times 4$	**6** $4 \times 4 \times 4$		

Shortening the question

As you may have noticed by now, mathematicians like writing everything down in as short a way as possible. Let's look closely at a way of doing this in the next section.

$$x + x^2 + (y - 2) + z^2$$
$$+ 3z + 2y - z^2 - 2$$
$$- y + y^2 - (2y + 2z)$$
$$+ (4 - y^2) - (z + x^2)$$
$$= x$$

Powers and indices
Repeated continued products

(a) Find $2 \times 2 \times 2 \times 2 \times 2$.

Answer: 32.

(b) Find $5 \times 5 \times 5$.

Answer: 125.

(c) Find $23 \times 23 \times 23 \times 23$.

Answer: 279 841 (calculator).

The questions are still continued products but a *single number* is being continually *repeated*.

The number being repeated can be called the **base number**.

So these could be called **repeated continued products of a base number**.

Count the number of repetitions of the figure '2' in example (a).

It has **5** repetitions (2 is the base).

What about example (b)?

The figure 5 has **3** repetitions (5 is the base).

In example (c) the figure 23 has **4** repetitions (23 is the base).

As you might imagine, we have a special word for the number of repetitions:

● *The number of repetitions is called the **power** and is written smaller and up to the right of the base number. It points out the number of repetitions of this base number.*

Look carefully at this example:

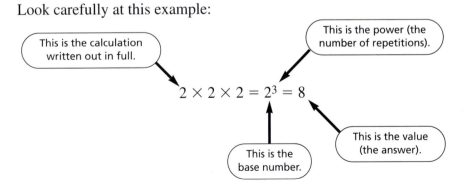

This is the calculation written out in full.

This is the power (the number of repetitions).

$$2 \times 2 \times 2 = 2^3 = 8$$

This is the base number.

This is the value (the answer).

We write:

$2^1 = 2$

$2^2 = 2 \times 2 = 4$

$2^3 = 2 \times 2 \times 2 = 8$

$2^4 = 2 \times 2 \times 2 \times 2 = 16$

$2^5 = 2 \times 2 \times 2 \times 2 \times 2 = 32$

⋮

Read 2^1 as 'two to the **power of one**'.

Read 2^2 as 'two to the **power of two**'.

Read 2^3 as 'two to the **power of three**'.

Read 2^4 as 'two to the **power of four**'.

⋮

Indices

The Latin word **index**, which can mean 'forefinger', is also used for the word 'power', since if you point at something you use your forefinger or index finger.

Putting all this together we can say

5^3 means $5 \times 5 \times 5$ which works out to 125.

It can be read as 'five to the power of three' where the small number 3 is also called 'the index'. The number '5' is called the 'base'.

Note that the whole process can be called **raising a number to a power** or **writing a number in index notation**.

$7^2 = 7 \times 7 = 49$ which is read 'seven to the power of two is forty-nine' (the index is 2).

$10^4 = 10 \times 10 \times 10 \times 10 = 10\ 000$ which is read 'ten to the power of four is ten thousand' (the index is 4).

$4^3 = 4 \times 4 \times 4 = 64$ is read: 'four to the power of three is sixty-four' (the index is 3).

The plural of 'index' is **indices**.

Exercise 10.3

Write the following in index notation. Do not find their values yet.

1 $2 \times 2 \times 2 \times 2 \times 2$ **4** $7 \times 7 \times 7 \times 7$ **7** 9×9 **9** $8 \times 8 \times 8$

2 3×3 **5** $10 \times 10 \times 10$ **8** $6 \times 6 \times 6 \times 6 \times 6$

3 $2 \times 2 \times 2$ **6** $5 \times 5 \times 5 \times 5 \times 5$ **10** $14 \times 14 \times 14 \times 14$

Exercise 10.4

Work out the values of the repeated products in the previous exercise. You will need to use your calculator for some of them.

Exercise 10.5

Write out these repeated products in full *without* indices. Do not evaluate them yet.

1 2^7 **4** 7^2 **7** 10^6 **9** 6^8

2 3^5 **5** 5^4 **8** 9^3 **10** 13^2

3 4^3 **6** 8^1

Exercise 10.6

Evaluate the continued repeated products in the previous exercise.

Using a calculator, graphics calculator or computer

Many scientific calculators have a special key for raising numbers to a power.

Graphics calculators and computers also have special methods. But beware, different machines work in different ways! Ask your teacher.

Other uses for indices

Can you guess what $2^3 \times 3^2$ means?

Written out it is $2 \times 2 \times 2 \times 3 \times 3$ or 8×9 or 72.

Try $4^3 \times 2^2 \times 3$.

It is $4 \times 4 \times 4 \times 2 \times 2 \times 3$ or 768 (calculator).

Exercise 10.7

Write out the following products in full, then find the answers.

1 $3^3 \times 2^2$ **4** $2^2 \times 7$ **7** $2^2 \times 3 \times 5$ **9** $2^2 \times 3^2 \times 5^2$

2 2×3^2 **5** $3^2 \times 5$ **8** $2 \times 3^2 \times 5$ **10** $3^2 \times 5^3 \times 7$

3 3×2^3 **6** $2 \times 3 \times 5^2$

Using the index '1'

It isn't necessary to use an index of '1'. If you mean 2^1, you can just write a 2 on its own because you can see there's only one of them.

Factors

Can you think of a number which divides exactly into 24? There are several. Write them down: 2 will divide; 3 will divide; so will 6, 4, 8, 12, and 1.

● *When one number divides exactly into another, the first one is called a **factor** of the second. So 6 **is a factor of** 24; 8 **is a factor of** 24 and so on. Note that 1 **is** counted as a factor of 24 and 24 **is** counted as a factor of 24.*

Is 3 a factor of 10? No.
Is 3 a factor of 15? Yes.
Is 5 a factor of 10? Yes.
Is 6 a factor of 15? No.
Is 1 a factor of 10? Yes.
Is 15 a factor of 15? Yes.

You need to know your multiplication tables well to be good with factors!

Exercise 10.8

Write 'yes' or 'no' as appropriate.

1 Is 5 a factor of 20?
2 Is 4 a factor of 21?
3 Is 7 a factor of 21?
4 Is 7 a factor of 20?
5 Is 2 a factor of 20?

6 Is 3 a factor of 20?
7 Is 3 a factor of 21?
8 Is 10 a factor of 21?
9 List all factors of 20.
10 List all factors of 21.

Exercise 10.9

List all the factors of the following numbers.

1 12 (Answer: 1, 2, 3, 4, 6, 12.)
2 14
3 16
4 13

5 6
6 23
7 9

8 28
9 30
10 36

Check the answers. Count the *number* of factors in your answers. For example, 12 has six factors. Which of the numbers in the exercise have *only two* factors? 13 and 23.

Can you think of other numbers with only two factors?
Can you remember the word for numbers with only two factors?
They are called **prime numbers**.

Prime numbers

Prime numbers have only the number 1 and the number itself as factors. Therefore they have *two*, and *only two*, factors (*exactly two factors*).
    Some other numbers which fit this description are 7, 11 and 29.

- *Note that the number 1 is **not** a prime number since it has only **one** factor and so doesn't fit the description.*

So the smallest prime number is 2. Which is the next?
    3 has only factors 1 and 3 so *is* a prime number;
    4 has factors 1, 2, 4 so is *not* a prime number;
    5 has only factors 1 and 5 so *is* a prime number;
    6 has factors 1, 2, 3, 6 so is *not* a prime number;
    7 has factors 1 and 7 so *is* prime;
    8 has factors 1, 2, 4, 8 so is *not* prime;
    9 has factors 1, 3, 9 so is *not* prime;
and we could go on for ever, testing each number to see if it is prime.

Exercise 10.10

List the prime numbers less than 30.

For thousands of years, mathematicians have considered prime numbers rather special. It's something to do with not being able to break up a prime number into simpler bits (factors).
    Perhaps you can get something of the feeling by looking at **prime factors**.

Prime factors

We have found out what a *factor* is and also what a *prime number* is. So a *prime factor* is a *factor* which is a *prime number* as well.
    For example: the factors of 12 are 1, 2, 3, 4, 6 and 12. But, of this list, only 2 and 3 are prime, so the prime factors of 12 are 2 and 3.
    The factors of 14 are 1, 2, 7 and 14. But only 2 and 7 are prime, so the prime factors of 14 are 2 and 7.
    Find the prime factors of 30.
    Now, since $6 = 2 \times 3$, and both 2 and 3 are prime numbers, you can see that 6 can be split into a product of prime numbers.
    Have a look at 12:

$$12 = 2 \times 6$$
$$= 2 \times 2 \times 3$$

and that splits 12 into a product of primes.

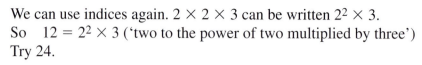

We can use indices again. $2 \times 2 \times 3$ can be written $2^2 \times 3$.

So $12 = 2^2 \times 3$ ('two to the power of two multiplied by three')

Try 24.

$$
\begin{aligned}
24 &= 2 \times 12 \\
&= 2 \times 2 \times 6 \\
&= 2 \times 2 \times 2 \times 3
\end{aligned}
$$

So $24 = 2^3 \times 3$.

We can work out a little routine for this. Divide by the prime numbers in order, smallest first, dividing by each one again until it won't divide anymore. The process stops when you get to 1.

$$
\begin{array}{c|c}
2 & 24 \\
\hline
2 & 12 \\
\hline
2 & 6 \\
\hline
3 & 3 \\
\hline
& 1
\end{array}
$$

Split 36 into its prime factors.

$$
\begin{array}{c|c}
2 & 36 \\
\hline
2 & 18 \\
\hline
3 & 9 \\
\hline
3 & 3 \\
\hline
& 1
\end{array}
$$

So $36 = 2^2 \times 3^2$.

Split 300 into its prime factors.

$$
\begin{array}{c|c}
2 & 300 \\
\hline
2 & 150 \\
\hline
3 & 75 \\
\hline
5 & 25 \\
\hline
5 & 5 \\
\hline
& 1
\end{array}
$$

So $300 = 2^2 \times 3 \times 5^2$.

You can use a calculator to help with the larger divisions.

There are some rules which help with spotting which numbers divide by 2, 3 or 5:

- if the *number is even*, ending in 0, 2, 4, 6 or 8, the whole number divides by 2;
- if the *sum of the digits* of the number divides by 3, the whole number divides by 3;
- if the *number ends in 0 or 5*, the whole number divides by 5.

Exercise 10.11

Split each of the following numbers into its prime factors, expressing the answer in index form.

1 18	**4** 45	**7** 350	**9** 490
2 72	**5** 75	**8** 1617	**10** 273
3 63	**6** 105		

If a whole number splits up into factors it is called **composite**. What's more, you can see that once you have found its *prime* factors it's the *only* way it will split up (apart from the order of the factors, which isn't important).

So a whole number (greater than 1) is either prime or composite and if composite has a unique prime factorisation.

Mathematicians have always found this a rather nice fact – like seeing a difficult pot in a snooker match drop neatly into the pocket!

Multiples

Any number which has 2 as a factor is a multiple of 2.

Numbers on the 3 times table are multiples *of 3*. So 3, 6, 9, 12, 15, 18, ... are all multiples of 3. And so on.

Remember:

*Numbers on the 2 times table are called **multiples** of 2. For example the numbers 2, 4, 6, 8, 10, 12, ... are all multiples of 2.*

Is 29 a multiple of 7? No.
Is 28 a multiple of 7? Yes.
Is 250 a multiple of 5? Yes.
Is 36 a multiple of 3? Yes.
Is 14 a multiple of 6? No.

Exercise 10.12

Write out a list of natural numbers starting 2, 3, 4, 5, ... up to and including 50 and then pick out the following multiples from it. Write them in separate lists. Label the lists M2, M4, M3, etc. so that you can talk about them more easily.

a Multiples of 2
b Multiples of 4
c Multiples of 3
d Multiples of 9
e Multiples of 6
f Multiples of 5
g Multiples of 15

Now examine your lists of multiples and try to see any connections between them. Write a few sentences about any connections you can see. Make other lists of multiples of your own. Investigate!

Exercise 10.13

1 Get several copies of a hundred number square and on one of them colour in all the multiples of 2.
2 On a different copy of a hundred square, colour in the multiples of 3.
3 Using a different square each time, colour in separate multiples of 4, 5, 6 etc. up to (say) 13.
4 Have a close look at the patterns you get.
5 Put two patterns of different multiples on top of each other and hold them up to the light.
   Compare with other patterns of multiples.
   Compare with results from the previous exercise.
   Investigate!

1	2	3	4	5	6	7	8	9	10
11	12	13	14	15	16	17	18	19	20
21	22	23	24	25	26	27	28	29	30
31	32	33	34	35	36	37	38	39	40

SUMMARY

■ Repeated multiplication by the same number is called **raising to a power**.
■ The number of repetitions of the starting number is called the **power** or **index**.
■ The plural of index is **indices**.
■ A number raised to the power 1 is written as the plain number.
■ When one (whole) number divides exactly into another, the first number is called a **factor** of the second.
■ **Prime numbers** have only two factors, the number 1 and the number itself.
■ The number 1 is not a prime number.
■ A number which is not prime is called **composite**.
■ A composite number can be split into powers of **prime factors** in only one way.
■ Numbers on a particular multiplication table are called **multiples**.

Exercise 10A

Write these using index notation.

1 $2 \times 2 \times 2 \times 2$
2 $3 \times 3 \times 3 \times 3$
3 $5 \times 5 \times 5 \times 5$
4 10×10
5 $10 \times 10 \times 10$
6 $10 \times 10 \times 10 \times 10$
7 4×4
8 $4 \times 4 \times 4$
9 7×7
10 17×17

Exercise 10B

Write these out in full then evaluate them.

1 3^7 **4** 6^1 **7** 9^4 **9** 3^{13}

2 5^3 **5** 8^2 **8** 13^3 **10** 10^6

3 15^2 **6** 2^8

Exercise 10C

Finding prime numbers

There is a very well-known way of finding prime numbers.

First get a hundred number square.

We are going to cross out the composite numbers and leave the prime numbers showing, like this:

- cross out 1 (it's not a prime number);
- leave 2 (it is a prime number);
- every second number after 2 is a multiple of 2 so cross out 4, 6, 8, 10, 12, 14, . . . up to 100 (that's half of the numbers gone!);
- leave 3 (it is a prime number);
- every third number after 3 is a multiple of 3 so cross out 6, 9, 12, 15, 18, . . . (some, which are multiples of 2 as well, have been crossed out already);
- notice that all the multiples of 4 have been crossed out;
- leave 5 (it is a prime number);
- cross out the few remaining multiples of 5;
- all the multiples of 6 have gone (why?);
- leave 7 (it is a prime number);
- cross out the few remaining multiples of 7.

Because $11^2 = 121$, and 121 is greater than 100, all the multiples of 11 have been crossed out and you should now have only prime numbers left.

Make a list of the 25 prime numbers less than 100.

> This method of finding prime numbers can be extended as far as you have patience to go, and was the idea of a Greek mathematician called Eratosthenes who lived from 275 BC to 194 BC. Eratosthenes was also an astronomer who worked out a measurement for the circumference of the Earth.

This method is rather like using a garden sieve because you shake out the composite numbers and are left with the primes, so it is called **the sieve of Eratosthenes**.

Exercise 10D

Proof in mathematics

You can learn to tell the time from a clock without ever knowing how it works. But if you take it apart and examine it carefully you can see, step by step, how one part connects to the other, and then perhaps eventually see how everything happens.

'Proof' in mathematics is a bit like that. See if you can follow this imaginary discussion.

Is there a largest prime number?

I met this Greek gentleman, Euclid, the other day who said there was no largest prime number.

Me: I think the largest prime number is 3.

Euclid: That can't be right, because if I work out 2 × 3 + 1 that makes 7, which is a prime number greater than 3.

Me: Oh! Very well, so **7** is the largest prime number.

Euclid: I'm sorry! No good. Work out 2 × 3 × 5 × 7 + 1. That makes 211 which is a new prime number much more than 7.

Me: Oh yes, you're right, but why do all that multiplication? And then add 1 as well?

Euclid: It makes sure I get a number definitely larger than your supposed largest prime number and which can't be divided either by that number or any of the smaller prime numbers.

Me: Yes, I see that now. You will always get a remainder of 1 if you divide 211 by 2 or 3 or 5 or 7, which means it can't be divided exactly by any of these numbers.

Euclid: Yes, including the one you just said was the largest!

Me: But hang on! You couldn't always be sure the number you get after you do your calculation is a new *prime* number. For example, work out 2 × 3 × 5 × 7 × 11 × 13 + 1. That's 30 031 which has factors of 59 and 509, making 30 031 *not* prime.

Euclid: And 59 and 509 are prime themselves. You lose again!

Me: But try 2 × 3 × 5 × 7 × 11 × 13 × 17 + 1 which equals 510 511. Now 510 511 has prime factors 19, 91 and 277 and each of these is more than 17!

Me: This looks as if it's going on for ever! If I think I have the largest prime number, you multiply all the prime numbers together (including this largest) and add one. Either it is a new prime number, so larger than the previous one, or it has a prime factor larger than the one I thought I found!

Euclid: Absolutely! Heads I win, tails you lose!

Me: Very clever. So there is *no* largest prime number. You seem to have thought it through very carefully!

Euclid: I've had long enough [he said, fading out of sight] I lived in the third century BC!!

11 Measuring surface

Area

Paint is used to cover the **surface** of things. Can you think of other materials which are also used to cover surfaces?

But it's not good enough just to think about *covering* a surface. You have to be able to measure it, otherwise you don't know how much paint or other materials to get, nor can you compare different qualities of materials.

Exercise 11.1

1 Make a list of different materials which are used to cover a surface.
2 Try to think of other circumstances where surfaces need to be measured.
3 Can you think of any different jobs where people need to measure surfaces?

It's difficult to think about a surface on its own! You can't take off the top layer of something without it having *some* thickness, however small. Think of a piece of tracing paper.

Even so, surfaces *can* be measured.

One way of protecting a bathroom wall from splashing is to use tiles. The wall above the bath at home looks like this:

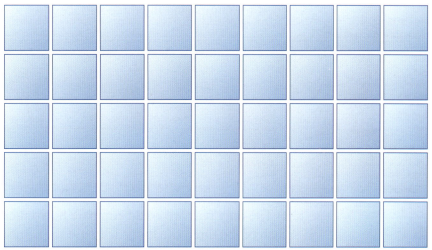

Count the number of tiles needed for this part of the wall.

In the kitchen, we had to replace the floor tiles.
When finished, the floor looked like this:

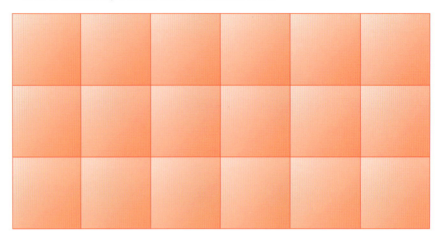

Count the number of tiles needed for this job.
Behind the sink there was a covering of plain and patterned tiles like this:

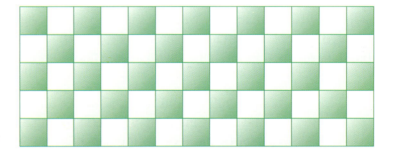

Count the total number of tiles used to cover this surface.

So, we used 45 tiles for the bathroom wall, 18 tiles for the kitchen floor and 65 tiles behind the sink. But why aren't these numbers much good for comparing the three surfaces?

The only way we could compare how much surface is covered in each of the three situations is to use the same size of tile in each case.

Real tiles are made in several different sizes for different purposes, so we *invent a standard tile* which can be used to measure any surface.

This standard tile is a square which measures 1 cm along each edge. It is called 'a one centimetre square' and written:

$$1 \text{ cm}^2$$

But the measure of a surface is also called its **area**.

So the area (in cm²) of a surface is the *number of standard tiles needed to cover that surface* (without overlaps or gaps).

It is important to remember that area can only be measured in square measure:

cm² ← note

never

cm   (which is the measure of the **length** of a line)

The index ² is *absolutely essential*.

Exercise 11.2

On a sheet of centimetre squared paper, draw these shapes full size, shade them in and write down their areas. They are all made from standard tiles.

Remember:

cm² each time

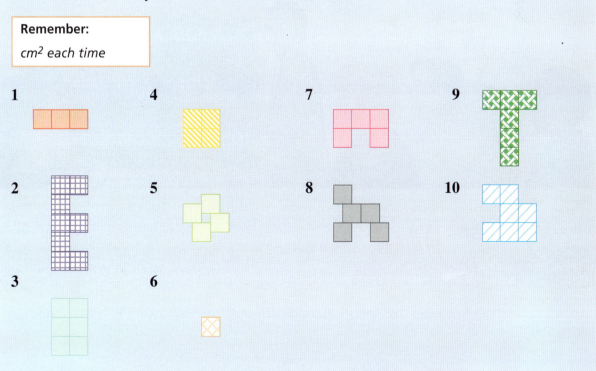

1

4

7

9

2

5

8

10

3

6

Latin *area*:
vacant piece of
level ground

If the shape whose area you are finding is a rectangle, there is a quick way of getting the answer.

Find the area of this rectangle:

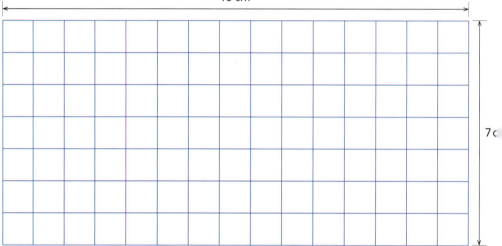

15 cm

7 c

Since there are seven rows of fifteen squares, it is quicker to multiply 15×7 than to count the squares. Work out the answer now yourself.

$15 \times 7 = 105$ so the area is 105 cm^2
'one hundred and five square centimetres'.

Make sure *you* get it right!

105 ✗ WRONG

105cm ✗ WRONG

105cm^2 ✓ CORRECT

Exercise 11.3

Draw these shapes full-size on centimetre squared paper and write down their areas.

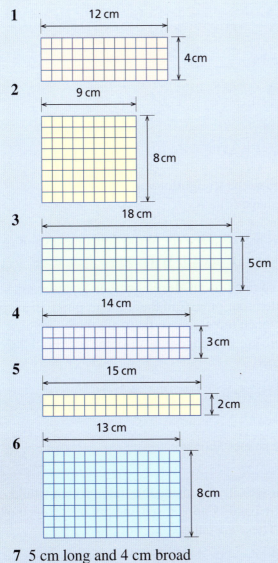

1 12 cm / 4 cm

2 9 cm / 8 cm

3 18 cm / 5 cm

4 14 cm / 3 cm

5 15 cm / 2 cm

6 13 cm / 8 cm

7 5 cm long and 4 cm broad

8 6 cm long and 8 cm broad

9 20 cm high and 3 cm wide

10 19 cm by 5 cm

Irregular shapes

It's easy enough to calculate areas of rectangles. You multiply the number of centimetres in the length by the number of centimetres in the breadth, which is just a short way of counting the squares.

But what about shapes that aren't made exactly of squares? Let's have a first look at the problem.

These shapes are drawn on centimetre dotted paper. Draw them full-size on centimetre squared paper:

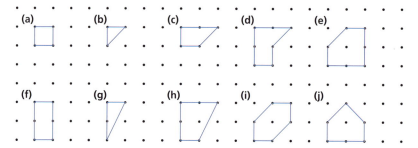

- (a) is easy: the area is 1 cm².
- (b) is half of (a) so the area is $\frac{1}{2}$ cm².
- What is the area of (c)?
- The area of shape (d) should be straightforward too.
- Write down the area of shape (e).
- (f) should be easy.
- Look carefully at (g). It is half of shape (f). Write down the area of (g).
- Look carefully at shapes (h), (i) and (j). Write down their areas.

Look again at shape (a). Imagine it is an elastic band on a pin-board. The elastic band would touch four pins. Call these 'edge-pins'. In shape (b) the elastic band would touch three pins so there are three 'edge-pins'. Can you see that there are five edge-pins in shape (c)? Find the seven edge-pins in shape (d).

Exercise 11.4

Make a note of the number of edge-pins in all the shapes above.

Look at shape (e). Can you see one pin inside the shape which would not be touched by the elastic band? Can you see one pin inside each of the shapes (h), (i) and (j)? These are called 'interior pins'.

Exercise 11.5

Make a chart with the following headings and complete it:

If you can't see a connection yet, do the next exercise.

edge-pins	interior pins	area (cm²)

Investigate the connection between the edge-pins, interior pins and the area of these shapes.

Exercise 11.6

First investigate shapes which have no interior pins. Here are a few suggested shapes:

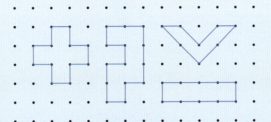

Invent others of your own. Then draw shapes with only one interior pin, like these:

If you still can't find the connection – ask your teacher for another hint!

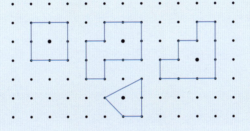

Invent more of your own. Then draw shapes with only two interior pins; then three, etc. Make a new chart each time with the same headings.

More irregular shapes

If you needed to find the area of a leaf, which is important when studying the growth of plants, the only way would be to spread the leaf out on centimetre squared paper and count the number of squares it covers.

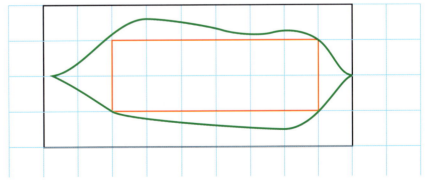

This is not easy to do since you would have to estimate the area of bits of squares. In order not to give a really silly answer, you could find the area of the largest rectangle which fits inside the leaf and the smallest rectangle which fits outside the leaf.

Do this for the leaf illustrated above.

Give a closer estimate for the area of the leaf.

Exercise 11.7

Collect some real leaves and estimate their areas.

Exercise 11.8

Estimate the areas of the following shapes. First draw a rectangle inside and outside the shape.

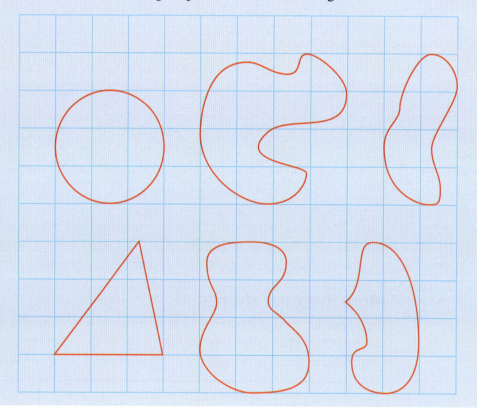

SUMMARY

- ■ You need to be able to compare the surfaces of things for practical reasons.
- ■ The measure of a surface is called its **area**.
- ■ In order to compare surfaces you need a standard unit.
- ■ A good unit for measuring area is the cm^2.
- ■ You must be careful to measure area in 'squared' units.
- ■ To find the area of a rectangle in cm^2, multiply the number of centimetres in the length by the number of centimetres in the breadth.
- ■ To find the area of irregular shapes, you sometimes have to draw them on centimetre squared paper and count squares.

Exercise 11A

Draw these shapes full-size on centimetre squared paper, shade them in and write down their areas.

1

2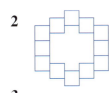

3

4

5

6

7

8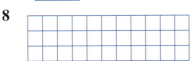

9

10

Exercise 11B

Calculate the areas of these shapes.

1

2

3

4 4 cm

4 cm

5 6 cm

6 cm

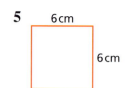

6 A rectangle, 12 cm long and 7 cm broad
7 A square, 7 cm long and 7 cm broad
8 A square of side 17 cm
9 A rectangle, 2 cm wide and 3.5 cm high
10 A rectangle, 5 m long and 3 m broad (Be careful about the units.)

Exercise 11C

Find the areas of these shapes, giving your answers in numbers of squares.

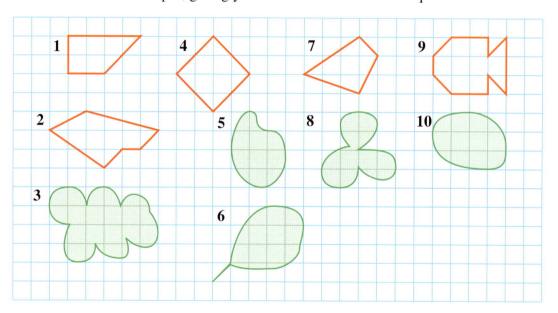

Exercise 11D

Look at this group of equilateral triangles:

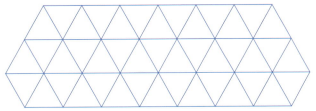

    Get some paper which is ruled out like this. It is sometimes called 'isometric' paper.
    Look at this rectangle drawn on the isometric paper. Count the number of equilateral triangles which fill this rectangle.

    You can see that the area of the rectangle could be described using equilateral triangles. We would have to invent a new measurement for the area of one equilateral triangle, say 'an arequil'. So I would then say the area of the rectangle is '12 arequils'!

1 Draw some shapes of your own invention on isometric paper and ask a friend to write down their areas in 'arequils'. Or you could even invent your own units!

2 Write a few sentences to say why it wouldn't be such a good idea actually to measure area using equilateral triangles.

3 Try to think of shapes other than squares or equilateral triangles which could be used as a unit of area. Invent names for them. Draw some shapes of your own and ask someone else to find their areas in terms of these new units.

4 In the building trade, people used to measure area in terms of the 'foot super'. Look up the word 'superficial' and explain why using the words 'foot super' is a good way of describing area.

5 Get some squared paper *ruled in millimetres*, draw some *simple* shapes on it *using centimetres* and write down their areas in both cm^2 and mm^2.

12 Measuring turning

There are a very large number of situations where, to get something done, an object needs to be **turned**.

Exercise 12.1

Make your own list of situations where something turns. Compare your list with those of others in the class.

There are some situations where the *amount* of turn isn't important. If you were filling a kettle with water, for example, you only need to know that the tap needs to be turned, but a rambler or orienteer following a map in the country needs to know *exactly* in which direction to turn when going on a walk.

Exercise 12.2

Choose one pupil in the class to stand up, face the front and then to turn all the way round (ending up facing the front again!)

*The pupil has moved through **one complete turn**.*
Ask them now to turn so they face the back wall.
*The pupil has moved through **half a turn**.*

Starting from facing the front again, what directions would you give so that the pupil ends up facing the left-hand wall?

Angles

An amount of turn is called an **angle**.

Many watches have a 'seconds' hand. In one minute it moves through a complete turn. In half-a-minute (30 seconds) it moves through half a turn.

In how many seconds does it move through a quarter-turn?

When people in ancient times settled to an agricultural life they needed to be able to predict when the seasons were due. By observing the moon and the stars and the changing lengths of shadows, it was gradually realised that a year was approximately 360 days.

So it became useful to divide a complete turn into 360 parts, one for each day, and this is the reason why we still divide one complete turn into 360 degrees.

Exercise 12.3

Write down the number of degrees in the following fractions of a complete turn.

Degrees are usually written using the degrees sign °.

1 One whole turn
2 Half a turn
3 Quarter of a turn
4 Three quarters of a turn
5 A third of a turn
6 Two thirds of a turn
7 A sixth of a turn
8 A twelfth of a turn
9 A tenth of a turn
10 One fifth of a turn

Attach two strips of cardboard or plastic together with a paper-fastener near one end, like the hands of a clock.

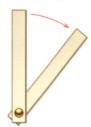

Arrange one strip to be vertical and rotate the other in a clockwise direction as shown in the diagram.

Exercise 12.4

Using your joined strips, and keeping one strip vertical, rotate the other strip (approximately) through the fractions of turns in the last exercise. Work in pairs, checking each other's answers.

Did you have any problems checking the answers?

If the lines used to draw the angles on the answer sheet are not the same lengths as your strips, it's awkward to compare them.

Equal angles

Try to guess by eye which of these two angles is the bigger:

Did you guess correctly?

They are equal: *both* are the same number of degrees.

Some people think that, if the lines used to draw an angle are made longer, then the angle gets bigger. Just to make sure that this isn't true, trace one of the angles above and place the tracing over the other angle.

Describing angles

The lines used to draw an angle are called the **arms** of the angle

and the point of the angle, where the two arms meet, is called the **vertex**.

Latin *vertere*: turn

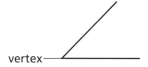

There is no need to make both arms of an angle the same length.

● *In drawing angles, what is important is the amount of turn to move from one arm to the other:*

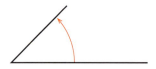

Exercise 12.5

Try to guess which, if any, of the following angles are equal to each other.

1 **2** **3** **4**

Check by tracing.

Measuring angles

'Protractor' may come from the Latin *trahere*: to draw.

There are several instruments which can be used to measure angles. But the most accurate (and the cheapest!) is the **protractor**.

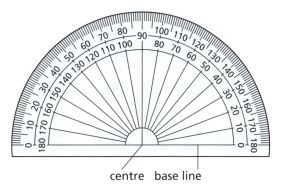

centre base line

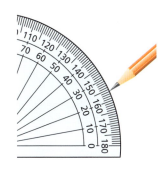

Measuring angles accurately is not an easy thing to do.

One problem is that a single degree is a very small quantity. So you need a very sharp pencil and you need to look very carefully.

Another problem is that you need to be very precise in measuring from the centre of the protractor; make sure it is exactly over the vertex of the angle.

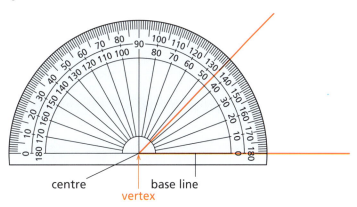

centre base line

vertex

A third problem is to know which of the two sets of figures round the edges of the protractor is the one to use; the *outside* set measures *clockwise* angles and the *inside* set measures *anti-clockwise* angles.

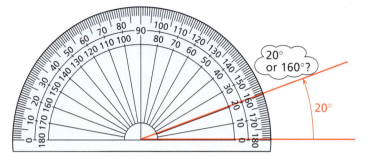

A fourth problem can be to confuse the **base line** of the protractor with the edge of the extra piece of plastic at the *bottom* of some protractors.

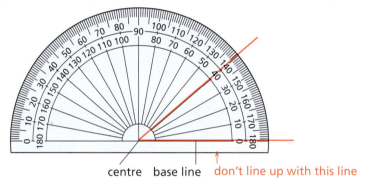

A fifth problem can arise if the arms of the angle being measured don't reach the edge of the protractor.

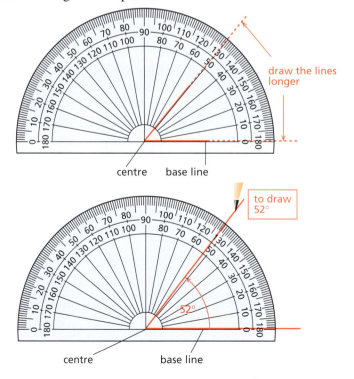

Exercise 12.6

Use your protractor to measure these angles.

1 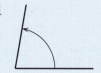 4   7   9

2   5   8   10

3   6

Exercise 12.7

Draw these angles in a *clockwise* direction, starting from any line drawn on your book.
Make sure you leave enough space for each one!

1 50°	**3** 30°	**5** 10°	**7** 60°	**9** 20°
2 70°	**4** 25°	**6** 45°	**8** 80°	**10** 90°

Exercise 12.8

Draw the same angles as the last exercise but in an *anti-clockwise* direction.

Types of angle

Because a complete turn is such a big movement, it is convenient to describe angles in relation to *parts* of a complete turn, such as a quarter-turn or half-turn.

The first of these to note is a quarter-turn, *an angle of 90°*, which is called a **right-angle**, since it is in a sense 'correct' or 'exact' (there's no such thing as a 'left-angle'!). Look round the room and notice the number of right-angles you can see.

Latin *acus*: needle
Latin *obtusus*: blunt

- Angles *less* than a right-angle are called **acute**.
- Angles *more* than a right-angle, but less than 180° (a half-turn), are called **obtuse**.
- Angles *greater than 180°* are called **reflex**.

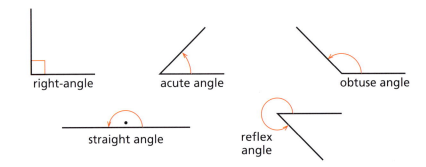

right-angle   acute angle   obtuse angle

straight angle   reflex angle

An angle of 180° is sometimes called a straight angle. Why?

Exercise 12.9

Classify these angles using the words acute, obtuse, right, straight and reflex.

1 120°	**3** 180°	**5** 91°	**7** 90°	**9** 270°
2 37°	**4** 236°	**6** 89°	**8** 10°	**10** 360°

Drawing and measuring reflex angles

The simplest way to draw a reflex angle is to use a 360° protractor.

But, if you don't have a 360° protractor, either draw a straight line and add on the difference from 180° to the angle; or subtract the reflex angle from 360°, draw this angle and note the remaining part.

For instance, to draw 200°, either take 180° from 200° (20°) and add this on to a straight line; or work out 360° − 200° (160°), draw this and note the angle 'left over'.

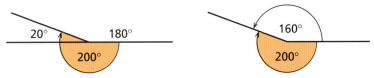

20°   180°   200°   160°   200°

Exercise 12.10

Draw these angles.

1 300°   **2** 260°   **3** 190°   **4** 200°   **5** 320°

Exercise 12.11

Measure these angles.

1    2   3   4 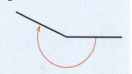   5

Make sure your pencil is sharp.

Exercise 12.12

Draw these angles carefully in a clockwise direction.

1 68°   **3** 53°   **5** 185°   **7** 236°   **9** 77°
2 37°   **4** 120°   **6** 46°   **8** 100°   **10** 321°

Exercise 12.13

Measure these angles to the nearest degree.

1   4   7   9

2   5    8   10

3    6

Calculating with angles

Sometimes you can work out the size of an angle without measuring.

Get a long strip of card or plastic and a shorter strip. Fasten the shorter strip to the middle of the longer one with a paper-fastener.

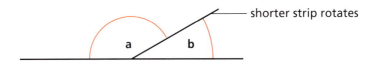

shorter strip rotates

Rotate the shorter strip slowly, watching the angles marked **a** and **b** in the diagram.

Because the longer strip is kept still, as the shorter strip is moved, the angles **a** and **b** will always add up to a straight angle or 180°.

● *When the sum of two angles is 180°, the angles are called* **supplementary**. *Each is the* **supplement** *of the other.*

For instance:

- the supplement of 80° is 100°,
- the supplement of 30° is 150°,
- the supplement of 28° is 152°,
- the supplement of 140° is 40°.

Are 123° and 57° supplementary? Yes, since 123 + 57 = 180.
Are 132° and 49° supplementary? No, since 132 + 49 = 181.

Exercise 12.14

Calculate the missing angles. The diagrams are *not* drawn to the correct size.

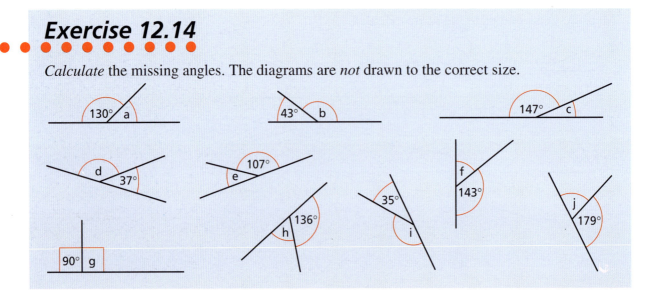

Opposite angles

Fasten two strips of card or plastic together at their centres with a paper-fastener.

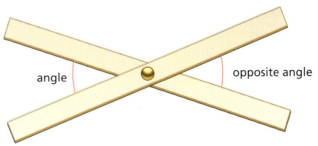

Rotate the strips slowly, watching how the opposite pair of angles made by the strips change.

Exercise 12.15

Place your strips flat on the desk and measure with a protractor the pair of opposite angles between the strips.

Do this for five different positions (it's difficult to do accurately because of the thickness of the strips).

Record the results in a table.

angle	opposite angle

Can you come to any conclusion about these pairs of angles?

If you have measured accurately, your results should suggest that opposite angles are equal. Now let's test this by calculating.

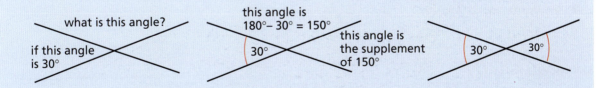

Repeat these calculations for an angle of 20°.

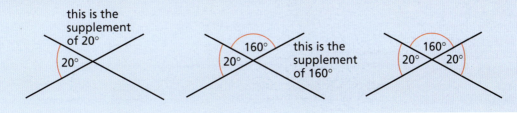

Exercise 12.16

Calculate the opposite angles in each diagram using supplements. (Not drawn as correct size.)

1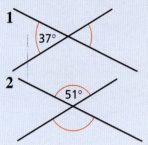

3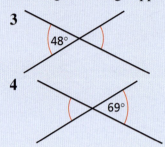

5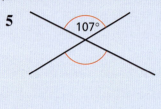

2

4

You can see that this calculation would work whatever angle you started with, so we conclude that:

● *If two straight lines cross, the opposite angles so formed are always equal.*

What we have called 'opposite angles' are usually called **vertically opposite** angles because they are 'opposite at a vertex'.
So we should really say:

● *When two straight lines cross, the vertically opposite angles so formed are equal.*

Exercise 12.17

Use your knowledge of supplementary and vertically opposite angles to *calculate* the lettered angles in the following diagrams.

1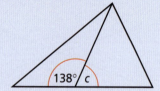

2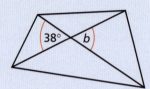

3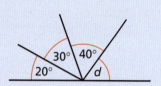

4 Explain why the points *A*, *B* and *C* in the diagram below must be in a straight line if the diagram were drawn accurately. Find angle *e*.

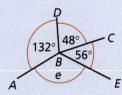

SUMMARY

- To get from one position to another, an object sometimes needs to be turned.
- It is often important to measure the amount of turn.
- An amount of turn is called an **angle**.
- It was once thought that a year was 360 days, so a complete turn was divided into 360°.
- The lines used to draw an angle are called its **arms**, and where the arms meet is called its **vertex**.
- The size of an angle does not depend on the length of its arms.
- Angles are drawn and measured using a **protractor**.
- An **acute** angle is less than 90°.
  A **right-angle** is equal to 90°.
  An **obtuse** angle is between 90° and 180°.
  A **reflex** angle is more than 180°.
- **Supplementary** angles add to 180°.
- If two straight lines cross, the **vertically opposite** angles so formed are equal.

Exercise 12A

1 Write down the number of degrees in one ninth of a complete turn.
2 Sketch an angle and mark its vertex.
3 Sketch a protractor and indicate its base line.
4 Write down whether these angles are acute, right, obtuse, straight or reflex:
  a 100°
  b 230°
  c 30°
  d 180°
  e 90°
5 Draw and mark an angle of 35°.
6 Draw and mark an angle of 310°.
7 Draw and mark an angle of 73°.
8 Measure this angle.

9 Measure this angle.

10 Measure this angle.

Exercise 12B

1 Write down the number of degrees in one eighth of a complete turn.
2 Sketch an angle and mark in its arms.
3 Sketch a protractor and indicate its centre.
4 Write down whether these angles are acute, right, obtuse, straight or reflex:
  a 132°
  b 213°
  c 13°
  d 31°
  e 231°
5 Draw and mark an angle of 43°.
6 Draw and mark an angle of 85°.
7 Draw and mark an angle of 135°.
8 Measure this angle.

9 Measure this angle.

10 Measure this angle.

Exercise 12C

1 Write down the supplementary angle to 30°.
2 Write down the supplementary angle to 98°.
3 Write down the supplementary angle to 153°.
4 Calculate angle a in this diagram.

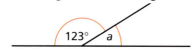

5 Calculate angles p and q in this diagram.

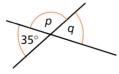

6 Calculate angles *r* and *s* in this diagram.

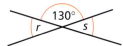

7 Calculate angles *u* and *v* in this diagram.

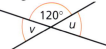

8 Calculate angle *x* in this diagram.

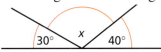

9 Calculate angle *y* in this diagram.

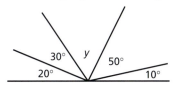

10 If this diagram were drawn accurately, which line would be straight?

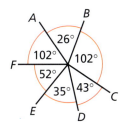

Exercise 12D

1 If a reflex angle is subtracted from 360° is the answer always obtuse? Investigate and explain!

2 Draw any triangle and measure its separate angles. Add your three answers together. Repeat for several other triangles. Comment.

3 Repeat question 2 for a quadrilateral.

13 Counting in tenths

This line is 1 cm long. ▬ Check with a ruler.
This line is 2 cm long. ▬▬ Check again.
But this line is *between* 1 and 2 cm long. ▬▬

To measure a line which is not an exact number of centimetres, we break each centimetre into ten equal parts and call the new divisions millimetres (mm).

Measure the last line. It is 1 cm and 7 mm long.

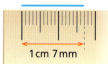

1 cm 7 mm

Since the second centimetre has been broken into ten equal parts, each part could be written as $\frac{1}{10}$ cm.

So 1 mm is equal to $\frac{1}{10}$ cm, and 7 mm can be written as $\frac{7}{10}$ cm.
The length of the line can now be written as $1\frac{7}{10}$ cm.
Check that the next line measures $1\frac{4}{10}$ cm. ▬

Remember chapter 8!

Exercise 13.1

Measure these lines using centimetres and **tenths** of a centimetre.

1 ▬▬▬▬
2 ▬▬▬▬▬
3 ▬▬▬▬
4 ▬
5 ▬▬

Exercise 13.2

Draw lines in your exercise book of the following lengths using centimetres and tenths of a centimetre. Then change books with a partner and check each other's measurements.

1 $3\frac{2}{10}$ 2 $4\frac{1}{10}$ 3 $6\frac{9}{10}$ 4 $5\frac{4}{10}$ 5 $7\frac{7}{10}$

From common fractions to decimal fractions

The 'unit' we are using for measuring these lines is the centimetre.

As above, to measure 'bits' of a centimetre we break the unit into ten equal parts – tenths of a centimetre – and call each tenth a millimetre (mm).

So the lines in exercise 13.2 could be written

3 cm 2 mm,   4 cm 1 mm,   6 cm 9 mm,   5 cm 4 mm,   7 cm 7 mm

These lengths can also be written

3.2 cm,   4.1 cm,   6.9 cm,   5.4 cm,   7.7 cm

where the dot (or **decimal point**) is used to separate the centimetre and millimetre (tenths of a centimetre).

So 3.2 is really another way of writing $3\frac{2}{10}$,
4.1 is another way of writing $4\frac{1}{10}$,
6.9 another way of writing $6\frac{9}{10}$, etc.

Latin *decimus*:
tenth

- A number written as $3\frac{2}{10}$ is a mixed number involving a **common fraction**.
- A number written with a decimal point (a dot) as 3.2 is a **decimal fraction**.

When a number is less than a unit, always put a **zero** before the decimal point to show there is no 'units' figure. For example, $\frac{9}{10}$ is written as 0.9.

$$\frac{9}{10} = 0.9$$

fraction less   always put a zero if
than 1   fraction is less than 1

Exercise 13.3

Write these as decimal fractions.

1 $\frac{6}{10}$	**3** $1\frac{1}{10}$	**5** $\frac{2}{10}$	**7** $3\frac{9}{10}$	**9** $5\frac{4}{10}$
2 $2\frac{3}{10}$	**4** $\frac{8}{10}$	**6** $\frac{5}{10}$	**8** $\frac{7}{10}$	**10** $\frac{10}{10}$

Exercise 13.4

Write these as common fractions, using mixed numbers where necessary.

1 1.1	**3** 2.3	**5** 7.5	**7** 6.8	**9** 8.6
2 3.2	**4** 0.7	**6** 0.9	**8** 0.4	**10** 10.1

Decimals and place value

1 a Enter the number '23' into the display of your calculator.
 b Multiply by 10 and press =.
 c Multiply by 10 again (and press =).

Notice that the '23' moves one position to the left each time you multiply by ten

		2	3	
	2	3		
2	3			

empty places
are filled
by zeros

		2	3	
	2	3	0	
2	3	0	0	

2 a Keep '2300' on the display and **divide** by 10.
 b Divide by 10 again.

Notice how the '23' moves one position to the *right* each time you *divide* by 10.

3 a Keep the '23' where it is and divide by 10 again.
 b Observe the result.

2	3	0	0		
	2	3	0		
		2	3		
			2 • 3		

the '3' represents three hundreds

the '3' represents three tens

the '3' represents three units

what does *this* '3' represent?

Since each move to the right *divides* by 10, the 3 in the last row represents three *tenths*.

Note that when you do this on the calculator, a dot appears between the '2' and the '3' for the last division.

This dot is the decimal point again.

So all approaches lead to the same labelling of the columns:

• the decimal point separates units and tenths,
• moving to the right, each position becomes one tenth of the value of the previous position.

			TENS	UNITS	•	tenths	
(a)				6			
(b)						6	
(c)			6				

this '6' represents 6 *units*

this '6' represents 6 *tenths*

this '6' represents 6 *tens*

But if you don't use this **decimal grid**, you must put zeros or decimal points (or both) to make the size (value) of the number clear.

So (a) is written as '6', (b) is written as '0.6' and (c) is written as '60'.

WARNING. It is sometimes convenient to write '6' as '6.0' or even '6.00' (for example, when adding decimals). It still means 'six **units**'.

Exercise 13.5

Copy the following decimal grid into your exercise book.

			TENS	UNITS • tenths	
				•	
				•	
				•	
				•	
				•	

Put these numbers in their correct places on the decimal grid.

1 0.7

2 7.0

3 7.7

4 70

5 70.7

Write these numbers as decimal fractions without the decimal grid.

			TENS	UNITS • tenths	
6			4	•	
7				• 4	
8			4 •		
9			4	• 4	
10			4 • 4		

Order with decimal numbers

On a **number line**, decimals get bigger moving from left to right.

So, for example, 2 is greater than 0.2; 2.3 is less than 3.2; 2.3 is greater than 0.8.

To write the numbers

$$2, \quad 0.8, \quad 3.2, \quad 0.2, \quad 2.3$$

in order of size with the least first, you follow the order on the number line, left to right. The correct order for these numbers then becomes:

$$0.2, \quad 0.8, \quad 2, \quad 2.3, \quad 3.2$$

Exercise 13.6

Sort the following sets of numbers into **ascending order**.
Illustrate your answers to questions 1, 4 and 7 on a decimal number line.

1 1, 0.7, 0.9, 0.3, 0.5, 0.2, 0.4, 0.1
2 2.7, 2.5, 2.6, 2.9, 2.8
3 4.1, 2.1, 5.1, 3.1, 1.1
4 10, 1, 11.1, 11, 1.1, 0.1, 10.1
5 9.2, 2.9, 29, 92, 9, 2, 90, 90.2, 20.9
6 50, 0.5, 55, 5.5, 55.5, 5, 50.5
7 5, 0.3, 13, 1.5, 0.8, 5.1, 0.5, 3.5, 3, 15.1
8 7.5, 5.7, 1.4, 14, 4.1, 0.7, 3.6, 6, 6.3, 41, 0.2
9 27.8, 87, 28.7, 78, 78.2, 20.8, 70.2
10 46, 6.4, 4.6, 60.4, 40.6, 46.4, 64, 46.6, 66.4, 60.6

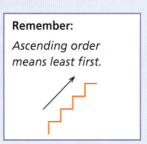

Remember:

Ascending order means least first.

WARNING. A dot between numbers doesn't *always* mean a decimal point!

Hundredths

Everyone is used to writing amounts of money in pounds and pence. For example, £2.35 means 'two pounds and thirty-five pence'. Here the dot *is* a decimal point.

What does £2.50 mean? No problem – it stands for 'two pounds and *fifty* pence'.

But how about £2.05? This is different – it means 'two pounds and *five* pence'.

If I owed you £2.50 and offered you £2.05 you would soon complain!

The '5' at the end of the number means 'five *pence*' and, since *there are one hundred pence in a pound*, this '5' means 'five **hundredths** of a pound'. This could be written using common fractions as $£\frac{5}{100}$.

Or we could write £2.05 as $£2\frac{5}{100}$.

This must mean that $0.05 = \frac{5}{100}$. So how could this be written on a decimal grid?

	HUNDREDS	TENS	UNITS	•	tenths	hundredths	
				•		5	this '5' represents 0.05
			£2	•	5	0	this is 'two pounds fifty'
			£2	•	0	5	this is 'two pounds five'

● *The first position to the right of the decimal point represents **tenths** and the second position to the right of the decimal point represents **hundredths**.*

  So $\quad 0.5 = \frac{5}{10} \quad 0.05 = \frac{5}{100}$

  Notice this fits with dividing by 10 since a digit moves one more place to the right.

Exercise 13.7

Write the numbers in this decimal grid as decimal fractions without using the grid. Make sure you put in all the necessary zeros.

	HUNDREDS	TENS	UNITS	•	tenths	hundredths	
1				•	3		
2			3	•			
3				•		3	

	HUNDREDS	TENS	UNITS	•	tenths	hundredths
4			3	•		
5	3			•		
6		3		•	3	
7		3		•		3
8	3		3	•		3
9	3		3	•	3	
10	3			•		3

Exercise 13.8

Use the same decimal grid from exercise 13.7 to write the numbers as common fractions, using mixed numbers where necessary.

Exercise 13.9

Draw a decimal grid like the one above and write the following on it in the correct places.

1 $12\frac{7}{100}$ **3** $20\frac{6}{100}$ **5** $6\frac{2}{100}$ **7** $10\frac{1}{10}$ **9** $101\frac{1}{10}$

2 $2\frac{7}{10}$ **4** $2\frac{6}{10}$ **6** $10\frac{1}{100}$ **8** $101\frac{1}{100}$ **10** $100\frac{1}{10}$

Exercise 13.10

Write these as decimals. There is no need to use a decimal grid.

1 $\frac{9}{100}$ **3** $\frac{3}{10}$ **5** $4\frac{8}{100}$ **7** $48\frac{8}{100}$ **9** $700\frac{7}{100}$

2 $\frac{9}{10}$ **4** $\frac{3}{100}$ **6** $8\frac{4}{100}$ **8** $48\frac{8}{10}$ **10** $700\frac{7}{10}$

Exercise 13.11

Write these as fractions, using mixed numbers where necessary.

1 0.01	**3** 10.01	**5** 10.1	**7** 20.02	**9** 22.2
2 0.05	**4** 2.09	**6** 20.2	**8** 22.02	**10** 202.02

Remember:

Fractions are obtained by breaking up some unit into equal parts.

Decimal order with hundredths

It's not very practical to measure one hundredth ($\frac{1}{100}$) of a centimetre because it's so small. But, if you start with a larger unit, hundredths become quite manageable.

Imagine a metre rule . . .

Exercise 13.12

1 What measurement is the same as 0.01 of a *metre*?
2 What measurement is the same as 0.1 of a metre?

1 could be written
1.0
1.00
0 could be written
0.0
0.00

Put these numbers into ascending numerical order.

3, 0.03, 0.3, 3.3, 3.03, 3.33

Answer: 0.03, 0.3, 3, 3.03, 3.3, 3.33

Exercise 13.13

Sort these sets of numbers into ascending numerical order.

1 0.01, 1, 0.02, 2, 1.01, 1.2, 1.02
2 2.7, 2.37, 2.73, 2.08, 2.18
3 23.32, 20.32, 32.32, 32.23, 30.03, 23.02
4 0.63, 0.06, 0.72, 0.09, 0.53, 0.84, 0.45
5 1.10, 1.11, 1.01, 0.01, 0.10
6 123.62, 103.62, 120.62, 101.26, 100.06, 100.02
7 107.4, 104.7, 170.04, 17, 170, 104.07, 117.17, 14.07, 14.7
8 Draw a line numbered 0, 1, 2, spreading out the numbers as shown.

0	1	2

Indicate roughly, by vertical arrows (↑), where the decimals in question 1 would come on this number line.

9 Draw a line numbered every 0.1 as shown

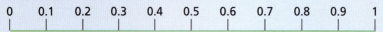

Represent the numbers from question 4 on this line.

10 Draw a line numbered every 0.1 from 0 to 1.2 as shown.

0   0.1   0.2   0.3   0.4   0.5   0.6   0.7   0.8   0.9   1.0   1.1

Represent the numbers in question 5 by arrows on this line.

Thousandths

Tenths are smaller than units.

Hundredths are smaller than tenths.

And we can go on breaking the unit into smaller and smaller parts. The next smaller division after hundredths would be **thousandths**.

Look at a metre rule again. There are *ten* millimetres in one centimetre and a *hundred* centimetres in one metre. So there are a *thousand* millimetres in one metre.

How would this be represented on a decimal grid? It's the next position to the right after hundredths.

Putting all this together means that 1 millimetre could be written as 0.001 of a metre.

And 0.001 is the same as $\frac{1}{1000}$.

$$0.1 \quad = \frac{1}{10}$$
$$0.01 \quad = \frac{1}{100}$$
$$0.001 = \frac{1}{1000}$$

Also

$$0.3 \quad = \frac{3}{10}$$
$$0.03 \quad = \frac{3}{100}$$
$$0.003 = \frac{3}{1000}$$

What about 0.13?

0.13
one three
tenth hundredths

This is one tenth and three hundredths or

$$\frac{1}{10} + \frac{3}{100} = \frac{10}{100} + \frac{3}{100}$$
$$= \frac{13}{100}$$

So

$$0.13 = \frac{13}{100}$$

In the same way, for example,

$$0.47 = \frac{47}{100}$$
$$0.93 = \frac{93}{100}$$
$$0.41 = \frac{41}{100}$$
$$\frac{23}{100} = 0.23$$
$$\frac{37}{100} = 0.37$$

You should be able to work out yourself how this extends to thousandths.

Exercise 13.14

Write these decimal fractions as common fractions.

1 0.51	**4** 0.163	**7** 0.453	**9** 0.81
2 0.63	**5** 0.9	**8** 0.081	**10** 0.009
3 0.063	**6** 0.89		

Exercise 13.15

Write these common fractions as decimal fractions.

1 $\frac{17}{100}$	**4** $\frac{9}{100}$	**7** $\frac{99}{1000}$	**9** $\frac{27}{100}$
2 $\frac{31}{100}$	**5** $\frac{9}{1000}$	**8** $\frac{27}{1000}$	**10** $\frac{327}{1000}$
3 $\frac{9}{10}$	**6** $\frac{99}{100}$		

Other ways to change fractions to decimals

Decimal fractions are common fractions with **powers of 10 in the denominators**. So the problem arises of writing common fractions as decimal fractions when the common fraction *doesn't* have a power of 10 in the denominator.

Write $\frac{2}{5}$ as a decimal fraction.

The problem here is that the denominator of 5 is not a power of ten. But it's an easy one to overcome since $10 = 5 \times 2$.

So write

$$\frac{2}{5} = \frac{2 \times 2}{5 \times 2} = \frac{4}{10} = 0.4$$

Write $\frac{1}{5}$ as a decimal fraction.

Answer: $\dfrac{1}{5} = \dfrac{1 \times 2}{5 \times 2} = \dfrac{2}{10} = 0.2$

What if the original denominator is not a factor of ten? You could then try using a denominator of a hundred.

Write $\frac{3}{4}$ as a decimal fraction.

Notice that $100 = 4 \times 25$, so

$$\frac{3}{4} = \frac{3 \times 25}{4 \times 25} = \frac{75}{100} = 0.75$$

Exercise 13.16

Write these common fractions as decimal fractions.

1 $\frac{3}{5}$ **2** $\frac{4}{5}$ **3** $\frac{1}{4}$ **4** $\frac{3}{25}$ **5** $\frac{1}{2}$

Notice that, since $\frac{2}{5} = 2 \div 5$, there is another way of changing the fraction to a decimal. We could first write 2 as $\frac{20}{10}$ and then say:

'twenty tenths broken into five equal parts is four tenths and that's written as 0.4'

This is usually written out like this, first writing 2 as 2.0:

$$5\overline{)2.0}^{\,0.4}$$

> 5 doesn't divide into 2 so put a zero above 2 in the answer; 5 divided into 20 is 4, but that's actually 4 tenths: answer 0.4.

Try $\frac{1}{5}$ in the same way:

$$5\overline{)1.0}^{\,0.2}$$

> 5 doesn't divide into 1 so put a zero in the answer; 5 divided into 10 is 2, but that's actually 2 tenths: answer 0.2.

Consider $\frac{3}{4}$:

$$4\overline{)3.00}^{\,0.75}$$

> 4 doesn't divide into 3 so put zero in the answer; 4 divided into 30 is 7 but that's actually 7 tenths; the 2 remaining is 20 hundredths; 4 divided into 20 hundredths is 5 hundredths exactly: answer 0.75.

Exercise 13.17

Do exercise 13.16 again but as division sums.

- *To change a common fraction to a decimal fraction, **divide the denominator into the numerator**, keeping all the figures in their correct places.*

Sometimes you need to go three (or more) places before the process stops.

Change $\frac{3}{8}$ to a decimal fraction.

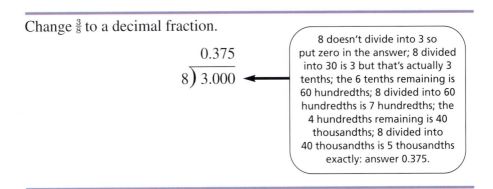

$$8 \overline{\smash{)}\, 3.000} \quad \begin{array}{c} 0.375 \end{array}$$

> 8 doesn't divide into 3 so put zero in the answer; 8 divided into 30 is 3 but that's actually 3 tenths; the 6 tenths remaining is 60 hundredths; 8 divided into 60 hundredths is 7 hundredths; the 4 hundredths remaining is 40 thousandths; 8 divided into 40 thousandths is 5 thousandths exactly: answer 0.375.

If you can't remember the remainders then set the working out like a 'long' division sum.

Exercise 13.18

Change these common fractions to decimal fractions by division.

1 $\frac{5}{8}$ **2** $\frac{1}{8}$ **3** $\frac{6}{25}$ **4** $\frac{7}{40}$ **5** $\frac{7}{8}$

The description of how to do the division is of course an explanation; when you actually do it, it's much shorter!

Using a calculator

Some of you will have already discovered that you can change common fractions to decimal fractions very easily on the calculator: just divide the numerator by the denominator directly and press '='.

But you shouldn't do this until you understand what's going on! Ask your teacher.

You can also change a decimal fraction to a common fraction very easily if you have a fraction button.

Change 0.225 to a common fraction.

You first have to realise that $0.225 = \frac{225}{1000}$; then enter 225 in the display; press the fraction button; enter 1000; press '='; the answer is $\frac{9}{40}$.
   Otherwise you have to realise that

$$\frac{225}{1000} = \frac{25 \times 9}{25 \times 40} = \frac{9}{40}$$

which is the same thing but you need to know your multiplication tables very well!

Ask your teacher which you should do.

Exercise 13.19

Change these decimal fractions to common fractions, giving the answer in its lowest terms.

1 0.12   **2** 0.175   **3** 0.02   **4** 0.325   **5** 0.22

SUMMARY

- Lines which are not an exact number of centimetres can be measured with the help of millimetres.
- One millimetre is a tenth of a centimetre which can also be written as '0.1 of a centimetre'.
- A number written as $4\frac{1}{10}$ involves a **common fraction**.
- When a dot is used to separate *units* and *tenths of a unit*, it is called a **decimal point**.
- If you keep on dividing a number by 10, it appears to move one position to the right on each division, including past the decimal point.
- **Decimal fractions** can be represented on a **decimal grid**.
- If a decimal fraction is *less than* 1, put a zero in the units place.
- The *first* position to the right of the decimal point represents **tenths**, the *second* position represents **hundredths**, and the *third* position represents **thousandths**.
- Decimal fractions can be represented on a **number line**.
- Common fractions and decimal fractions can be changed into each other.

Exercise 13A

1 Draw a line of length 3.4 cm, exchange with a partner and check the line.
2 Draw a line of length $4\frac{3}{10}$ cm, exchange with a partner and check the line.
3 Write 9.07 on a decimal grid.

4 Draw a decimal grid and use arrows to illustrate on it that 38×10 is 380.

5 Draw a decimal grid and use arrows to illustrate that $38 \div 10 = 3.8$.

6 Write these decimal numbers as fractions, using mixed numbers where necessary.

    a 8.88

    b 0.08

    c 8.08

    d 80.8

    e 80.08

7 Write these mixed numbers using decimals.

    a $9\frac{9}{100}$

    b $90\frac{9}{100}$

    c $90\frac{9}{10}$

    d $\frac{9}{100}$

    e $9\frac{9}{10}$

8 Change these common fractions to decimal numbers without using a calculator.

    a $\frac{1}{5}$

    b $\frac{1}{50}$

    c $\frac{9}{25}$

    d $\frac{1}{2}$

    e $\frac{3}{4}$

9 Change these decimal numbers to common fractions in their lowest terms.

    a 0.25

    b 0.33

    c 0.625

    d 0.425

    e 0.375

10 Sort these numbers into ascending numerical order. Illustrate on a number line.
1.3, 0.4, 1.4, 0.48, 1.01, 0.04, 1.89, 0.42, 0.57, 1.98, 1.1, 0.8, 1.9, 1.35, 1.11.

Exercise 13B

1 Draw a line of length 2.3 cm.

2 Draw a line of length $3\frac{2}{10}$ cm.

3 Write 7.9 on a decimal grid.

4 Illustrate on a decimal grid that 3.8×100 is 380.

5 Illustrate that $3.8 \div 10$ is 0.38 on a decimal grid.

6 Write these decimal numbers as fractions using mixed numbers where necessary.

    a 10.1

    b 0.01

    c 1.1

    d 10.01

    e 1.01

7 Write these mixed numbers using decimals.

a $30\frac{1}{10}$

b $4\frac{7}{100}$

c $5\frac{6}{10}$

d $6\frac{5}{10}$

e $20\frac{4}{100}$

8 Change these common fractions to decimal numbers.

a $\frac{7}{4}$

b $\frac{7}{50}$

c $\frac{7}{25}$

d $\frac{7}{40}$

e $\frac{7}{8}$

9 Change these decimal numbers to fractions in their lowest terms, using mixed numbers where necessary.

a 0.15

b 0.05

c 0.35

d 1.55

e 0.325

10 Sort these numbers into ascending numerical order. Illustrate on a number line.

1.09, 0.34, 1.17, 0.09, 1.43, 0.53, 1.35, 1.9, 0.7, 0.17, 1.7, 1.34, 0.9, 0.43, 1.53

Exercise 13C

1 Write the following using decimals:

a $9 + \frac{3}{10} + \frac{7}{100}$

b $1 + \frac{1}{10} + \frac{1}{100}$

c $700 + \frac{7}{100}$

d $403 + \frac{3}{1000}$

e $304 + \frac{3}{10} + \frac{4}{1000}$

2 Write out the following in full using whole numbers and fractions, as in question 1.

a 4.05

b 41.15

c 38.51

d 5.004

e 40.0004

Exercise 13D

The table of the full metric system of lengths (not all of which is used) is as follows:

- 10 millimetres is 1 centimetre   (cm)
- 10 centimetres is 1 decimetre   (dm)
- 10 decimetres is 1 metre   (m)
- 10 metres is 1 dekametre   (Dm)
- 10 dekametres is one hectometre   (Hm)
- 10 hectometres is one kilometre   (km)

Note the capitals 'D' and 'H'.

1 Rewrite the table in terms of a metre using fractions like this.

1 mm $= \frac{1}{1000}$ metre

1 cm =   metre

1 dm =   metre

1 Dm =   metres

1 Hm =   metres

1 km =   metres

2 Rewrite the table in terms of the metre using decimals.

1 mm =   m

1 cm =   m

1 dm =   m

1 Dm =   m

1 Hm =   m

1 km =   m

3 Note that 5 km 2 Hm 7 m (for example) could be written 5.207 km or 52.07 Hm or 5207 m, etc.

Write each of the following as decimals of a kilometre.

a 1 km 7 m 2 dm

b 4 km 5 m 4 cm

c 6 Hm 2 m 5 dm

d 2 Dm 5 m 3 dm

e 3 Dm 4 dm 7 mm

4 A decimal grid could be rewritten using the headings km, Hm, Dm, m, dm, cm, mm. Rewrite the lengths for question 3 on such a grid.

14 Algebraic expression

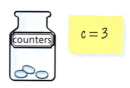

Do you remember the 'code' used in chapter 5 for the things found in the maths cupboard?

We decided that if we wrote '$c = 3$', we took it to mean that we had a single jar containing three counters.

And if we wrote '$2c$, where $c = 3$' this would mean we had two jars, each containing three counters, making six counters in all.

Exercise 14.1

1 Work out $3c$ if $c = 5$.
2 Evaluate $4c$ if $c = 7$.
3 Find $2c$ if $c = 3$.
4 Calculate the value of $5c$ if $c = 10$.
5 What is $8c$ if $c = 6$?

Using different letters

We soon realised in chapter 5 that the situation became confused if we tried always to use the first letter of the things in the jars or boxes. The letter really stands for the *number* of things and not the *name* of the things.

It is quite reasonable to talk about 'a jar labelled x' or 'a jar labelled y' or 'a jar labelled s' or 'a box labelled n', just using the different letters to distinguish between the number of things in the different jars or boxes.

We could use any letter at all. *The letter is a label for a particular container and represents the number of objects in that container.*

● *If we write '$x = 9$', it means no more than having something labelled 'x' containing nine objects.*

We can also say that x 'has the **value** 9' or that 'x has been replaced by 9' or '9 is substituted for x'.

All of these statements mean the same.

Exercise 14.2

Work these out.

1 $3x$, if $x = 5$ **2** $3x$, if $x = 7$ **3** $7y$, if $y = 3$ **4** $7y$, if $y = 10$ **5** $7z$, if $z = 10$

We can change the value of the *same* letter from question to question. It means that the *label* on the jar stays the same but we have a *different number of things* in that jar.

Exercise 14.3

Calculate these.

1 $7x$, if $x = 5$ **4** $10x$, if $x = 7$ **7** $9y$, if $y = 5$ **9** $6z$, if $z = 0$
2 $5x$, if $x = 2$ **5** $9x$, if $x = 1$ **8** $4u$, if $u = 1$ **10** $201t$, if $t = 26$
3 $8x$, if $x = 14$ **6** $3a$, if $a = 11$

Left-overs

The situation could easily arise where we have too many counters to go in a jar. Some would be left over. They might be left on the table.

Suppose the jar will only hold *seven* counters but we have nine counters altogether. How could this be written?

Let's use n for the label so that $n = 7$. Then we could write $n + 2$ for the number of counters, the extra '2' being the two counters left over.

If we have 11 counters (the jar will still hold only seven), it could be written $n + 4$, the '4' describing the four counters left on the table.

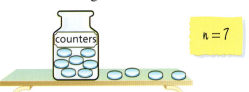

Still with seven in a jar, how many counters would $n + 6$ mean?
One jar of seven and six left over, or 13 counters.

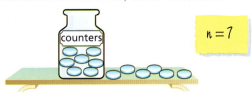

If we have 15 counters, and the jar holds seven we would have two jars of seven and one left over.
We would write $2n + 1$.

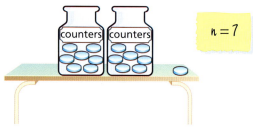

Say we now have 23 counters and the same-sized jars.
That would be $3n + 2$.

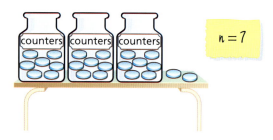

Exercise 14.4

If each jar can hold *only seven counters*, write down the number of jars which could be filled, and the number of counters left over, if I have the following numbers of counters.

1 8 counters [Answer: $n + 1$]
2 10 counters
3 17 counters
4 29 counters
5 47 counters

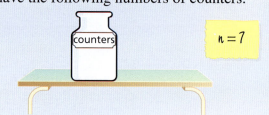

Exercise 14.5

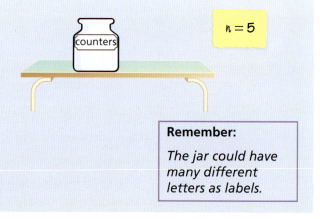

If one jar can hold only five counters, say how many counters I have altogether if I write down these expressions.

1 $3n + 2$
2 $2n + 4$
3 $n + 4$
4 $5n + 1$
5 $4n + 3$

Remember:

The jar could have many different letters as labels.

Exercise 14.6

> In words, if one jar has four counters in it and each jar is labelled '*x*', find the total number of counters I have in five of these jars, together with three extra counters which are on the table. Algebra certainly shortens things!

1 Find $5x + 3$, if $x = 4$. ←

2 Find $2c + 3$, if $c = 5$.

3 Work out $7v + 6$, where $v = 3$.

4 Calculate $3j + 1$, if $j = 4$.

5 Evaluate $4w + 5$, $w = 1$.

6 Find $9s + 7$, $s = 3$.

7 What is $12m + 13$, when $m = 15$? (Use a calculator?)

8 Find the answer to $23e + 43$, $e = 57$.

9 Find the value of $96g + 452$, $g = 46$.

10 Calculate $2x + 1$, $x = 0$.

Algebraic 'stories'

> let x be the number of drawing pins in each box; to start with $x = 6$

If I had five boxes, each originally containing six drawing pins, but I spilled four drawing pins on the floor, I would now have only 26 left in the boxes altogether. We would write that as

$$5x - 4, \text{ where } x = 6 \text{ [originally]}$$

The minus sign shows that four drawing pins have been 'lost'.

So, for example, $3a - 5$, where $a = 4$, would mean you were left with 7 drawing pins somewhere in the boxes

$$[3 \times 4 - 5 = 12 - 5 = 7]$$

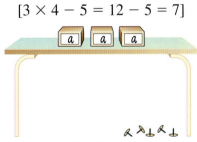

A 'story' about this might be: 'I had three boxes labelled "a", with four drawing pins in each box, but I lost five, which left me with seven altogether.'

Write the following statement in a shorter way using algebra:

'I had two boxes labelled t, with four counters in each, but I lost seven.'

'How many counters were left?'

Exercise 14.7

Describe these 'stories' using algebra.

1 I had three full boxes of counters, each box labelled *t*; then I lost five counters.
2 I had five full boxes of counters, each box labelled *n*; then I lost three counters.
3 I had six full boxes of counters, each box labelled *u*; then I *found* four counters.
4 I lost seven counters after having three full boxes, each labelled *x*.
5 I *found* eight counters after having five full boxes, each labelled *m*.

Exercise 14.8

Go back to exercise 14.7 and work out the number of counters for each question if each box contained:
a four counters,
b seven counters.

Exercise 14.9

Describe these 'stories' using algebra. You will need to choose your own letter to label the box in each example. Choose a different letter for each one.

1 I had five full boxes (choose a letter for a label); then I lost nine counters.
2 I had three full boxes; then I found five counters.
3 I lost six counters after having two full boxes.
4 I found one counter after having had three full boxes.
5 I had five full boxes. I lost seventeen counters.

In this exercise you have to choose your own labels.

Exercise 14.10

Go back and work out the number of counters in each question in exercise 14.9 if each box contained:
a three counters,
b two counters.

Exercise 14.11

Describe these 'stories' using algebra. Choose a different letter to label the box in each case.

1 I had eight boxes and found three counters.
2 I had twelve boxes but lost seven counters.
3 I had thirteen boxes, then found 23 counters.
4 I had seventeen boxes, then lost 52 counters.
5 After counting my boxes and finding they numbered sixteen, I lost 431 counters.

Exercise 14.12

Invent 'stories' to fit this algebra.

1 $5x + 1$ **2** $7a - 3$ **3** $24z - 23$ **4** $23u + 24$ **5** $19c - 19$

Exercise 14.13

Evaluate the following, when $x = 3$.

1 $5x + 2$ **3** $5x - 2$ **5** $2x + 1$ **7** $4x + 7$ **9** $100x - 299$
2 $3x + 5$ **4** $3x - 5$ **6** $7x - 4$ **8** $4x - 7$ **10** $3x - 9$

SUMMARY

■ A *letter* could be thought of as a *label* for a container. The letter represents the number of things in that container, it has replaced the number. Any letter could be used.
■ The *same* letter can have *different* **values** in different situations.
■ Objects may not always fill a box completely.
■ A piece of algebra can tell a 'story'.

Exercise 14A

1 Find $23x$ if $x = 5$.
2 Work out $14c$ if $c = 3$.
3 Calculate $6v$, when $v = 8$.
4 Evaluate $19x$, where $x = 1$.
5 Find $13c$, $c = 6$.
6 I have 23 counters with four counters in each box and some left over. Write this using algebra if each box is labelled z.
7 I have 15 counters with four in each box. Write this using algebra if each box is labelled y.
8 Describe the situation in algebra: I had six boxes, each with five counters, and I found three counters.

9 Describe the situation in algebra: I had nine boxes, each with seven counters, but I lost five counters.

10 Write using algebra, then evaluate: I lost seven drawing pins from five packets each labelled d, with 10 pins originally in each packet.

Exercise 14B

1 Find $14y$ if $y = 3$.
2 Work out $8u$ if $u = 7$.
3 Calculate $7s$, when $s = 4$.
4 Evaluate $28q$, where $q = 1$.
5 Find $31z$, $z = 5$.
6 If one box contains five counters, write down the situation using algebra if I have 23 counters altogether (use your own label for a box).
7 If one box contains five counters, and I have 103 counters altogether, describe the situation using algebra.
8 Describe the situation in aglebra: I had seven boxes, each with three counters and I found four more.
9 Describe the situation in algebra: I had four boxes, each with 17 counters but I lost 13 counters.
10 Write using algebra then evaluate: I lost 13 drawing pins from five packets each labelled c. There were originally 12 pins in each packet.

Exercise 14C

Evaluate the following where $n = 5$.

1 $7n$	3 $7n - 1$	5 $n - 1$	7 $5n - 5$	9 $1001n$
2 $7n + 1$	4 $n + 1$	6 $5n + 5$	8 $100n$	10 $n - 5$

Exercise 14D

A boy helped with the family shopping one weekend. At the superstore, he bought two boxes, each containing 48 packets of crisps. On the way back in the car, one of the boxes was opened and three packets of crisps were eaten. When the family reached their house, the dog rushed out to meet them, jumped up and knocked the boy over, spilling 15 packets of crisps which burst open into a muddy puddle. So that the family wouldn't run out of crisps that week (they did eat rather too many crisps) the boy was then sent round to the local shop to buy a smaller box of 24 packets, which he brought home safely.

a How many packets of crisps do the family have now?
b Describe the final situation using algebra, if instead of 48 packets the original box contained x packets of crisps.

15 Units of measurement

Metric units

The **metric** system is the official system of units of measurement in the UK, and should be used for most purposes.

Until 1995, Imperial units (inch, mile, pint, pound, gallon, etc.) were also widely used, and the names of some of these measures could well persist for a long time. But, in practical terms, everyone must now use **metric** measures.

Greek *metron*: measure

Units of length

The basic metric unit of length is the **metre** (pronounced 'meter'). After a survey in 1791 it was defined as one ten-millionth of a quarter of the distance round the earth and, to begin with, the standard metre was one kept in Paris. But now a more exact definition is used, based on the wavelength of light.

Handle a metre rule so that you become good at judging its size.

Also notice the metric measurements of some common objects.

The metric system of units was developed in France after the Revolution of 1789.

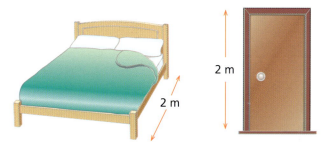

Exercise 15.1

Write down the names of the other metric units of length in common use.
Check your answers.

There are other metric units of length which are used to measure smaller or larger distances than would be practical with a metre.

Latin *centum*: one hundred
Latin *mille*: one thousand
Greek *khilloi*: one thousand

- *A **centi**metre is one hundredth of a metre.*
- *A **milli**metre is one thousandth of a metre.*
- *A **kilo**metre is one thousand metres.*

Conversions from one metric unit of length to another:

- 1 kilometre (km) is the same as 1000 metres (m)
- 1 metre (m) is the same as 100 centimetres (cm)
- 1 centimetre (cm) is the same as 10 millimetres (mm).

To get a rough idea of the size of these units,
 It takes about 15 minutes to walk 1 km.
 A bed is about 2 m long.
 A standard paper-clip is about 3 cm long.
 The point of a drawing pin is about 1 mm thick.

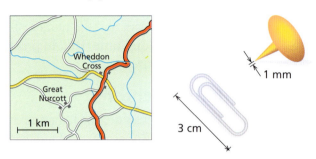

Look carefully at the centimetre and millimetre markings on your ruler.

Exercise 15.2

1 Write down the metric unit you would use to measure:
  a the length of a pencil
  b the distance from Birmingham to Liverpool
  c the height of a lamp-post
  d the length of an ant
  e the length of your foot.
2 Estimate the length of your classroom in metres.
3 Estimate the length and width of your exercise book in centimetres.
4 Use something straight, other than a ruler, to try to draw a line 6 cm long.
5 Use something straight, other than a ruler, to try to draw a line 15 mm long.
6 Use a ruler to check the lengths of your lines in questions 4 and 5.

It is important that you measure and draw lengths carefully, especially when working in millimetres, since a small error could make your answers very wrong!

Use a sharp pencil, and be careful to get your eye *directly* above the pencil and ruler.

Exercise 15.3

Use a ruler to draw these lines, getting a partner to check your answers.

1 A line 6 cm long
2 A line 21 cm long
3 A line 21 mm long
4 A line 76 mm long
5 A line 14 cm long

Measure these lines in centimetres.

6 _____

7 _____

8 _____

Measure these lines in millimetres.

9 _____

10 __

Greek *gramma*: small weight

Units of mass

The most common metric units of mass are the kilogram and gram. They must be used for all packaged foods.

Sometimes a unit larger than a kilogram is needed, for example, if you were weighing a full load on a large lorry. Then the tonne is used.

PUBLIC WEIGHBRIDGE

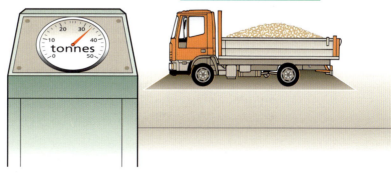

For very small objects, for example medicines in powder form, a tiny unit, the milligram, is used.

As a rough guide to the size of units of mass, sugar is usually sold in bags of 1 kilogram.

Conversions from one metric unit of mass to another:

- 1000 kilograms (kg) is the same as 1 tonne (t)
- 1000 grams (g) is the same as 1 kg
- 1000 milligrams (mg) is the same as 1 g.

Exercise 15.4

Which metric unit would be suitable to measure the mass of the following?

1 An elephant
2 A bag of potatoes
3 A bar of chocolate
4 A tiny spider
5 A baby

Converting from one unit to another

There are times when people need to convert from one unit to another, for example to compare two lengths or masses which were originally in *different* units.

● *You could end up making terrible mistakes about the sizes of objects if you don't take proper account of the **units**!*

Here are three examples. Read them and discuss them!
    Your aunt needs to order a fitted carpet for her front room which is 20 m long. The sales assistant asks for the measurement in centimetres. Your aunt gives the measurement as 200.

Your uncle decides to make a new garden path which will need $\frac{1}{2}$ tonne of concrete. He orders 5000 kg from a ready-mix supplier which they deliver into the front garden.

You are sent to buy $2\frac{1}{2}$ m of material for a skirt. You ask for 2500 cm in the shop.

Here are some correct conversions:

Convert 4 m into centimetres.

Each 1 m is the same as 100 cm.
So 4 m = 4 × 100 cm = 400 cm.

Change 5.6 kg to grams.

You know that 1 kg is the same as 1000 g.
So 5.6 kg = 5.6 × 1000 g = 5600 g.

The last two examples went from a larger unit to a smaller one.
Suppose you needed to convert the other way.

Change 26 mm to centimetres.

Since each 10 mm is the same as 1 cm, this time you need to *divide* by 10.
26 mm = 26 ÷ 10 cm = 2.6 cm.

If you're not sure about the divisions look back to chapter 13.

Try converting 7630 kg into tonnes.

1000 kg is the same as 1 tonne.
So 7630 kg = 7630 ÷ 1000 t = 7.63 t.

Exercise 15.5

For each question, convert the given amount to the new unit.

1 Write 50 cm in millimetres.
2 Write 6 kg in grams.
3 Express 25 t in kilograms.
4 Convert 6.7 g into milligrams.
5 Express 1.78 m in centimetres.
6 Write 45.8 km in metres.
7 Convert 21.4 kg to grams.
8 Write 0.65 m in centimetres.
9 Express 9.06 km in metres (be careful!).
10 How many milligrams is the same as 0.065 g?

Exercise 15.6

1 Convert 6700 mg into grams.
2 How many metres is the same as 200 cm?
3 Write 865 mm in metres.
4 Express 8724 kg in tonnes.
5 Convert 56 mm into centimetres.
6 Convert 56 mm into metres.
7 Write 436 g in kilograms.
8 How many kilometres is the same as 150 m?
9 Express 12 300 m in kilometres.
10 Write 3 mg in grams.

> This exercise converts from smaller units to larger ones. Remember to divide, not multiply.

Exercise 15.7

If you are not sure whether to multiply or divide, ask yourself first if the number should get bigger or smaller.

Convert!

1 Five tins weigh 450 g, 78 g, 230 g, 315 g, and 425 g. Find their total weight in kilograms.
2 I walked 5 km 345 m one morning. How many metres is that?
3 A pharmicist had 2 g of a particular drug. She needed to split it into 5 mg portions. How many portions could she make?
4 A businessman was travelling to Berlin by aeroplane. He was allowed to take 35 kg of luggage with him. His bags weighed 495 g less than the limit allowed. How much did his bags weigh?
5 A sunflower plant grew 15 cm per day one summer. How tall was it, in metres, after 30 days?

Litre from French litra (via Latin), from Greek litra, a unit of money

Units of capacity

Capacity is the measure of liquids (fluids) such as water, milk, beer or petrol. The standard metric unit of capacity is the litre. For example, a large carton of fruit juice is usually a litre.

For smaller amounts (such as a can of cola) the millilitre (ml) is used.

Conversion:

• 1000 millilitres (ml) is the same as 1 litre (l).

Exercise 15.8

1 Find out the size of a standard cola can in millilitres.
2 How many small cartons of orange juice make up a litre?
3 Measure the amount of air in your classroom in litres.
4 How much medicine will a standard teaspoon hold?
5 Find out how much more water you use in a bath than in a shower, on average.

Imperial units

Imperial units are the older system which was used in the UK for several centuries before the metric system was adopted.

Try to find a cookery book which is written only in Imperial units.

Find out about King Canute.

The Imperial system is much more complicated than the metric system since the numbers used to convert from one unit to another are not just multiples of 10 as in the metric system.

Exercise 15.9

Find out the names of some Imperial measurements, their conversions to each other and their approximate metric equivalents. You will need some of these for the next exercise.

Exercise 15.10

1 Roughly how many pounds are there in 6 kg?
2 My bedroom is about 12 feet long. Roughly how many metres is that?
3 If a neighbour asked you to buy 4 pints of milk, how many litres would you need to buy to be sure you had enough?
4 An American penfriend wrote that their baby daughter now weighed 25 lb. Roughly how many kilograms is that?
5 My father's old tape measure is marked only in feet and inches. The space for a bookcase measures 4 feet 6 inches. How big, roughly, is the space in centimetres?

Remember:

*Thirty days hath September
April, June and November
All the rest have thirty-one
Excepting February alone
Which has but twenty-eight days clear
And twenty-nine in each leap year.*

Time

Time does not use metric measurements, because it depends on the rotation of the earth and the movement of the earth around the sun.

Conversions:

- 100 years is the same as 1 century
- 10 years is the same as 1 decade
- 365 days is the same as 1 year
- 366 days is the same as 1 leap year (every fourth year)
- 7 days is the same as 1 week
- 24 hours is the same as 1 day
- 60 minutes is the same as 1 hour
- 60 seconds is the same as 1 minute.

You can use a rhyme to help you remember the number of days in each month.

Exercise 15.11

1 Use your calculator to work out:
   a the number of hours in a week
   b the number of minutes in a day
   c the number of seconds in January.
2 You go to the cinema to see a film which starts at 8 o'clock. The film is 90 minutes long. What time does the film finish?
3 You are asked to put the dinner on so that it is ready for half-past seven. The food takes 40 minutes to cook altogether. When do you need to start cooking?

SUMMARY

- The commonest system of units in use today is the **metric** system.
- An older system is the Imperial system.
- Metric units of length are the kilometre (km), metre (m), centimetre (cm) and millimetre (mm).
- Metric units of weight are the tonne (t), kilogram (kg), gram (g) and milligram (mg).
- Metric units of capacity are the litre (l) and millilitre (ml).
- Imperial units of length include the mile, foot and inch.
- Imperial units of weight include the stone, pound and ounce.
- Time is not measured using a metric or Imperial system.

Exercise 15A

1 What metric unit is best for measuring your weight?
2 Use a straight edge to draw a line which is about 67 mm long. Now measure it using a ruler. How close were you?
3 Which Imperial unit is best for measuring distances between cities?
4 Write 6 cm in millimetres.
5 Write 6 cm in metres.
6 Roughly how many inches is 6 cm?
7 I bought 250 g of plums in a supermarket. They cost £2.45 per kilogram. How much did my plums cost?
8 An American cookbook asks you to use one quarter of a pound of flour in a recipe. How much flour should I weigh on my (metric) scales?

Exercise 15B

1 What metric unit is best for measuring the length of your arm?
2 Use a straight edge to draw a line which is about 14 cm long. Now measure it using a ruler. How close were you?
3 Which Imperial units are best for measuring your height?
4 Write 27 g in kilograms.
5 Write 27 g in milligrams.
6 Roughly how many kilometres is 25 miles?
7 A doctor told me to drink about three extra pints of water a day. How many litres, roughly, is that?
8 When moving house, each box had to weigh no more than 0.4 t. One box still had some space in it, and weighed 235 kg. How much more weight could be put in the box?

Exercise 15C

1 Fabric costs £2.75 per metre. I want to buy 345 cm of fabric. How much will it cost?
2 A group of friends went to see a film. They bought 750 g of loose sweets to eat in the cinema. The sweets cost £2.50 per kilogram. How much did their sweets cost?
3 Saffron (an expensive spice) costs £2.50 per gram in one shop. In one year, the shopkeeper sold 3.45 kg of saffron. How much money did he make?
4 There are 12 inches in 1 foot. My height is 1.72 m. What is that in feet and inches?
5 There are 14 lb in 1 stone. My old scales show that my dog weighs 3 stones and 5 pounds. The vet says that my dog must not weigh more than 22 kg. Is my dog overweight?

Exercise 15D

1 The carpet in a dining room measures 13 ft by 15 ft. How many square metres (m²) is that?
2 An old gardening book instructs you to add 1 fl oz (fluid ounce) of fertiliser to each gallon of water when feeding plants. There are 20 fl oz in 1 pint, and 8 pints in 1 gallon. I want to add the correct amount of fertiliser to 6 litres of water. Roughly how much fertiliser do I need to add in millilitres?
3 Some other Imperial units are quart, hundredweight, perch, fathom, furlong. Find out what they were used for! Can you find any others?

16 Types of fraction

Fractions less than 1

Remember:

*Fractions are about breaking **units** into **equal** parts.*
*Each fraction has a **numerator** and a **denominator**.*
A particular fraction may be represented in many different ways.

The shaded part represents a fraction of the whole circle.
Write down its denominator.
Write down its numerator.
Write down the fraction.

If all the parts were shaded, what fraction is represented?

This is $\frac{8}{8}$, which is the whole unit.
As we found in chapter 8, it is represented by the number 1.

Exercise 16.1

To remind you that a unit can be broken into any number of equal parts, draw three differently shaped diagrams so that:

- the first one can be broken into three equal parts
- the second into four equal parts
- the third into five equal parts.

Shade each diagram to illustrate the number 1.

What fraction is represented here?

Answer: $\frac{7}{8}$
Since fewer than eight equal parts are shaded, $\frac{7}{8}$ is less than the whole unit.
Or we could say that $\frac{7}{8}$ **is less than 1.**

Exercise 16.2

Draw your own diagram to show that $\frac{5}{7}$ is less than 1.
Write a sentence to say how your diagram shows this.
Do the same for $\frac{5}{8}$ and $\frac{3}{5}$.

● *Any fraction which is less than 1 has its numerator less than its denominator.*

Write down five fractions which are less than 1.

A fraction which has its numerator less than its denominator is called a **proper fraction**. Proper fractions are less than a unit.

Fractions more than 1

We can illustrate fractions less than 1 and fractions equal to 1. What about fractions more than 1?

At first, there may seem something wrong here. All our fractions have been illustrated by breaking a unit into smaller parts. So how can we have a fraction more than a unit?

If the unit is a brick, for example, you just use several bricks. It's no problem to have (say) one brick and another quarter of a brick. But in the same way as you have to be careful to break the brick into *equal* parts, you have to be careful to have *equal bricks* for this situation.

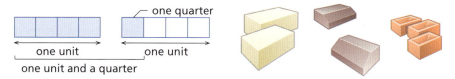

We can write 'one unit and a quarter' as $1\frac{1}{4}$. But we can also write it as $\frac{5}{4}$, and read it as 'five quarters'.

Count the five shaded quarters in the diagram. So

$$1\frac{1}{4} = \frac{5}{4}$$

$\frac{5}{4}$ is called an **improper fraction**.

Illustrate $\frac{4}{3}$. This is read as 'four thirds'.

The shaded parts of the diagram could also be read as 'one and one third'. So

$$\frac{4}{3} = 1\frac{1}{3}$$

The number $1\frac{1}{3}$ is called a **mixed number**.

Let's illustrate the mixed number $1\frac{3}{5}$.

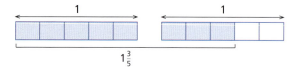

Count the number of shaded fifths. There are eight. So

$$1\frac{3}{5} = \frac{8}{5}$$

In a similar way, any mixed number can be written as an improper fraction.

Write $2\frac{3}{4}$ as an improper fraction.

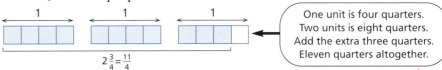

One unit is four quarters.
Two units is eight quarters.
Add the extra three quarters.
Eleven quarters altogether.

$2\frac{3}{4} = \frac{11}{4}$

Counting the number of quarters, you can see that two and three quarters is the same as eleven quarters.

Write $4\frac{2}{3}$ as thirds.

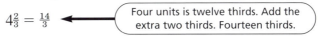

$4\frac{2}{3} = \frac{14}{3}$

Four units is twelve thirds. Add the extra two thirds. Fourteen thirds.

Write $2\frac{4}{5}$ as fifths.

Two units is ten fifths and together with four more fifths that makes fourteen fifths.

● *Always use the denominator of the fractional part to change the units.*

Write $3\frac{1}{2}$ as halves.

The denominator of the fraction is 2 so write the three units as halves. Three units is six halves and one more half makes seven halves. So

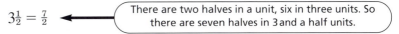

$3\frac{1}{2} = \frac{7}{2}$

There are two halves in a unit, six in three units. So there are seven halves in 3 and a half units.

Exercise 16.3

Write the following mixed numbers as improper fractions.
    Change to the denominator of the fractional part.

1 $2\frac{3}{5}$ (in fifths)

2 $1\frac{4}{5}$

3 $3\frac{3}{4}$ (in quarters)

4 $1\frac{2}{3}$ (decide on the denominator first)

5 $3\frac{1}{7}$

6 $2\frac{1}{2}$

7 $1\frac{3}{10}$

8 $5\frac{7}{10}$

9 $2\frac{2}{7}$

10 $4\frac{1}{8}$

Fractional parts of quantities

The 'unit' could be a quantity. For example, it could be a mass, say 20 kg.

Find $\frac{1}{5}$ of 20 kg.

Again we have the idea of breaking a unit into equal parts.

Put 20 kg into five equal parts. $20 \div 5 = 4$ so $\frac{1}{5}$ of 20 kg is 4 kg.

You could also find $\frac{2}{5}$ of 20 kg. Since this is twice $\frac{1}{5}$ of 20 kg the answer is 2×4 kg or 8 kg.

What is $\frac{3}{5}$ of 20 kg?

Since one fifth of 20 is 4, three fifths of 20 kg is 12 kg.

What is $\frac{4}{5}$ of 20 kg?

It is four lots of one fifth of 20 kg, or 16 kg.

Find $\frac{2}{3}$ of 15 min.

$\frac{1}{3}$ of 15 min is 5 min, so $\frac{2}{3}$ of 15 min is 10 min.

Find $\frac{3}{8}$ of 24 cm.

First find $\frac{1}{8}$ of 24 cm, which is 3 cm, so $\frac{3}{8}$ of 24 cm is 9 cm.

Find $\frac{3}{4}$ of 1 hour in min.

First, $\frac{1}{4}$ of 1 hour is $\frac{1}{4}$ of 60 min, which is 15 min, so $\frac{3}{4}$ of 60 min is 45 min.

Find $\frac{4}{5}$ of £2: which is $\frac{4}{5}$ of 200p.

First find $\frac{1}{5}$ of 200p, which is 40p, so $\frac{4}{5}$ of £2 is £1.60.

Exercise 16.4

Calculate these fractional parts.

1 Find $\frac{5}{8}$ of 32p.
2 Find $\frac{5}{6}$ of 1 hour in minutes.
3 Find $\frac{4}{9}$ of 27 cm.
4 Calculate $\frac{2}{7}$ of 2 weeks in days.
5 Work out $\frac{2}{3}$ of 1 day in hours.
6 Find $\frac{3}{4}$ of £2 in pence.
7 Find $1\frac{3}{4}$ of £2 in pence.
8 Calculate $2\frac{3}{5}$ of 20 kg.
9 Work out $\frac{3}{7}$ of 210 m.
10 Find $\frac{4}{5}$ of 1 litre in millilitres.

Equivalent fractions

Look at these examples carefully.

Work out $\frac{1}{3}$ of 18 kg.　Answer: 6 kg.

Work out $\frac{2}{6}$ of 18 kg.　Answer: $\frac{1}{6}$ of 18 kg; so $\frac{2}{6}$ of 18 kg is 6 kg.

Work out $\frac{3}{9}$ of 18 kg.　Answer: $\frac{1}{9}$ of 18 kg is 2 kg; so $\frac{3}{9}$ of 18 kg is 6 kg.

The last three answers are all the same! So there must be something the same about the fractions $\frac{1}{3}$, $\frac{2}{6}$ and $\frac{3}{9}$.

These three fractions are called **equivalent**.

> Sets of equivalent fractions are very important in future work!

Work out $\frac{3}{4}$ of 24 m.　Answer: 3 lots of 6, or 18 m.

Work out $\frac{6}{8}$ of 24 m.　Answer: 6 lots of 3, or 18 m.

Work out $\frac{9}{12}$ of 24 m.　Answer: 9 lots of 2, or 18 m.

So $\frac{3}{4}$, $\frac{6}{8}$, $\frac{9}{12}$ are also equivalent fractions.

Finding equivalent fractions

Look carefully at the fractions $\frac{3}{4}$, $\frac{6}{8}$, $\frac{9}{12}$. The numerators are on the three times table and the denominators are on the four times table. This gives us a clue to the next step.

Remember from chapter 10 that numbers on the *three* times table are called multiples of 3 and numbers on the *four* times table are called multiples of 4.

- 35 is the fifth multiple of 7 (35 is 5 × 7)
- 27 is the third multiple of 9 (27 is 3 × 9)
- 18 is the ninth multiple of 2 (18 is 9 × 2)

Exercise 16.5

1 Write down the third multiple of 5. (Answer: 15)
2 Write down the sixth multiple of 4.
3 Write down the eighth multiple of 3.
4 Write down the fourth multiple of 7.
5 Write down the fifth multiple of 2.
6 Which multiple of 7 is 42? (Answer: the sixth)
7 Which multiple of 3 is 15?
8 Which multiple of 2 is 16?
9 Which multiple of 9 is 45?
10 Which multiple of 4 is 28?

Now, apply these ideas to equivalent fractions.

Write $\frac{3}{5}$ as an equivalent fraction with denominator 30.

Think 'Which multiple of 5 is 30?' (the *sixth*), so which is the *sixth* multiple of 3? It's 18, so $\frac{3}{5} = \frac{18}{30}$.

> Six 5s are 30. The numerator is six 3s, or 18.

Write $\frac{2}{3}$ as an equivalent fraction with denominator 15.

Think 'Which multiple of 3 is 15?' (the *fifth*), so which is the *fifth* multiple of 2? It's 10, so $\frac{2}{3} = \frac{10}{15}$.

> Denominators 3, 15. Since $5 \times 3 = 15$ the numerator is $5 \times 2 = 10$.

Write $\frac{5}{7}$ with denominator 56.

Which multiple of 7 is 56? (the *eighth*), so which is the *eighth* multiple of 5? It's 40, so $\frac{5}{7} = \frac{40}{56}$.

> Eight 7s are 56, and eight 5s are 40.

Complete this. $\frac{3}{4} = \frac{}{24}$.

Answer: 24 is the *sixth* multiple of 4 so the numerator is the *sixth* multiple of 3 and this is 18 so $\frac{3}{4} = \frac{18}{24}$.

> Six 4s are 24 and six 3s are 18.

● *To change to an equivalent fraction you first decide which multiple of the denominator is needed and then find the same multiple of the numerator.*

Complete this: $\frac{5}{9} = \frac{}{36}$.

Answer: the fourth multiple of 9 is needed and then the fourth multiple of 5 is 20 so $\frac{5}{9} = \frac{20}{36}$.

> Four 9s are 36 and four 5s are 20.

Exercise 16.6

Write the equivalent fraction with the given denominator.

1 $\frac{1}{5}$, new denominator 20
2 $\frac{1}{9}$, new denominator 18
3 $\frac{2}{7}$, new denominator 35
4 $\frac{2}{3}$, new denominator 12
5 $\frac{7}{11}$, new denominator 44
6 $\frac{5}{6}$, new denominator 12
7 $\frac{3}{7}$, new denominator 21
8 $\frac{2}{5}$, new denominator 25
9 $\frac{3}{8}$, new denominator 32
10 $\frac{1}{4}$, new denominator 12

Consider again the equivalent fractions $\frac{1}{3}, \frac{2}{6}, \frac{3}{9}, \frac{4}{12}, \ldots$ and look at the following diagrams. Can you see why the fractions are called equivalent?

$\frac{1}{3}$ is shaded

$\frac{2}{6}$ is shaded

$\frac{3}{9}$ is shaded

$\frac{4}{12}$ is shaded

Exercise 16.7

Write the equivalent fraction with the given denominator for these.

1 $\frac{3}{7}$, new denominator 21

2 $\frac{2}{3}$, new denominator 15

3 $\frac{1}{6}$, new denominator 12

4 $\frac{4}{9}$, new denominator 36

5 $\frac{1}{3}$, new denominator 18

6 $\frac{4}{5} = \frac{}{20}$

7 $\frac{5}{6} = \frac{}{24}$

8 $\frac{6}{5} = \frac{}{30}$

9 $\frac{5}{3} = \frac{}{9}$

10 $\frac{5}{9} = \frac{}{27}$

The lowest representative

Equivalent fractions can be written in sets with equals signs between them like this: $\frac{2}{3} = \frac{4}{6} = \frac{6}{9} = \frac{8}{12} = \frac{10}{15} = \ldots$

The fraction $\frac{2}{3}$ is the **lowest representative** of the whole set, usually described as **reducing the equivalent fraction to its lowest terms**.

In this set of equivalent fractions, $\frac{4}{7} = \frac{8}{14} = \frac{12}{21} = \frac{16}{28} = \frac{20}{35} = \ldots$, the lowest representative for this equivalent set is $\frac{4}{7}$, which again is 'reduced to its lowest terms'.

Finding the lowest representative

Looking back you can see that the lists of equivalent fractions begin with the one we are calling the 'lowest representative'. So if you were given a list of equivalent fractions with the first one missing, you could work out the list's lowest representative.

For instance: $— = \frac{6}{8} = \frac{9}{12} = \frac{12}{16} = \frac{15}{20} = \ldots$

What is the lowest representative fraction for this list (the fraction in its lowest terms)?

> Since the numerators are multiples of 3 and the denominators are multiples of 4, the lowest representative fraction is $\frac{3}{4}$.

What is the lowest representative fraction for this list?

$— = \frac{10}{14} = \frac{15}{21} = \frac{20}{28} = \frac{25}{35} = \ldots$

> Since the numerators are multiples of 5 and the denominators are multiples of 7 the lowest representative fraction is $\frac{5}{7}$.

Exercise 16.8

Find the lowest representative fraction for each list, making sure the answers are the smallest numbers possible.

1 $— = \frac{6}{10} = \frac{9}{15} = \frac{12}{20} = \ldots$

2 $— = \frac{2}{6} = \frac{3}{9} = \frac{4}{12} = \ldots$

3 $— = \frac{10}{16} = \frac{15}{24} = \frac{20}{32} = \ldots$

4 $— = \frac{2}{14} = \frac{3}{21} = \frac{4}{28} = \ldots$

5 $— = \frac{4}{6} = \frac{6}{9} = \frac{8}{12} = \ldots$

You actually only need *one* member of the list in order to find the lowest representative fraction.

For instance, in the fraction $\frac{12}{20}$, since the numerator is a multiple of **3** and the denominator is *the same* multiple of **5** (the *fourth*) the fraction reduces to $\frac{3}{5}$.

You could also say that 3 is a factor (the fourth) of 12 and 5 is a factor (the fourth) of 20 (see chapter 10).

This is reversing what we did earlier in the chapter.

Try $\frac{15}{24}$.

You first have to notice that both 15 and 24 are multiples of 3 (or 3 is a factor of both 15 and 24). *Which* multiples of 3 are they? 15 is the *fifth* multiple of 3 and 24 is the *eighth* multiple of 3. So $\frac{15}{24}$ reduces to $\frac{5}{8}$.

Try $\frac{8}{36}$.

Notice that 8 and 36 are both multiples of 4 (have a common factor of 4). *Which* multiples of 4? 8 is the *second* and 36 is the *ninth* (divide 8 and 36 by the common factor). So $\frac{8}{36}$ reduces to $\frac{2}{9}$.

Reduce $\frac{6}{9}$ to its lowest terms.

6 and 9 are multiples of 3 (have a common factor of 3). 6 is the *second* and 9 is the *third* (divide by the common factor of 3). So $\frac{6}{9} = \frac{2}{3}$.

Reduce $\frac{18}{30}$ to its lowest terms.

18 and 30 are multiples of 6. 18 is the *third* and 30 is the *fifth* (divide by the common factor of 6). So $\frac{18}{30} = \frac{3}{5}$.

Reduce $\frac{7}{77}$ to its lowest terms.

7 and 77 are multiples of 7. 7 is the first and 77 the eleventh (divide 7 and 77 by the common factor 7). So $\frac{7}{77} = \frac{1}{11}$.

● *The quickest way of **reducing a fraction to its lowest terms** is to divide numerator and denominator by the **(highest) common factor.***

To be 'good at equivalent fractions' depends on *knowing your multiplication tables thoroughly!*

Learn your tables!

Calculators with a fraction button

Many calculators have a button which can do all the fraction calculations easily! But you will never be able to understand what is going on until you can follow the various steps on paper!

A calculator is useful *after* you understand. It won't teach you how the processes work.

Exercise 16.9

Reduce these fractions to their lowest terms.

1 $\frac{25}{30}$ (both multiples of 5, that is, highest common factor is 5)
2 $\frac{4}{12}$ (both multiples of 4, that is, highest common factor is 4)

3 $\frac{9}{15}$	**5** $\frac{10}{100}$	**7** $\frac{12}{21}$	**9** $\frac{20}{16}$
4 $\frac{21}{49}$	**6** $\frac{5}{45}$	**8** $\frac{23}{46}$	**10** $\frac{32}{12}$

Now go back over the whole chapter, pick out for yourself what appear to be the main important points, and write down your own summary of the chapter. How does it compare with the one below?

SUMMARY

■ A fraction has a **denominator** (the number of equal parts it's broken into), and a **numerator** (the number of those parts used).

■ The **unit** (written as the number 1) may be broken into *any* number of equal parts.

■ A **proper fraction** has its numerator *less* than its denominator.

■ An **improper fraction** has its numerator *more* than its denominator.

■ A **mixed number** has two parts: a whole number which is 1 or more, together with a proper fraction.

■ A mixed number can be written as an improper fraction (and vice versa).

■ To find a **fractional part of a quantity**, first find the value of one part, then multiply by the number of parts.

■ **Equivalent fractions** are those which have the same effect as each other.

■ To find a fraction equivalent to one given, write down the same multiple of the given fraction's numerator and denominator.

■ To **reduce a fraction to its lowest terms**, obtaining its **lowest representative**, divide its numerator and denominator by their **highest common factor**.

■ To be good at fractions you must know your multiplication tables very well!

Exercise 16A

1 Write $\frac{14}{5}$ as a mixed number.
2 Write $\frac{16}{9}$ as a mixed number.
3 Find $\frac{2}{5}$ of 140 m giving your answer in metres.
4 Work out $\frac{2}{3}$ of £1.80, giving your answer in pence.
5 Copy these fractions and fill in the missing numerators or denominators:
   a $\frac{7}{11} = \frac{}{44}$
   b $\frac{7}{9} = \frac{35}{}$
   c $3\frac{1}{4} = \frac{}{4}$
   d $2\frac{2}{3} = \frac{}{3}$
6 Write $\frac{8}{12}$ in its lowest terms.
7 Write $\frac{12}{20}$ in its lowest terms.

Exercise 16B

1 Write $4\frac{2}{7}$ as an improper fraction.
2 Write $2\frac{4}{13}$ as an improper fraction.
3 Find $\frac{7}{20}$ of 2 m, giving your answer in centimetres.
4 Work out $\frac{7}{10}$ of £2.50, giving your answer in pence.

5 Copy these fractions and fill in the missing numerators or denominators:

a $\frac{5}{9} = \frac{30}{}$

b $\frac{12}{5} = \frac{}{40}$

c $\frac{3}{10} = \frac{30}{}$

d $\frac{3}{7} = \frac{}{49}$

6 Write $\frac{18}{20}$ in its lowest terms.

7 Write $\frac{18}{30}$ in its lowest terms.

Exercise 16C

1 I have a full CD storage box containing twelve CDs. For my birthday I was given another CD storage box of the same size, and enough CDs to fill a quarter of it.

a How many CDs did I get for my birthday?

b How many CDs do I now have altogether?

2 A hotel has rooms enough to hold 350 people. During one week, the hotel is $\frac{5}{7}$ full. Calculate the number of guests in the hotel.

How many places are unfilled?

3 A recipe states that 75 g of butter and two eggs are needed as part of a cake mixture. A boy finds $\frac{1}{2}$ of a 250 g packet of butter and $\frac{1}{3}$ of a dozen eggs in the fridge. How much spare butter does he have and how many eggs are left after the cake is made?

4 One year it was announced that the cost of sending letters would be raised by $\frac{1}{10}$, rounded to the nearest penny. Work out the new postage on a letter previously costing 65p to send.

By how much has the cost risen?

5 An Old Wives' Tale says that a child is half their adult height at three years old. When I was three years old I was 95 cm tall. How tall should I now be according to the tale? My actual height is 172 cm. How wrong was the prediction?

Exercise 16D

1 Explain carefully what is wrong with the statement:

'I have the larger half of the cake'.

2 Which would you rather do, share (equally) your favourite cake with two other people or three other people?

Say how this explains which is larger, one third or one quarter.

3 'I have just eaten four thirds of my favourite cake.' Explain why this is impossible.

I meant to say 'I have eaten three quarters of the cake.' What fraction would be left?

17 Naming polygons

A closed shape drawn using several straight lines is called a **polygon**.
Polygon really means 'many angled'.

It is important that all of the sides are straight

not a polygon

and that the figure is closed.

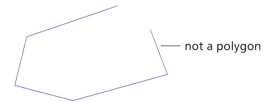

not a polygon

The following figures *are* polygons:

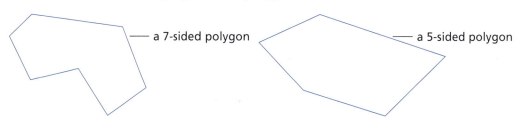

a 7-sided polygon

a 5-sided polygon

You probably already know the names of some polygons.
See how many you can remember.

Any three-sided polygon is a triangle.

Any four-sided polygon is a quadrilateral.

Any five-sided polygon is a pentagon.

Any six-sided polygon is a hexagon.

Any eight-sided polygon is an octagon.

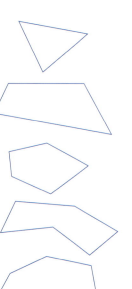

(Count the sides.) And so on.

Notice that squares and rectangles are polygons since they are both special sorts of quadrilateral:

Exercise 17.1

Draw four different squares and four different rectangles.
In each diagram mark in the sides which are equal to each other.
In each diagram mark in the angles which are equal to each other.

Regular polygons

Some of the other diagrams of polygons may not have looked quite as you expected. This is probably because we so often see diagrams of **regular polygons**, like these:

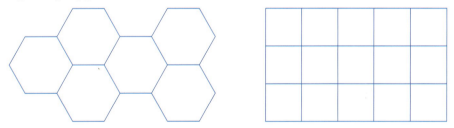

● *Each regular polygon has all its sides and all its angles the same size.*

So a square is a regular quadrilateral, because all its sides are the same length and all its angles are right angles.
But a rectangle is *not* a regular quadrilateral, because its sides are *not all* the same length.
A rhombus is *not* a regular quadrilateral. (Why not?)

Exercise 17.2

Go back to exercise 17.1 and on one of your squares mark the diagram to show why it *is* a regular polygon.
Mark one of your rectangles to show why it is *not* a regular polygon.

What is the special name for a regular three-sided polygon?
An **equilateral triangle**.

Other regular polygons do not have special names. So we talk of regular pentagons, regular hexagons, or regular octagons. But we usually say 'square' instead of 'regular quadrilateral' and 'equilateral triangle' instead of 'regular triangle'.

If a polygon is not regular, it is called **irregular**.

Exercise 17.3

Draw diagrams of the following polygons.
  Always assume that the polygons are irregular unless the question says otherwise.

1 A triangle
2 A hexagon
3 A regular quadrilateral (remember what that is?)
4 An octagon
5 A regular triangle

Drawing regular polygons that are not squares or equilateral triangles can be complicated.

Exercise 17.4

You will need:
- paper
- pair of compasses
- protractor
- sharp pencil
- rubber

Follow these instructions carefully. At first, draw all the lines lightly so that you can rub out some of them at the end.
  When you have finished, you should have drawn a regular octagon.

1 Draw a circle of radius about 6 cm.

2 Draw in one radius as in the diagram.

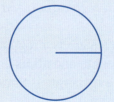

3 With your protractor, measure 45° from this line in an anti-clockwise direction. Draw in a second radius.

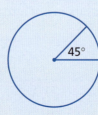

4 Repeat this, rotating the radius 45° and drawing a new one each time, until you come back to your original line. Your diagram should look like this:

5 Join up all the points on the edge of your circle (you should have eight points altogether).
6 Rub out the circle and the radius lines.

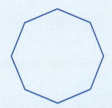

You should be left with a regular octagon!

Can you see why each angle had to measure 45°?
It's because you have split a complete turn (360°) into eight equal parts.

Polygons (especially regular ones) have been used a great deal throughout history for both building purposes and as decoration. You have probably seen examples using tiles, on floors, ceilings and walls.

Tessellations

If a shape can be repeated so that it fits together with itself without overlapping or leaving any gaps, then that shape is said to **tessellate**.
The pattern it forms is called a **tessellation**.
A chess board is an example of a tessellation of squares.

The patterns below are tessellations of other shapes. Many complicated patterns are possible!

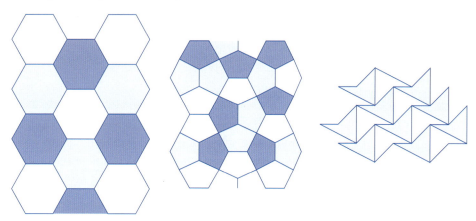

Exercise 17.5

1 By using different colours, create your own square tessellation.

2 Look at this irregular hexagon:

Make several copies of it on centimetre squared paper to show that it will tessellate. Colour the resulting pattern in some regular way.

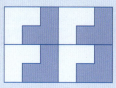

3 See if this irregular octagon will tessellate (use squared paper).

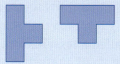

Try rotating the shape through a right-angle as illustrated.

4 See if you can invent a shape of your own which tessellates.

5 It is difficult to use a single regular shape to draw accurate tessellations on squared paper. Copy and colour this pattern. Note that the octagon is not a regular one.

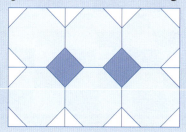

SUMMARY

- A closed shape with all its sides straight lines is called a **polygon**.
- If a polygon has all its sides the same length and all its angles the same size, then it is called a **regular polygon**. If not, then it is **irregular**.
- Three-sided polygons are called triangles. Regular triangles are **equilateral**.
- Four-sided polygons are called quadrilaterals. Regular quadrilaterals are called squares.
- Five-sided polygons are called pentagons.
- Six-sided polygons are called hexagons.
- Eight-sided polygons are called octagons.
- If a polygon (which doesn't have to be regular) can be fitted together to make a tiling pattern which doesn't overlap or have any gaps, then that polygon **tessellates**.
- Polygons are used in building and decorating.

Exercise 17A

Draw the following.

1 Three different irregular quadrilaterals
2 Two different irregular pentagons
3 A tessellation using a rectangle

Exercise 17B

Draw the following.

1 Three different irregular triangles
2 Two different irregular hexagons
3 A tessellation using an isosceles triangle

Exercise 17C

Following similar instructions to those in exercise 17.4, construct, on plain paper, the following regular polygons.
    First calculate the 'central' angle needed to make the figures.

1 A regular pentagon
2 A regular hexagon
3 Using your diagram from question 2 to help you, draw a tessellation using only a regular hexagon

Exercise 17D

1 Does a regular pentagon tessellate?
2 Do circles tessellate?
3 Using squared paper, demonstrate that *any* irregular quadrilateral tessellates!
4 Investigate the work of Escher, a Dutch artist whose work brings in many mathematical ideas. Can you create a tessellation of your own in the style of Escher's work?

18 Collecting data

Did it rain yesterday?
  If it did, does this mean that it will rain today?

How many pupils in your class came to school yesterday?
Will the same number come to school tomorrow?

You can't tell!
  What happened *yesterday*, is studied as part of the subject of **statistics**.
  What might happen *tomorrow* is a **prediction** and is more the study of **probability**.
  To be able to make good estimates of what might happen in the future, it helps to have good records of what has happened in the past. Records are often in terms of numbers and it helps to make sense of them by organising and sorting out what these numbers could mean.

Exercise 18.1

An athlete is training for a competition. His training times (in seconds) for seven weeks before his 100 m race are:

Week 1	15.2	14.8	15.1	15.2	14.9	15.1
Week 2	15.0	15.1	14.9	15.1	15.0	14.7
Week 3	14.9	14.8	15.0	14.6	14.6	14.7
Week 4	14.5	14.6	14.4	14.3	14.8	14.3
Week 5	14.2	14.2	14.0	14.2	13.9	14.1
Week 6	13.8	13.9	14.0	13.7	13.6	13.7
Week 7	13.5	13.6	13.4	13.5	14.0	13.5

1 What is the athlete's slowest time?
2 What is his fastest time?
3 How many times did he run 100 m in 14.2 seconds?
4 How many times did he run 100 m in 14.6 seconds?
5 Can you see any overall change to his times? If there is, are there any times which don't fit the pattern?
6 Do you think the athlete stands a chance of achieving the qualifying standard of 13.4 seconds to represent his school in the competition?
7 Can you think of a way of presenting these times that would make it easier to do parts (c) and (d) of this question?

Doing the last exercise, you may have thought about using some sort of table or graph for part (g).

There are many ways of presenting statistics.

Football results are statistics.

Soccer Results

EUROPEAN CUP
Semi-finals, second leg
Man Utd (0) 0   Borussla Dortmund (1) 1
53,606   Ricken 8
(agg: 0–2)
Juventus 4, Ajax 1 (agg: 6–2)
FA CARLING PREMIERSHIP
Derby (0) 0   Nottm Forest (0) 0
18,087
Leicester (0) 0   West Ham (0) 1
20,327

BOTTOM TEN	P	W	D	L	F	A	Pts
Derby	36	10	13	13	42	54	43
Everton	36	10	12	14	43	52	42
Blackburn	35	9	14	12	40	37	41
Leicester	35	10	10	15	39	50	40
Southampton	36	9	11	16	48	55	38
West Ham	35	9	11	15	34	45	38
Coventry	36	8	14	14	35	51	38
Sunderland	36	9	10	17	32	52	37

	P	W	D	L	F	A	Pts
Middlesbrough	33	9	9	15	44	53	33
Nottm Forest	36	6	15	15	30	53	33

NATIONWIDE LEAGUE
First Division
Crystal Palace (1) 3   Reading (0) 2
Linighan 13   Bodin 57
Hopkin 49   Williams 82
Shipperley 69   12,552
Wolverhampton (1)   1 Grimsby (1) 1
Gilkes 10   Oster 45
                                              25,474

TOP EIGHT	P	W	D	L	F	A	Pts
Bolton (C)	44	27	13	4	94	50	94
Barnsley	44	21	14	9	73	50	77
Wolverhampton	44	21	10	13	66	49	73
Ipswich	44	19	13	12	66	49	70
Sheff Utd	44	19	12	13	74	52	69
Crystal Palace	44	18	13	13	75	47	67
Port Vale	44	17	15	12	56	52	66
Portsmouth	44	19	8	17	58	52	65

Television viewing figures are statistics.

WHAT THE NATION WATCHED									
BBC1		**BBC2**		**ITV**		**C4**		**C5**	
1	EastEnders (Tue/Sun)	15.25	Absolutely Fabulous	4.21	Coronation Street (Mon)	15.48	Friends	5.30	Zena: Warrior Princess	1.06
2	Driving School	9.57	This Life (Thu/Sat)	4.12	Emmerdale (Tues/Wed)	10.33	Brookside (Fri/Sat)	4.72	Across 110th Street	1.01
3	Dalziel and Pascoe	8.97	The Vicar of Dibley	3.99	Wycliffe	10.23	Countdown (Tue)	3.45	Poltergeist: the Legacy	.95
4	Airport	8.78	The Travel Show	3.81	The Bill (Fri)	9.64	Frasier	3.28	Legacy of Evil	.93
5	National Lottery Live (Sat)	8.54	Gardeners' World	3.32	Home and Away (Mon)	8.81	Cybill	2.57	Blind Hate	.75
6	Only Fools and Horses	8.40	Ainsley's Barbecue Bible	2.99	Inspector Morse	8.73	The Deep (joint sixth)	2.53	French Lieutenant's Woman	.72
7	Neighbours (Mon)	8.29	Naked Spur	2.70	Bramwell	8.22	True Stories (joint sixth)	2.53	The Maid	.72
8	Crimewatch UK	8.14	Steptoe and Son	2.60	Wheel of Fortune	7.45	Ricki Lake (Tue)	2.50	Neighbours	.71
9	One Foot in the Grave	7.90	Reputations	2.49	News at Ten (Mon)	7.08	NYPD Blue	2.48	Family Affairs (Mon/Tue)	.67
10	Birds of a Feather	7.60	The Outer Limits	2.37	Staying Alive	6.73	Hollyoaks (Mon/Sun)	2.46	JAG	.61

Viewing figures for 7–13 July 1997. Source: Broadcasters' Audience Research Board (Barb)/RSMB. When more than one episode is broadcast in a week, the highest figure is given. If a programme is repeated, the audiences for the first and repeat broadcasts are combined.

Source: BARB

Weather details are statistics.

Around Britain Met Office report for 24 hours to 5pm yesterday																	
	Sun hrs	Rain ins	Temp H	L	Weather (day)		Sun hrs	Rain ins	Temp H	L	Weather (day)			Sun hrs	Rain ins		
Aberdeen	0.1	0.15	10	3	Rain	Hastings	10.2	––	13	2	Sunny	Poole	8.1	0.06		
Anglesey	9.7	––	13	8	Sunny	Hayling I	8.7	0.01	12	8	Sunny	Ross-on-Wye	5.8	––		
Aspatria	1.9	0.01	12	2	Rain pm	Herne Bay	6.2	––	15	2	Sunny	Ryde	7.5	0.01		
Aviemore	1.2	0.14	9	2	Rain	Hove	5.6	––	11	6	Sunny	Salcombe	8.9	0.02		
Belfast	0.8	0.01	13	2	Bright am	Hunstanton	––	––	15	–	Bright	Sandown	7.3	––		
Birmingham	2.4	0.01	14	4	Sh pm	Isle of Man	5.2	––	12	2	Bright	Saunton Sands	8.7	––		
Bognor Regis	7.0	––	13	4	Sunny pm	Jersey	9.6	––	15	7	Sunny	Scarborough	9.4	––		
Bristol	8.6	––	14	7	Sunny	Kinloss	0.3	0.03	13	4	Rain	Shanklin	8.6	0.01		
Buxton	5.8	0.01	12	3	Sunny	Leeds	8.2	0.01	15	5	Sh pm	Shrewsbury	4.9	0.01		
Cardiff	9.9	––	15	3	Sunny	Lerwick	2.7	0.03	5	0	Rain pm	Skegness	5.8	––		
Clacton	7.8	––	11	7	Sunny	Leuchars	1.2	0.02	11	0	Rain pm	Southend	2.8	––		
Colwyn Bay	6.5	0.09	15	5	Sunny pm	Littlehampton	7.3	––	13	–1	Sunny pm	Southport	8.4	––		
Cromer	5.7	0.01	15	7	Bright	London	5.8	0.01	15	7	Bright	Southsea	7.6	––		
Eastbourne	8.7	0.01	13	2	Sunny	Lowestoft	6.0	0.01	14	3	Bright pm	Stornoway	0.7	0.44		
Edinburgh	0.9	0.03	13	1	Rain pm	Manchester	6.3	0.01				Swanage	7.1	0.03		
Eskdalemuir	1.0	0.06	11	–4	Rain pm	Margate	8.4	––				Teignmouth	9.7	0.01		
Exmouth	9.9	––	14	6	Sunny	Morecambe	7.1	––				Tenby	7.5	0.01		
Falmouth	9.3	0.08	14	5	Sunny	Newcastle	6.5	––				Tiree	1.1	0.72		
Fishguard	5.6	0.01	13	5	Bright	Newquay	9.2	––				Torquay	9.9	0.01		
Folkestone	10.8	––	12	–2	Sunny pm	Norwich	5.8	0.02				Tynemouth	––	––		
Glasgow	0.6	0.22	10	1	Rain	Oxford	5.8	0.01				Ventnor	7.1	0.01		
Guernsey	9.5	––	16	7	Sunny	Penzance	––	––				Weston-s-Mare	8.0	––		
												Weymouth	8.1	0.01		

Frequency tables

The number of times something happens can be very important.

For instance, the number of sunny days in a year in Blackpool is very important to the Blackpool Tourist Office.

The number of times a goalkeeper lets in a goal is very important to the team manager!

The number of times a particular thing happens is called its **frequency**.

A table which records this is called a **frequency table**.

When you are drawing up your own frequency table from some data, it is quicker to record each result *in turn*, rather than count *all* the results which are the same.

Ten people were asked which sandwiches they prefer: chicken, tuna or egg (no other choices). Here are their answers:

chicken tuna chicken egg egg tuna egg egg chicken egg

We first make a **tally chart** of the results:

item	tally
chicken	|||
tuna	||
egg	||||

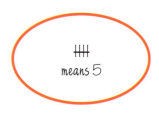

HH
means 5

You can see immediately that egg is the most popular sandwich and tuna is the least popular.

To present this as a proper frequency table, put the information in columns with headings and add a third column called frequency (which is just the number in the tally).

type of sandwich	tally	frequency
chicken	|||	3
tuna	||	2
egg	||||	5
Total:		10 (3 + 2 + 5)

Add up the frequency column to make sure all the results have been included.

Exercise 18.2

1 A supermarket manager wants to check the supermarket's sales of different types of bread, as it sometimes has a big surplus at the end of the day. She decides to look at how many loaves are sold on one particular day.

    She chooses four categories: brown (b), white (w), wholemeal (m), other (o)
    This is what she found:

w	w	m	b	o	o	o	o	w	o
m	b	b	w	m	b	w	w	b	m
w	b	m	w	b	o	o	o	w	m
w	b	m	w	o	o	b	b	m	w
m	w	b	o	o	w	w	b	b	m

    a Draw a frequency table to help the manager.
    b Which type of bread sold the most?
    c How many loaves were sold altogether?
    d What problems are there with the way the manager did her research? How could she improve this?

2 A class of 28 Year 7 pupils were asked how many brothers and sisters they had. Here are their answers:

2	0	1	1	1	2	0	3	0
1	2	4	2	1	0	2	1	1
3	1	2	0	1	0	2	1	0
5								

    a Show this information in a frequency table.
    b How many people had no brothers or sisters?
    c What was the largest number of brothers or sisters anyone in the class had?

3 Pupils in a class were asked which type of burger they preferred. They said they liked, beef (B), chicken (C), fish (F), vegetarian (V) or none (N).
  Here are their answers:

B	B	C	N	B	B	F	B	B	V
C	F	B	B	V	C	C	N	B	F
V	F	C	F	C	B	B	F	N	C

    a Which burger was the most popular? Is it easy to tell from the way the answers are presented above?
    b Design a frequency table to help you find the answer to part (a) more easily.
    c Ask the pupils in your class which type of burger they prefer (you may have to include other types). How do your results compare with the ones above?

Bar charts

Sometimes it can be useful to show information in a diagram instead of a table. The easiest sort of diagram to draw is a **bar chart**.

This is the bar chart for the 'sandwiches' frequency table.

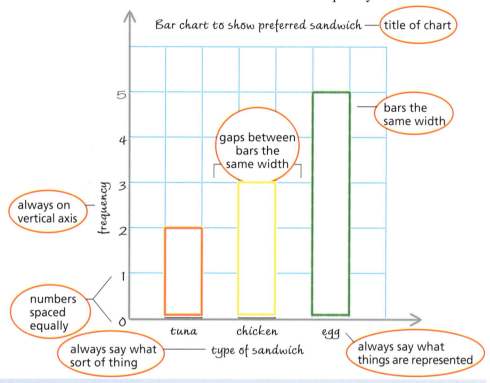

Exercise 18.3

Look carefully at the seven encircled pieces of text in the above diagram and then make a list of seven things you must remember when you draw a bar chart.

Exercise 18.4

Draw bar charts for the questions in exercise 18.2.

Exercise 18.5

1 A market research company was investigating the different ways local firms advertised their services. After conducting a survey, they put their results into a frequency table.

type of advertising	local papers	local radio	television	telephone directory	billboards	cinema	leaflets
number of firms	26	15	2	35	5	1	19

  a Can you think of any other ways of advertising?
  b Show this information in a bar chart.
  c Why is it impossible to know, just from this table, how many companies were interviewed?

2 To help its purchase of new stock, a local library investigated the types of fiction read by its members. All fiction books borrowed one Tuesday were recorded and divided into categories. These were the categories:

crime/thriller (C)   romance (R)   horror (H)
science-fiction (SF)   historical (P)   teenage (T)
literary classics (L)   children's (CH)

Here are the results.

type	C	R	SF	P	T	CH	H	L
frequency	51	97	38	31	17	21	8	11

  a Which category of books was borrowed the most?
  b Draw a bar chart to show this information.
  c What could the library do to make sure that its information was a really accurate picture of books borrowed?

There may be a problem with Tuesday. What might it be?!

Making and using databases

As well as using other people's data, you could also do some research of your own. You could make a class **database**.

In the past, databases were often stored on sets of cards but now computers are more often used.

A database is a set of different sorts of information collected together

A database can be as simple as the names and addresses of all the members of a club, or as complicated as the medical records of all the patients in a hospital.

If you make a list of the items of information you wish to collect and give each person a copy, this is called a **questionnaire**.

Exercise 18.6

1 Make your own class database using this questionnaire for each person. You may use other questions if you wish.

Questionnaire
Name:
Age (years and months):
Date of birth:
Place of birth:
Number of brothers/sisters:
Number of pets:
Height:
Shoe size:
Hair colour:
Eye colour:

2 Use your database to draw frequency tables and bar charts for:
   a the hair colour of the people in your class
   b the months of birth of the people in your class
   c some other category you have collected.

SUMMARY

■ **Statistics** is about recording, organising and sorting out information in number form.
■ **Frequency tables** and **bar charts** are used to make information easier to understand.
■ A bar chart must be properly numbered and labelled.
■ A **database** is information collection together.
■ A **questionnaire** is a form which is used to collect information.
■ A computer can be used to record a database.

Exercise 18A

1 In early 1997, a group of sixth-formers were asked which television channel they watched most often. At that time there were four 'terrestrial' channels, BBC1, BBC2, ITV and C4, and one main satellite network (counted as one channel).
The channels were coded like this: BBC1 (1), BBC2 (2), ITV (3), C4 (4), Satellite/cable (5).
Here are their answers:

1	3	3	1	2	1
3	4	1	1	3	3
5	1	2	1	1	3
3	3	4	1	1	1
2	1	1	3	1	5
3	3	4	1	3	5
2	3	1	2	1	1
3	4	3	3	3	1

a How many sixth-formers were asked?
b Draw a frequency table and bar chart to show these results.
c Which channel was watched most often?
d Ask your own class the same question (don't forget to include any new channels!).
How do your results compare with those of the sixth-formers?

2 A building firm decided to investigate popular sorts of heating before installing heating systems into new houses. A mixture of young and old people were asked which sort of heating they preferred, central heating (C), night storage heaters (N), electric fires (E), gas fires (G) or other types (O).
Here are the results:

C	O	G	N	N	C	C	C	C	G
E	G	O	N	N	C	N	N	C	N
E	O	N	N	C	C	C	N	N	N
O	G	N	N	C	N	C	N	C	O
N	N	C	C	C	C	E	C	C	E

a Draw a frequency table and bar chart to show these results.
b Which form of heating was most popular?
c Do you think younger and older people gave different answers? Explain your answer.
d What sort or sorts of heating do you think the building firm should use?

Exercise 18B

1 This frequency table shows the ways in which workers in a small factory in London travelled to work.

walk	bus	car	train	tube	cycle
6	12	5	2	9	4

a How many workers are there altogether at the factory?
b Which method of transport is least popular?
c Draw a bar chart to illustrate this information.

2 A travel agent surveyed a group of people one winter to help decide what sorts of holiday to offer the next year.
People were asked about their main holiday the previous year.
Holidays were split into six categories.

Here is the result of the survey.

hotel abroad	self-catering abroad	hotel in UK	self-catering in UK	with friends	none
256	451	204	390	158	97

a Which category was most popular?
b Find the total number of people questioned.
c Draw a bar chart illustrating this information.
d How could the survey be improved?

19 Symmetry

You will need:
- several small pieces of tracing paper
- a small mirror

Trace this figure carefully.

Fold the figure about the vertical line shown in the diagram and notice that both halves match exactly.

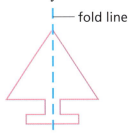

— fold line

Start again by drawing only half the shape

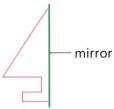

— mirror

and place a mirror along the line shown.

Look in the mirror from the left, and notice that the reflection together with the original half-figure looks just like the first drawing!

Whenever a figure can be reflected like this, or can be folded so that one part matches the other, the figure is said to be **symmetrical**.

You need to be good at recognising **symmetry** wherever it might occur.

Exercise 19.1

Look at these drawings and say which ones are symmetrical. If you are not sure, check using tracing paper or a mirror or both.

1

3

5

7

2

4

6

8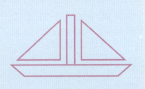

Exercise 19.2

Collect some pictures of objects which are symmetrical and stick them in your book.

Lines of symmetry

When a figure is symmetrical, the fold line is called a **line of symmetry**. It can also be called an **axis of symmetry**.

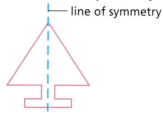

Since it's also the place you would put the mirror in order to see the symmetry, the line of symmetry can also be called the **mirror line**.

Exercise 19.3

Trace the symmetrical figures from exercise 19.1 and fold them to show their lines of symmetry.

Use a mirror to check they are the mirror lines.

Draw them in your book and put in the lines of symmetry.

Exercise 19.4

Draw these shapes on centimetre squared paper and complete them so that the heavy line is a mirror line. Try to do them without using tracing paper or a mirror.

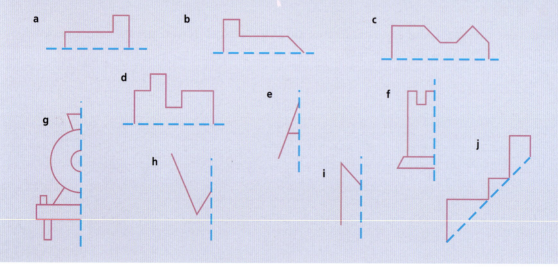

Exercise 19.5

Invent five half shapes of your own and give them to a partner to complete as if using a mirror.

Exercise 19.6

You will need:
- some small pieces of plain paper or thin card
- scissors

Fold a small sheet of paper or card and cut out a shape of your own invention starting and finishing on the crease.

Notice that both the cut-out piece and the shape left behind are symmetrical. You could use the shape left behind as a stencil to make an imaginative picture!

Try several different shapes. Combine them in a picture. Work with a partner. You could ask your art teacher for help.

You will need:
- pieces of plain paper (some square in shape)
- scissors

More than one line of symmetry

Each of the shapes we have used so far has had *one and only one* line of symmetry. Try this.

Fold a piece of paper or thin card *twice*, so that the second fold is perpendicular to the first:

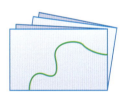

Cut through all four thicknesses and unfold. You get a shape with *two* lines of symmetry. (This is the cut-out piece.)

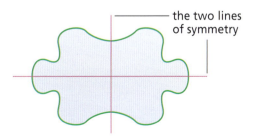

the two lines of symmetry

Try this several times, folding twice and cutting out a different shape each time.

Also try folding a *square* piece of paper twice and then folding the square 'packet' along a diagonal line and cutting across a corner.

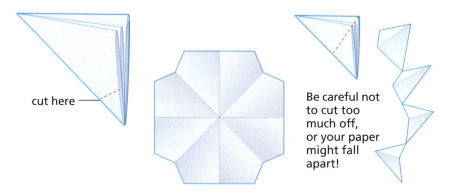

cut here

Be careful not to cut too much off, or your paper might fall apart!

When it works you get *four* lines of symmetry. Check with a mirror. It is possible to draw a shape with any number of lines of symmetry you would like! This shape has *five* lines of symmetry.

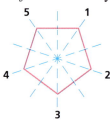

Exercise 19.7

By tracing or by using a mirror, find the number of lines of symmetry of the following shapes.

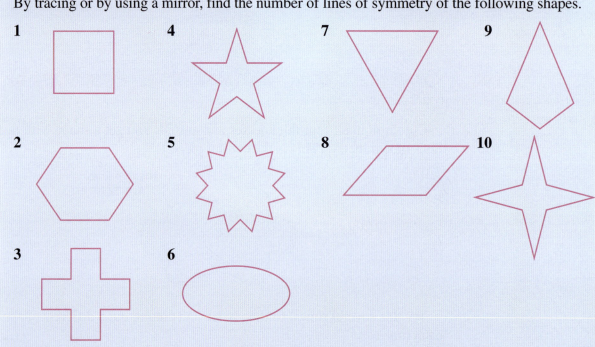

Exercise 19.8

Extend your collection of symmetrical objects and drawings to include some natural ones.

Symmetry in nature

Many natural objects have lines of symmetry. Look at these pictures and notice the symmetry.

Natural objects are not often *exactly* symmetrical. You could ask your biology teacher about this.

Rotational symmetry

On centimetre squared paper, draw a large capital 'N'.

Try this a few times – until you are totally convinced.

Make a tracing and try to find any lines of symmetry by folding. You could also use a mirror.

After some experimentation you should realise *that it hasn't got any*!

But the letter 'N' *does* have a *different sort of symmetry*.

If you turn the letter upside-down it still looks the same as it did before (try it).

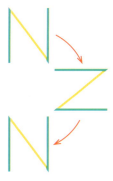

What has happened is that you have **rotated** the shape through *half a turn* or 180°. When this occurs, we say the shape has **half-turn** symmetry.

Try the same thing with the letter 'Z'.

Z

It also has half-turn symmetry.

Consider the next shape:

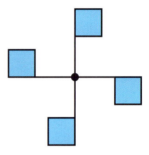

Copy it onto squared paper and make a tracing of it.

Place the tracing over the drawing and put the point of a pencil on the heavy dot. Now, keeping the squared paper still, rotate the tracing clockwise so that it covers the drawing again.

You should have rotated through an angle of 90°.

Rotate 90° again – the shape is covered again. Turn another quarter-turn clockwise and another and the shape is back where it started.

● *If you can rotate a shape **four times**, covering the shape again each time, this figure is said to have **rotational symmetry of order 4**.*

Check that this shape has rotational symmetry of order 3.

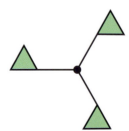

Exercise 19.9

Decide which of the following shapes have rotational symmetry and state the order of rotation for those which do.

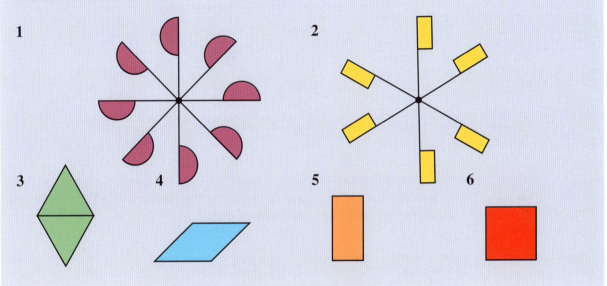

1   2

3   4   5   6

Some shapes have both line and rotational symmetry.
   A rhombus shape like this

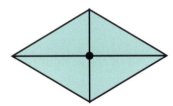

has two lines of symmetry *and* rotational symmetry of order 2.
   Check with tracing paper.
   A square has rotational symmetry of order 4 and also four lines of symmetry.

Centre of rotation

The point about which a figure can be turned so that it fits back on itself is called its **centre of rotation**.

Exercise 19.10

Draw the capital letters of the alphabet and, under each one, put its order of rotational symmetry.
   Put a dot to show the centre of symmetry and also draw in any lines of symmetry.

Congruence

When a figure is reflected in a mirror, the original and its reflection are exactly the same shape and size.

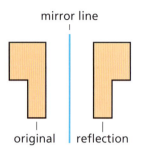

mirror line

original · reflection

You can see this in the above diagram even though the shape becomes 'turned over'.

But there are many ways of changing the position of a figure without changing its shape or size. Look at these:

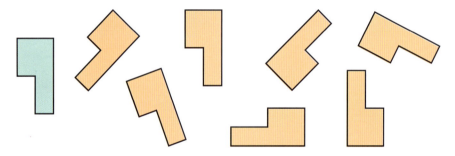

All of these figures are exactly the same as the original, apart from being moved about in some way.

● *When figures are identical (apart from position), they are said to be* **congruent** *to each other.*

Exercise 19.11

In each of the following pairs of shapes, say whether the shapes are congruent. If you're not sure, check by tracing.

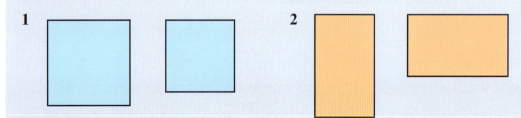

1

2

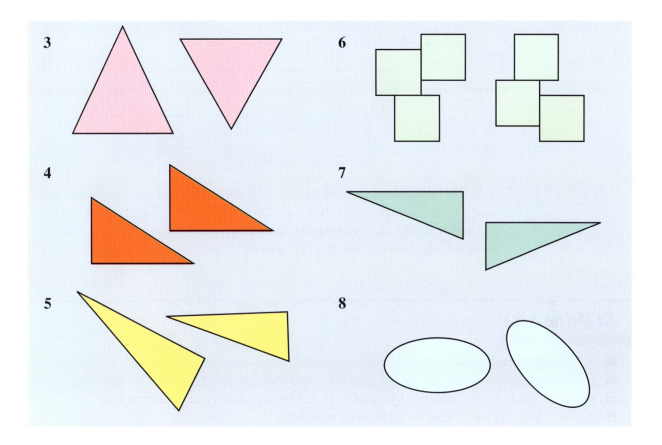

Symmetry in 3D

The previous examples of symmetry have been in two dimensions (2D). But you can get symmetry in 3D as well.

Look at this drawing of a cube. If a cut were made through the middle of the cube it would separate the two halves as if one were a reflection of the other.

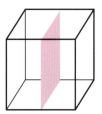

This cut is called a **plane of symmetry** and is like the mirror line in 2D.

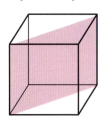

This illustrates another plane of symmetry of a cube.

You have to be careful with symmetry in three dimensions since not every cut into halves is a plane of symmetry.

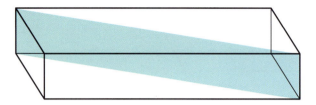

This does *not* illustrate a plane of symmetry since the two halves are *not* mirror images of each other. You could see this if you made one half from some suitable material such as clay, alloplast, polystyrene, balsa wood, etc. and looked at it in a mirror.

SUMMARY

- A 2D **symmetrical** shape looks the same as itself when reflected in a mirror.
- A 2D symmetrical shape can be folded about a line so that one half matches the other.
- The fold line is called a **line of symmetry** or **axis of symmetry** or a **mirror line**.
- A shape may have any number of lines of symmetry.
- Many natural objects are symmetrical, though often not exactly.
- Some shapes look the same after rotation about a point and have **rotational symmetry**.
- The number of times a shape can be turned round and still fit is called the **order of rotation**.
- The point around which you turn a shape is called its **centre of rotation**.
- A shape can have both line symmetry and rotational symmetry.
- When shapes are identical apart from position they are **congruent** to each other.
- 3D shapes can have **planes of symmetry**.

Exercise 19A

Copy these shapes onto centimetre squared paper and mark any lines of symmetry and centres of symmetry.

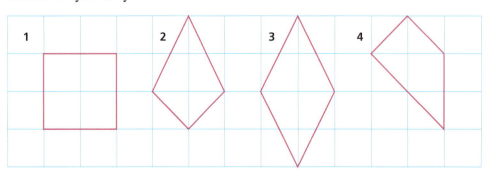

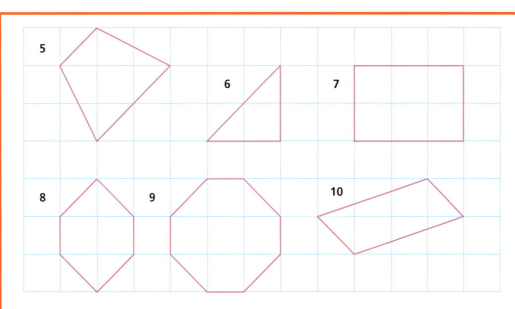

Exercise 19B

Group together the numbers of the following shapes which are congruent to each other.

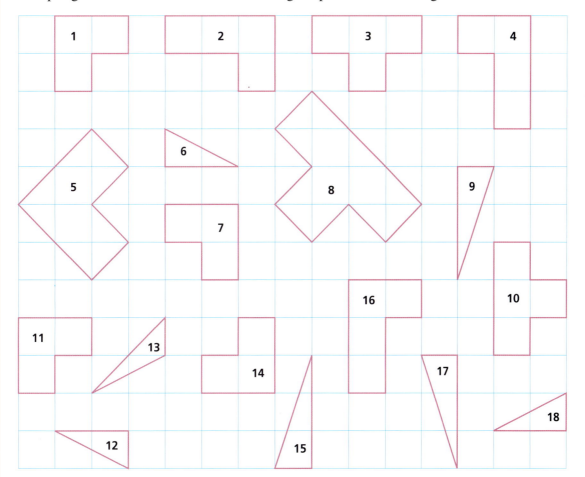

Exercise 19C

1 Make separate drawings of a cuboid with none of its edges equal to show all possible different planes of symmetry.
   If you can, make a solid but transparent model of these.

2 Make drawings of a cone, a sphere, a cylinder and a square-based pyramid to show a plane of symmetry of each.

3 Make five separate drawings like the one below, which represents a cuboid with a square base, to show its five planes of symmetry.

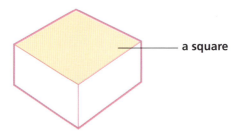 

a square

4 How many planes of symmetry has a cube altogether?

There are more than you think!

Exercise 19D

Invent shapes of your own (2D, 3D or both), some of which have line symmetry, some of which have rotational symmetry, some of which have both and some of which have no symmetry at all.
   Mark in any lines, planes and centres of symmetry.
   Write down any orders of rotation.

20 Directed numbers

Negative and positive

Have you ever been to an athletics match or seen one on television?

Many numbers are used to describe and record both track and field events.

Perhaps you have noticed that for short races like the 100 m the wind speed is sometimes flashed up on the screen? This is because a strong wind interferes with the race; in fact if it's too strong athletes' times don't count for records.

The commentator will talk about a 'head wind' or a 'following wind'. A **following wind** blows in the same direction as the runners and is shown on the screen by a **plus** (+) sign. A **head wind** blows against the direction of the runners and slows them down. Head winds are shown on the screen using a **minus** (−) sign.

Who else do you think might need to know about 'following' and 'head' winds?

Another place where a minus sign is used is when a frosty night is expected by the weather forecasters after news broadcasts.

Temperatures below zero are called **negative** or 'minus'. You can see the minus sign on television screens and in newspapers throughout the winter.

Temperatures above zero are **positive**.

The 'negative' or 'minus' sign has been used for a very long time. One of its first recorded uses is from Babylonian times, about 3000 years ago!

The Hindu mathematician Brahmagupta wrote about it around 500 BC and another Hindu mathematician, Bhaskara, wrote down the rules for using negative numbers around AD 1100. He talked about them to do with 'debt' or 'loss'.

During medieval times it was common for plus and minus signs to be used in warehouses, chalked on sacks, to show if the sacks had too much or too little in them.

The idea of negative quantities became widespread in the seventeenth century when Italian bankers allowed people to borrow more money than was in their account, writing the amounts on the opposite side of the ledger in red.

This is why, even today, if you owe money it's called 'being in the red'.

Exercise 20.1

Write a few notes about the history and uses of negative numbers.
Use a library to find out more, or think of uses of your own.

Describing movement and position

If 'moving north' were called *positive*, how could you describe the corresponding *negative* direction?

moving south

If 'climbing a ladder' were described as *positive*, what would be the corresponding *negative* direction?

descending a ladder

Exercise 20.2

If each of the following describes a *positive* direction, describe the corresponding *negative* direction.

1 Moving east
2 Moving up
3 Rotating anti-clockwise
4 Pushing
5 Counting forwards

Exercise 20.3

Write down some pairs of opposite directions of your own. In each pair, say which is to be positive and which negative.

The language of mathematics

As you become older you must begin to use more precise language to discuss mathematics since this helps to sort out the ideas.

For example, it is better to say 'subtract' rather than 'take away'.

The words 'negative' and 'minus' actually mean different things, in the same way as 'positive' and 'plus' mean different things.

- *Positive refers to the number itself, like 'positive three'.*
- *Plus describes the **operation** of addition (something you do). So you should say 'add **positive** three', not 'add **plus** three'.*

When we want to show that we mean the number 'positive three', it will be written in brackets like this:

$$(+3)$$

When we mean to add, it will be written with the plus sign on its own like this:

$$+ (+3)$$

and read: 'plus positive three' or 'add positive three'.

(-3) is read as 'negative three' and
$- (-3)$ is read as 'subtract negative three' or 'minus negative three'.

We shall look more closely at the addition and subtraction of positive and negative numbers in chapter 24.

Exercise 20.4

Say these to yourself in your head.

Ten minus four means subtract four from ten.

1 'Ten *minus* four' means '*subtract* four from ten'.
2 '*Subtract* negative three from positive six' means the same as 'positive six *minus* negative three'.
3 $5 - 3$ should be read 'five minus three'.
4 $(+5) - (-3)$ should be read 'positive five minus negative three'.
5 'What is $6 - 7$?' should be read 'What is six minus seven?'.

Exercise 20.5

Read these correctly to yourself in your head.
 Then take it in turns to read them aloud to the class.

1 $7 - 4$
2 $(+8) - (+3)$
3 $(+8) - (-3)$
4 $(-8) - (+3)$
5 $(-8) - (-3)$

More about positive and negative numbers

In most uses of positive and negative numbers:

- *up* is the positive direction and *down* is negative
- *to the right* is the positive direction and *to the left* is negative.

A rise of 5 °C would be $(+5)$ °C, and a fall of 5 °C would be (-5) °C.
 A walk of 2 km east would be $(+2)$ km, and a walk of 2 km west would be (-2) km.

Exercise 20.6

Rewrite the number mentioned using a positive or negative sign and brackets.

height of
cliff edge

1 I fly a kite 50 metres above the cliff edge (I am standing on the cliff edge). [Answer: (+50) m]
2 I look at a rock, 50 m below the cliff edge (I am on the cliff edge).
3 I see a nest, 25 m below the cliff edge (I am looking over the cliff edge).
4 I notice that a balloon bursts, 30 m above the cliff edge (I am on the cliff edge).
5 A helicopter passes 200 m over my head (measured from where I am).
6 A dolphin leaps 1 m out of the sea (measured from sea level).
7 A diver tells me he has just been to the sea floor, 15 m below sea level (measured from sea level).
8 A ship lowers its anchor 10 m (measured from the ship).
9 A flag flutters at the top of the ship's mast, 10 m above the deck (measured from the deck).
10 I throw a stone which lodges 5 m below the cliff edge.

Exercise 20.7

Write down which of these pairs of degree Celsius temperatures is the higher (warmer).

1 $(+5), (-5)$
2 $(+4), (+3)$
3 $(-3), (+1)$
4 $(-2), (-5)$
5 $(-4), (+4)$
6 $(+2), (+4)$
7 $(0), (-3)$ (notice that zero doesn't have any sign)
8 $(0), (+3)$
9 $(-3), (-2)$
10 $(-1), (-2)$

Exercise 20.8

Write the answers to these using positive or negative numbers.

1 Write a debt of £24.
2 My pocket is empty and I find 20p.
3 Write a temperature 3 °C warmer than −2 °C.
4 I owe 35p.
5 Which is colder, −2 °C or −1 °C?
6 The valley was 60 m below the path.
7 How much is left after depositing £30 and withdrawing £50 from my bank account?
8 Write a temperature 3 °C colder than 2 °C.
9 I walk five steps to the left then three to the right; where am I?
10 I walk three steps to the left then five to the right; where am I?

Exercise 20.9

Ask your teacher for this exercise (in Teacher's Resource File 1).

SUMMARY

- Positive and negative numbers have had a long history.
- Using the correct words helps you understand the ideas.
- The word **plus** means 'add', something you *do*.
- The word **minus** means 'subtract', something you *do*.
- The word **negative** describes the *position* of a number (often 'below' or 'to the left').
- The word **positive** describes the *position* of a number (often 'above' or 'to the right').
- Negative temperatures are below zero (°C).
- 'Negative money' could be described as a 'loss' or 'debt'.

Exercise 20A

Rewrite these statements using positive or negative signs.

1 I dig a hole in the sand 50 cm deep.
2 I build a sandcastle 50 cm tall.
3 The foundations of the building were ten metres deep.
4 My bank account is £5 in the red.
5 What is the deepest point of the Channel Tunnel? [Find out!]
6 This sack is 700 g too heavy.
7 I got home quicker because of a following wind of 10 miles per hour.
8 How much is left if I withdraw £35 after depositing £10 in my empty bank account?
9 Write a temperature 2 °C colder than −1 °C.
10 Has the weather become warmer or colder when the temperature changes from −4 °C to −1 °C?

Exercise 20B

Rewrite these statements using positive or negative signs.

1 I look at the roof of a house 20 m above street level.
2 I raise the window-blind 3 m above the window-sill.
3 I drop a stone down a well 10 m deep.
4 This sack is 3 kg too light!
5 I had to ride my bicycle more carefully because of a head wind of 20 km per hour.
6 Write a temperature 3 °C warmer than −4 °C.
7 I put £2.50 into my savings account.
8 The hole in the road was 2 m deep.
9 I owed £2 and borrowed another £1. I then owed £3.
10 Has the weather become warmer or colder when the temperature changes from −1 °C to −4 °C?

Exercise 20C

Rewrite these statements using positive or negative signs. You may have to change several words to get the statement to make sense!

1 I dug a hole in the sand 20 cm deep and then made it 30 cm deeper. The hole was then 50 cm deep. (Draw diagrams to illustrate.)
2 I dug a hole in the sand 40 cm deep and then filled it in 10 cm. The hole was then 30 cm deep. (Draw diagrams to illustrate.)
3 I dug a hole in the sand 20 cm deep and then made a sand-castle 60 cm tall in the hole. The sand-castle ended up 40 cm above the original level of the sand. (Draw diagrams to illustrate.)
4 I made a sand-castle 40 cm tall but my younger sister stamped on it reducing it by 50 cm. The resulting hole was 10 cm deep. (Draw diagrams to illustrate.)
5 A boy weighed 40 kg and now weighs 35 kg. He has lost 5 kg in weight.
6 A girl weighed 32 kg but she gained 3 kg. She now weighs 35 kg.
7 I was sent to get groceries from a new shop the other day. At the end of my road I should have turned 120 m to the right but turned left instead. How far am I from the correct place? If 'to the right' is considered positive, describe my position from the end of the road.
8 If in the same situation as question 7, I first go 40 m to the left from the end of my road, realise my mistake and walk 100 m to the right, describe my position from the end of the road.
9 On another occasion I walk 40 m to the right and then turn round and walk 60 m to the left, describe my position from the end of the road.
10 Describe a situation of your own using positive numbers.

Exercise 20D

Ask your teacher for this exercise (in Teacher's Resource File 1).

21 : Angles and parallel lines

A reminder from chapter 12

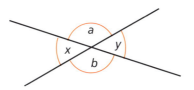

a and *b* are vertically opposite
x and *y* are vertically opposite
b and *y* are supplementary
x and *a* are supplementary
x and *b* are supplementary
a and *y* are supplementary

Exercise 21.1

1 Which angles are vertically opposite each other in this diagram?

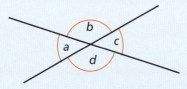

2 Which angles are supplementary to each other in the diagram above?

3 *Calculate* the angles marked with letters in the diagrams below.

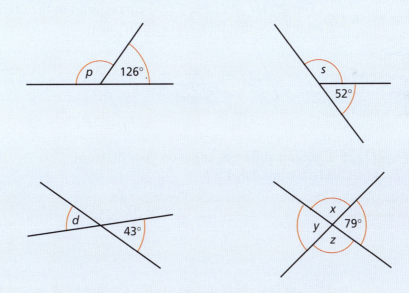

Corresponding angles

1 Using the lines in your exercise book, draw a set of three parallel lines:

2 Now draw a line using a ruler so that it crosses all three lines:

this line is called a **transversal**

3 Take a separate piece of paper, align it with the transversal, and fold the corner down to align with the top horizontal line. This fits the shape of the *supplement* of angle *a*.

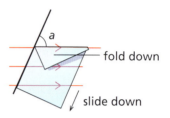

fold down

slide down

4 Move the edge of your paper down the transversal line and notice that the folded edge fits onto the next parallel line. Notice that it also fits a second time. Mark the equal angles with the letter '*a*'.

The angles you have found **correspond** to the original angle *a*. Can you see that they make an 'F' shape?

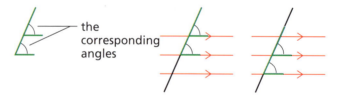

the corresponding angles

5 Choose a different angle on your diagram. Mark it and label it *b*.

6 Mark in two other angles corresponding to '*b*'.

Corresponding angles *are always equal* because they are the same angle moved further along the transversal.

Find four pairs of corresponding angles in this diagram.

Look for 'F' shapes.

Exercise 21.2

1 Copy the following diagrams and mark in the angle(s) which correspond to *p* and *q*.

2 Remembering that corresponding angles are equal, find the size of the angles marked with a letter in the following diagrams. (You may need angle facts you have learnt before.)

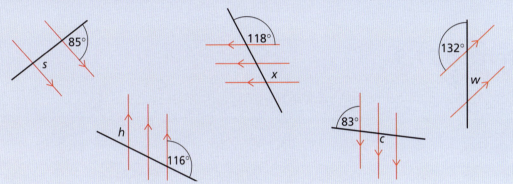

Alternate angles

Look at this diagram.

The problem is to find the size of angle *f*.
Using corresponding angles, angle *g* must be 65°.
But angles *f* and *g* are vertically opposite, so angle *f* is also 65°.
There is also a direct way of working out angle *f*.
Can you see the 'Z' shape in this diagram?

If you gave this diagram a half-turn, the *f* would end up where the 65° is now (try it using tracing paper!).

The *f* and the 65° are on opposite sides of the transversal, so they are called **alternate angles**. (If you alternate between two things you go from one to the other.) Here the angles are on alternate sides of the transversal.

This shows that *alternate angles are always equal*.

The 'Z' shapes, just like the 'F' shapes for corresponding angles, might be turned round, turned over or even stretched out.

Remember:

Look for the arrows showing parallel lines.

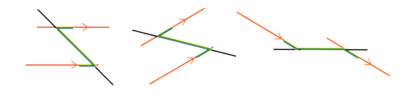

Exercise 21.3

1 Copy the diagram below and mark in the two pairs of alternate angles.

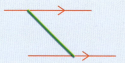

In questions 2–5, find the size of the angles marked with a letter. You may need to use other angle facts.

2

3

4

5

6 Copy the diagram below. Mark in as many angles as you can find which are equal to angle *p*.

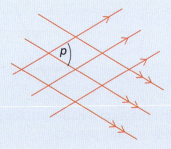

Interior angles

There is one other sort of pair of angles connected with parallel lines. Suppose you had to find out the size of angle *m* in the diagram below.

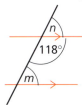

Angles *m* and *n* are corresponding angles, so they will be the same size.

But angle *n* and 118° make a straight line, so are supplementary (add up to 180°).

So angle *m* and 118° must also be supplementary.

So angle *m* is 62°.

This time, the two angles (118° and *m*) are both *inside* a pair of parallel lines, and on the *same side* of the transversal.

They are called **interior angles**.

Because the transversal is a straight line, and the other lines are parallel, *interior angles always add up to 180°*.

This time, the shape to look for is a 'U' turned on its side.

Exercise 21.4

In questions 1 and 2, copy the diagram and label the pair(s) of interior angles.

1

2 (two pairs)

In questions 3–7, find the size(s) of the marked angle(s). You may need to use any of the angle facts you have learnt so far, as well as interior angles.

3

4

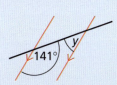

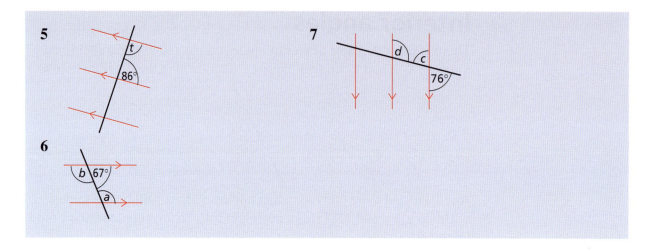

5

6

7

Angles in triangles

Follow these instructions exactly – or this WILL NOT WORK!

1 On fairly stiff plain paper draw a large triangle. Make sure it is not isosceles or right-angled.

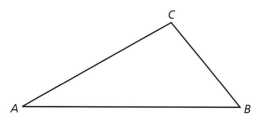

2 Cut the triangle out very carefully with scissors or a cutting knife.
3 Fold the triangle by sliding point *B* along line *BA* until the top of the fold reaches *C*. Crease the fold.

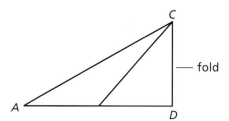

4 Unfold *B*. Mark the point *D*.

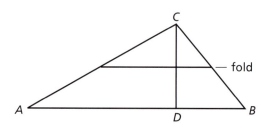

5 Fold *C* down to meet *D*.

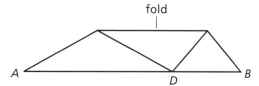

6 Fold *B* to meet *D*.

7 Fold *A* to meet *D*.

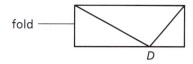

Unfold the triangle and as you fold it up again notice how the original angles come together along the straight line *AB*.

What does this tell you about the sum of the angles of the triangle?
Does this happen with your neighbour's triangle?
Glue the 'packet' into your exercise book so that it can still be unfolded.
This has demonstrated a very important fact of geometry:

● *The sizes of the three angles in any triangle add up to 180°.*

For example, suppose you were asked to work out the size of the missing angle in this triangle:

Remember:

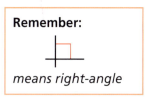

means right-angle

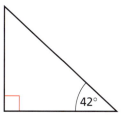

The sizes of the angles given are 90° and 42°, which add up to 132°.
So work out the size of the last angle by 180° − 132° = 48°.

Exercise 21.5

Calculate the size of the missing angle in each of these triangles.

1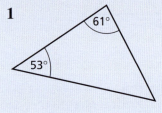

5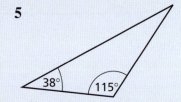

8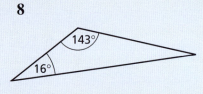

2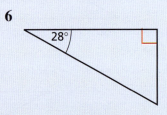

6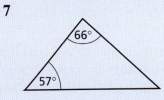

9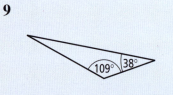

3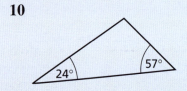

7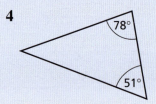

10

4

Exercise 21.6

1 Sketch an **equilateral triangle**. What is special about its sides? What is special about its angles?

2 Sketch an **isosceles triangle**. What is special about its sides? What is special about its angles?

3 Write down a general statement about the angles of an equilateral and an isosceles triangle.

Angles in quadrilaterals

Follow these instructions exactly.

1 Draw a quadrilateral but *don't* draw a square or rectangle!

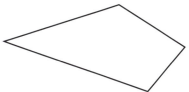

2 Draw a line going from one corner of your quadrilateral to the opposite corner (its diagonal).

3 What shapes has your quadrilateral been split into?

4 How can you use your drawing to calculate what the sizes of the angles of the quadrilateral add up to? Compare with your neighbour; draw some more yourself!

● *The sizes of the four angles in a quadrilateral add up to 360°.*

Exercise 21.7

Calculate the size of the missing angle in each of these quadrilaterals.

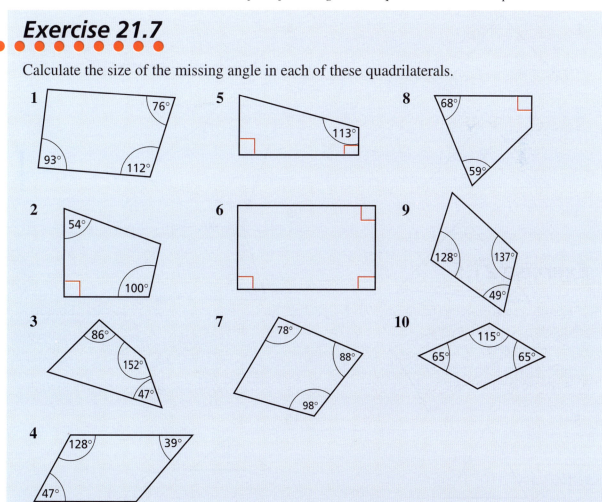

SUMMARY

■ When a transversal crosses two or more parallel lines, corresponding, alternate and interior angles can be identified.
■ **Corresponding angles** are equal (look for an 'F' shape).
■ **Alternate angles** are equal (look for a 'Z' shape).
■ **Interior angles** add up to 180° (look for a 'U' shape).
■ The sizes of all the angles in a triangle add up to 180°.
■ The sizes of all the angles in a quadrilateral add up to 360°.
■ All angles in an equilateral triangle are 60°.
■ In an isosceles triangle, the two angles at the base of the equal sides are equal.

Exercise 21A

Use all the angle facts you know to help you in this exercise.

For each question, find the size of angle *w*.

1

6

2
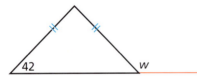

7
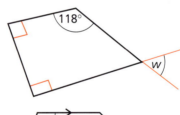

3
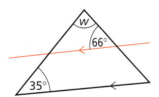

8
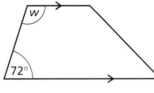

4

9
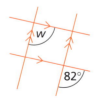

5
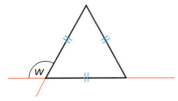

10
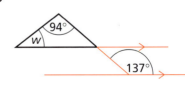

Exercise 21B

Use all the angle facts you know to help you.
For each question, find the size of angle *b*.

1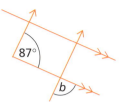

2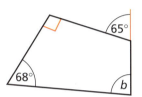

3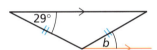

4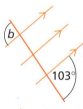

5

6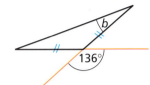

7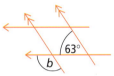

8

9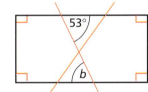

10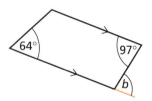

Exercise 21C

Find the size of the angles marked with letters.
You may need to find out the size of other angles as well.

1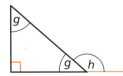

2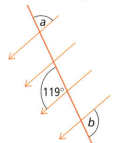

3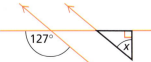

4

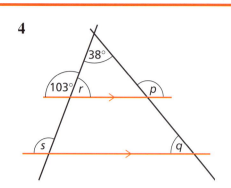

5

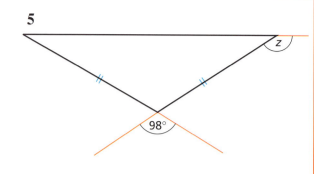

Exercise 21D

In questions 1 to 3, find the size of the angles marked with a letter. You may need also to find other angles.

1 Find the size of the equal angles f.

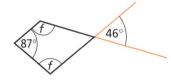

2 If $a = 41°$ find b.
If $b = 104°$ find a.

3

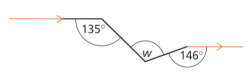

4 Construct an equilateral triangle with sides 6 cm long. Label it *DEF*. Now construct equilateral triangles *DEG*, *DFH* and *EFI* using the sides of your original triangle.
Giving explanations, mark any lines in your diagram which are parallel.
Mark in the sizes of as many angles as you can in your diagram.
What is special about triangle *HGI*?

5 Construct an isosceles triangle *ABC* with $AB = AC = 5$ cm and $BC = 7$ cm.
Construct triangle *BCD* underneath *ABC*, with $BD = CD = 5$ cm.
Giving reasons for your answers, mark in as many equal angles and parallel lines as you can.
What is the special name of quadrilateral *ABDC*?

22 Doing investigations

At several places in this book you have been asked to 'investigate' a piece of mathematics.

You can also be asked to do a complete investigation as an exercise on its own. It could be as part of your class work, or homework, or for an examination.

This chapter looks at some of the things you should bear in mind when you do this sort of work.

Investigation

Imagine you found an old game in a box in a cupboard.

Let's say there is a game-board, some counters and a dice, but the instructions have been lost.

You can't be sure you have the correct number of pieces; you won't know the purpose of the game nor the rules by which it is played!

To do a good maths investigation is like describing a game – you have to say exactly what is going on.

Preparing a report of an investigation

1 Say clearly what the investigation is about.

Say exactly what is required in order to carry out the investigation.
Give a precise description of what to do.

For example, if you were describing the well-known 'Frogs' investigation you might describe it like this.

This investigation requires a pegboard and equal numbers of red and blue pegs.

The pegs are placed in a straight line separated by one space, like this:

red pegs on the left of the space, blue pegs on the right.

The red pegs can either:

a move *one* space *to the right* if that space is empty

or

b jump (to the right) over *one* blue peg if the space to the right of the blue peg is empty.

The blue pegs obey the same rules but can move only to the *left*.

The purpose of the game is to change over the red and blue pegs in the least possible number of moves.

2 The next step is to try the investigation.

If you can get it done successfully, you should write down how you did it.

This sometimes means you have to invent a new way of your own to describe what you do.

For example, with 'Frogs' you might say 'Move the red, jump the blue, move the blue, jump the red, . . .'

You might not, however, be able to do the problem!

If not, try to simplify the original problem.

With 'Frogs', for instance, you could start with fewer pegs.
  And when you have done that try two pegs of each colour, and so on …

3 When you have several results, make a record.

With 'Frogs', you could make a table like this:

the number of pegs of one colour	the number of moves taken
1	.
2	.
3	.
4	.
5	
6	
7	
.	
	.

4 Look for a pattern in the results.

If you think you can see one, **predict** the next answer before you do it and then check to see if you were correct.

  Making a prediction is like going to the light switch in a room and asking yourself 'What do I expect to happen if I press this'; and then pressing it and seeing if the light *does* come on.

5 Write a conclusion.

With 'Frogs' for instance, you might try to connect the number of moves with the number of pegs.

6 Finally, try to extend the problem.

With 'Frogs' you could put more than one space between the different colours or you could use a different number of pegs each side of the space. You could perhaps use three (or more) colours with one or more spaces between. You could even try to go into two or three dimensions with the game!

It's a good idea to use books if it helps, but if you do you must say which books and how you used them. Otherwise it's cheating!

Proof in mathematics

Consider this investigation.

You may have come across words which read the same backwards as forwards:

noon, level, pop, radar, … Try to find some more of your own.

Words like this are called **palindromes**.

There are palindromic sentences:

MADAM IM ADAM
WAS IT A CAT I SAW

and even palindromic poems and stories.

In the same sort of way, there are palindromic numbers.

For instance, 22, 353, 1771, 43634, 241142, etc. are palindromic.

The investigation is to try to find out if these numbers have any special properties.

First notice that there are only a few two-digit palindromic numbers like 11, 22, 33, …

List them all. What do you notice about them?

Try some three-figure ones like 454, 393, 626, etc.

Do they have this common factor?

Now try some four-digit palindromic numbers like 4334, 5225, 6116, etc.

Write down ten four-digit palindromic numbers and see if any of them have a factor of 11.

They all do! Does this *always* happen? Can we explain this?

11, 22, 33, 44, …
They all have the same factor.

How many two-digit palindromic numbers are there? How many three-digit palindromic numbers are there? Investigate.

Look at 2882.

$$2882 = 2002 + 880$$
$$= 2 \times 1001 + 8 \times 110$$

Look at 5335.

$$5335 = 5005 + 330$$
$$= 5 \times 1001 + 3 \times 110$$

Look at 6446.

$$6446 = 6006 + 440$$
$$= 6 \times 1001 + 4 \times 110$$

Split 3223 this way; and 5665; and 6116, . . .

Split up all of your ten four-digit palindromic numbers like this.

You can see that, because the first and fourth digits are the same, you can always split off a number with 1001 as a factor.

And because the second and third digits are the same, you can always split off a number with 110 as a factor.

Divide 1001 by 11. Eleven is a factor!

Divide 110 by 11. Eleven is a factor!

Can you see that

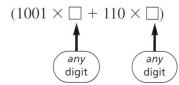

has a factor of 11?

Because *every* four-digit palindromic number can be split up like this (look back at your own list again), this **proves** that

● *every four-digit palindromic number has 11 as a factor.*

Being sure

Proof in mathematics is about *being sure* that something is *always* going to be true. If something is **proved** it means that there isn't even *one* exception!

You have to be careful.

For instance, try dividing 979, 616, 737 or 858 by 11.

You might be tempted to think that *all three*-digit palindromic numbers have a factor of 11! But they don't.

Try some five-digit palindromic numbers like 83138, 75757, 32923, 86768, …

Try six-digit palindromic numbers …

INVESTIGATE!

Here is a *sketch* of another investigation.

Investigate sums and products of odd and even numbers.

Odds and evens investigation

This is a dot pattern for the number 7.

This is a dot pattern for the number 6.

Using two rows only for each dot pattern for 5, 8, 9, 10, 11, 14, we have:

You can see that an even number always looks like a complete rectangle:

(even)

but an odd number has an extra 'piece' jutting out

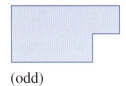

(odd)

It doesn't matter how big a number is, it will *always* have one or other of these shapes.

Investigating sums of odd and even numbers

Add some even numbers together to see what happens:

$$2 + 4 = 6 \qquad 10 + 12 = 22 \qquad 28 + 162 = 190 \qquad 48 + 64 = 112$$

Notice the answers are even. But will this *always* happen?

You can see that it does from this diagram:

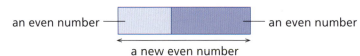

an even number — an even number

a new even number

And, because two rectangles will always fit together like this, we can say 'even + even = even'.

Next, try adding even and odd numbers.

$$2 + 3 = 5 \quad 9 + 4 = 13 \quad 123 + 46 = 169$$

The answers are all odd numbers. A diagram proves this is always so:

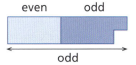

Odd plus even would be similar if the odd number shape were turned round:

Try adding odd numbers together:

$$3 + 5 = 8 \quad 7 + 11 = 18 \quad 23 + 47 = 70$$

The answers seem to be even.

This might seem puzzling at first, and a diagram doesn't seem to help.

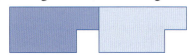

But you can turn one of the diagrams round and it still represents an odd number. Now the two jutting out bits fit together like a jigsaw making an overall shape of a rectangle.

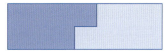

This proves that odd + odd = even.

Collect these results together:

$$\text{even} + \text{even} = \text{even}$$
$$\text{even} + \text{odd} = \text{odd}$$
$$\text{odd} + \text{even} = \text{odd}$$
$$\text{odd} + \text{odd} = \text{even}$$

Present the conclusions in a table:

+	odd	even
odd	even	odd
even	odd	even

Investigating products of odd and even numbers

Multiply some even numbers:

$$2 \times 4 = 8 \quad 6 \times 10 = 60 \quad 12 \times 4 = 48 \quad 112 \times 96 = 10\,752$$

The answers seem to be even. But how can we prove this? There are always an even lot of even numbers:

an even number of these ...

but an even number of rectangles could be put into pairs without any left over, making one big even number.

So even × even = even.

Try multiplying even lots of odd numbers:

$$2 \times 3 = 6 \qquad 8 \times 5 = 30 \qquad 12 \times 7 = 84 \qquad 24 \times 53 = 1272$$

The answers seem to be even again. How can we prove this?

an even number of these ...

Each *pair* of odd numbers makes an *even* number with none left over.

So even × odd = even.

Finish this investigation off. You still have to find out about odd × even and odd × odd.

Present your conclusions in a table like the previous one.

Extension

Prove the following.

1 The square of an even number is even.
2 The square of an odd number is odd.

As a sort of extension to the palindromic number investigation, try writing down any three-digit number and multiplying by 7, then by 11 then by 13.

Comment on the result. Try other three-digit numbers. Prove what happens. Invent similar things.

Try multiplying a two-digit number by 3, then by 7, then by 13, then by 37. Investigate further.

23 Equations

Simple linear equations

Remember that $3x + 2$ can be thought of as: 'I have three boxes, each containing x counters, together with two extra counters.'

Finding the number of things in each box

If you're *not* told the number of objects in each box but instead the number *altogether*, it's still easy to work out how many there were in each box.

If there are three boxes of counters and two counters left over, making 14 counters altogether, you can work out the number in each box.

In these situations, we always assume that there are *equal numbers of counters in each box*.

How many are in each box?

Three boxes with 12 counters, with the same number in each box, means four counters in each box.

We can also write these steps down.

Label each box 'x'.

Three boxes and two extra counters can be written as $3x + 2$ counters. In this case $3x + 2$ comes to 14, so we write:

$$3x + 2 = 14$$

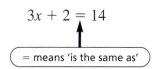

= means 'is the same as'

Put the two extra counters aside, leaving 12 for the three boxes, which we can write as:

$$3x = 12$$

This means there are 12 counters shared equally among three boxes, giving four counters in each box, which we write as:

$$x = 4$$

Five boxes of counters and three extra counters and it all comes to 38 counters: how many counters are in each box?

Remove the extra three counters leaving 35, giving 7 counters in each box.

You could write this down as:

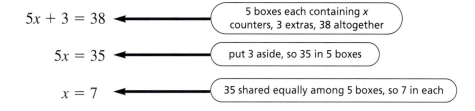

$5x + 3 = 38$ ← 5 boxes each containing x counters, 3 extras, 38 altogether

$5x = 35$ ← put 3 aside, so 35 in 5 boxes

$x = 7$ ← 35 shared equally among 5 boxes, so 7 in each

> I have 14 altogether. I can see there are 2 extra counters, so there must be 12 in the boxes.

Remember:

'x' stands for the number in each box.

Always assume there are the same number of counters in each box.

Notice how each line fits a step in the 'story'.

There could be 31 pins in nine boxes and four pins left over.
How many pins are in each box?
Put aside the four extras: this leaves 27.
27 pins to be shared equally amongst nine boxes: three in each box.
Write the algebra 'story' for this.

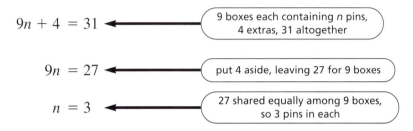

$9n + 4 = 31$ ← 9 boxes each containing *n* pins, 4 extras, 31 altogether

$9n = 27$ ← put 4 aside, leaving 27 for 9 boxes

$n = 3$ ← 27 shared equally among 9 boxes, so 3 pins in each

The last description involved pins and not counters. It doesn't matter what sort of object is in the boxes. It could have been three bricks or three five-pound notes(!). We're really concerned with the *number* of objects rather than the objects themselves.

But if you get in a muddle go back to thinking in terms of boxes.
Invent a description for this algebra 'story'

$$4m + 3 = 27$$
$$4m = 24$$
$$m = 6$$

A possible answer is:
'I have four boxes, each containing *m* pencils. I also have three extra pencils on the desk making 27 altogether. How many pencils in each box?'
'Move three pencils to one side, leaving 24 for the four boxes. This makes six in each box.'
You could have used any object at all!
Notice the neat appearance of the algebra on the page.
Always:

- line up the equal signs in a column
- keep your figures fairly small
- write clearly and tidily.

It's perhaps because we use so many equal signs when we write this sort of algebra that these particular 'stories' are called: **equations**. You have reached an important stage in mathematics when you understand what they are about.

> *Remember: equal numbers in the boxes.*

Exercise 23.1

Write these descriptions (stories) as equations. Do not work out the answers yet.

1 We have seven boxes of pens and three left over making 45 in all.
 (Answer: $7x + 3 = 45$, but you can use any letter you like.)
2 We have four boxes of eggs and five eggs extra making 29 altogether.
3 There are 57 apples in eight bags with one left over.
4 On my table there are three paper-clips together with two boxes of clips totalling 23 clips.
5 We have six boxes of counters and fifteen left over making 153 in all.

Exercise 23.2

Work out the number of pens, eggs, apples, paper-clips and counters in each box (or bag) in the situations described in exercise 23.1.

Lost counters found again

Suppose we had five boxes of counters but *lost* four counters.
 It would be written:
$5x - 4$, where each box contained x counters.
 If we knew that the total number of counters left after losing the four counters was 11, we could still work out the number in each box.
 Simply imagine that the lost counters had been found again. Then we would have not 11 but 15 counters and all the boxes would be full. Five full boxes totalling 15 counters means three counters in each box.

Remember chapter 14!

Still not quite sure? Try it with real boxes and counters.

$5x - 4 = 11$ (5 boxes each containing x from which 4 had been lost, leaving 11)
$5x = 15$ (return 4, making 15, and 5 full boxes)
$x = 3$ (so 3 in each box)

We have six boxes each containing z counters from which we have lost four counters leaving 26 remaining. This is written:

$$6z - 4 = 26$$

We now return the four missing counters so we have six full boxes containing 30 counters in all:

$$6z = 30$$

So there are five counters in each box:

$$z = 5$$

Write your own description for this:

$$8n - 3 = 29$$
$$8n = 32$$
$$n = 4$$

Solving equations

Finding the answer to an equation is called **solving** the equation, just like solving a puzzle. But, though we are beginning to use more of the words mathematicians generally use, it's still no more mysterious than finding the number of counters in a box!

Exercise 23.3

Write equations for these descriptions. Do not solve them yet.

1 We have five boxes each containing x counters from which we have lost four counters leaving 26.
2 We have two boxes each containing p counters from which we have lost five counters leaving three.
3 We have eight boxes each containing m counters and *find* four more ending up with 20.
4 We have eight boxes each containing m counters from which we have *lost* four leaving 20.
5 We have 31 counters in four bags, each containing q counters, plus three extra counters.

Exercise 23.4

Now go back and solve the equations you wrote in exercise 23.3.

The big step

The really big step in algebra is to solve equations without writing down the story each time.

$$\text{Solve:} \quad 9x + 4 = 67$$
$$\text{Answer:} \quad 9x + 4 = 67$$
$$9x = 63$$
$$x = 7$$

A bit stuck? Think of boxes . . .

Notice how each step is a sort of reversal of the previous one.

Because the '4' represents extra counters, you have to 'put them aside' which is the same as subtracting 4 from 67 to get the 63.

Then you divide the 63 by 9 to get 7.

Solve: $5x - 2 = 43$
Answer: $5x - 2 = 43$
$5x = 45$
$x = 9$

In this one, you add the '2' to the 43 to get 45 because this is 'putting back' the two counters which were lost.
Then divide the 45 by 5 to get 9.

See how quickly you can solve these equations.

1 $4x + 7 = 19$ **2** $4x - 7 = 17$

$4x + 7 = 19$ $4x - 7 = 17$
$4x = 12 \ (19 - 7 \text{ gives } 12)$ $4x = 24 \ (17 + 7 \text{ gives } 24)$
$x = 3$ $x = 6$

Some people make the step in brackets part of the explanation, like this:

$4x + 7 = 19$ $4x - 7 = 17$

$4x = 19 - 7$ $4x = 17 + 7$
$4x = 12$ $4x = 24$
$x = 3$ $x = 6$

Remember to set out your answers neatly lined up like this.
Further examples:

$3x - 7 = 5$ $5x + 2 = 47$
$3x = 5 + 7$ $5x = 47 - 2$
$3x = 12$ $5x = 45$
$x = 4$ $x = 9$

Exercise 23.5

Solve the following equations, setting them out like the examples.

1 $6x + 1 = 31$ **4** $2x + 3 = 31$ **7** $3x + 5 = 20$ **9** $6x - 5 = 19$
2 $8x - 5 = 19$ **5** $9x - 17 = 64$ **8** $3x - 5 = 1$ **10** $7x + 3 = 52$
3 $4x - 7 = 33$ **6** $5x + 3 = 43$

A story to fit the last equation in exercise 23.5 for instance, might be:
'I was making seven pizzas and each one was to be decorated with the same number of black olives. I put the required number of olives

into seven separate cups on the table but then noticed three extra olives on a saucer nearby. Altogether there were 52 olives. How many olives were used for each pizza?'

Exercise 23.6

Take any other one of the equations in the last exercise and make up an elaborate story to fit that equation! Read it out to the class.

SUMMARY

■ Stories using algebra can be re-arranged so that you can work out the number of things which started off the story.
■ These sorts of descriptions are called **equations**.
■ Finding the answer to an equation is called **solving** it.
■ Equations can be solved when you have either 'extra' things or 'lost' things.
■ Equations are solved by reversing the steps used originally to make up the equation.
■ Quite complicated situations can be solved using equations.

Exercise 23A

Solve these equations.

1 $5x = 35$ **4** $3a = 12$ **7** $7x - 3 = 60$ **9** $7n = 266$
2 $x + 5 = 35$ **5** $3a + 4 = 10$ **8** $7s + 3 = 45$ **10** $7 + n = 266$
3 $a + 3 = 12$ **6** $3b - 4 = 2$

Exercise 23B

Solve these equations.

1 $4t = 36$ **4** $7p = 21$ **7** $5y - 4 = 41$ **9** $13n = 91$

2 $t + 4 = 36$ **5** $5x + 7 = 47$ **8** $5u + 4 = 74$ **10** $13 + n = 91$

3 $p + 7 = 21$ **6** $5x - 7 = 23$

Exercise 23C

Write equations for these situations and solve them.

1 I have three boxes each containing x counters. I find 17 more counters, ending up with 23 altogether. Find the number of counters in each box.

2 I think of a number, multiply it by 3, add 17 and my answer is 23. Find my number.

3 I have five boxes, each filled with the same number of counters. I lose eight of the counters, ending up with 77 altogether. Find the number of counters in each box.

4 I think of a number, multiply it by 5 and then subtract 8. If my answer is 77, find the number.

5 I think of a number, multiply it by 11 and add 41. My answer is 140. Find the number.

6 I have four packets, each filled with the same number of paper-clips. I find six more paper-clips, making 206 altogether. How many paper-clips are in each box?

7 I think of a number, multiply it by 12 and subtract 21. If the answer is 147, what was the number I first thought of?

8 I have nine bookshelves, each holding the same number of books. I buy 12 more books in a sale, giving me 84 altogether. How many books were on each shelf originally?

9 My friend collects stamps. Her album has 15 pages, each with the same number of stamps. She swaps five stamps for a poster, leaving her with 175 stamps. How many stamps did she have on each page to start with?

10 I think of a number, which I multiply by 14. I then add 182. My answer is 308. What was my number?

Exercise 23D

1 Last Saturday, some friends came round at lunch-time. Mum said she was really busy and if I wanted to give them some lunch I could make omelettes – provided I did the cooking.

There were three boxes of eggs. They weren't full but had the same number of eggs in each box.

The trouble is, I'm not too good at breaking eggs properly and the first egg somehow ended up on the floor and the second had so much egg-shell in it I threw it away.

I don't know why Mum got so angry – she said the seven eggs we had left were more than enough for three people anyway.

Write down an equation for the number of eggs I now have, and solve it to find out how many eggs were in each box to start with.

Use your own label for the number in each box.

Next week we'll have fish fingers.

2 Make up a story of your own like the last one, leading to an equation. Give it to someone you don't like to solve!

24 The number line

Positive and negative numbers: integers

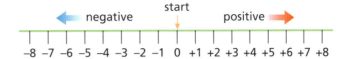

Notice that when you use a **number line**:

- moving from left to right *anywhere* on the line is in the positive direction,
- moving from right to left *anywhere* on the line is in the negative direction,
- the numbers get bigger moving to the right,
- the numbers get smaller moving to the left.

Exercise 24.1

Copy this number line into your book and use it to answer the following questions:

1 Which is larger, (-2) or $(+3)$?
2 Which is smaller, (-7) or (-1)?
3 Which is less, $(+5)$ or (-6)?
4 Which is more, (-3) or (-2)?
5 Do you move to the left or to the right from (-5) to (-1)?
6 Do you move to the left or to the right from $(+2)$ to (-4)?
7 Do you move in the positive or negative direction from (-1) to (-8)?
8 Do you move in the positive or negative direction from (-7) to $(+3)$?
9 Do the numbers get bigger or smaller in moving from $(+7)$ to (-1)?
10 Do the numbers get bigger or smaller in moving from (-1) to $(+7)$?

It is important always to use the correct words, so that other mathematicians are sure what you mean!

Integer
(pronounced 'in-ti-jer') from Latin meaning untouched, whole

- *The correct word for positive, negative (and zero) whole numbers is **integers**. Write it at the back of your exercise book, say it and spell it.*

Some mathematicians call them **directed numbers**. Can you see why?

Adding integers

You add integers using the number line.

Add positive three and negative five.

Start from zero, move three steps to your right (the positive direction) then move five steps to your left (the negative direction).

You can see that the finish arrow points to negative two.

So positive three and negative five is negative two.

Write this using numbers like this:

$$(+3) + (-5) = (-2)$$

It might be clearer at this stage to read the plus sign as 'followed by'.

Then you would say:

'Starting from zero, take three steps to the right, followed by five to the left, ending up at two to the left (of zero).'

Try $(-3) + (+5)$.

Three to the left followed by five to the right is two to the right.

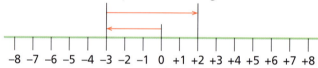

Don't forget that, when adding integers, you begin at zero and the answer is counted from zero. So $(-3) + (+5) = (+2)$.

$(-4) + (-2)$

Four to the left followed by two to the left is six to the left.

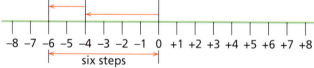

So $(-4) + (-2) = (-6)$.

$(+5) + (+2)$

Five to the right followed by two to the right is seven to the right.

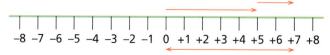

So $(+5) + (+2) = (+7)$.

● *To add integers, begin at zero; go left if negative, or right if positive, counting the correct number of steps; carry on counting from where you get to, moving left or right again according to the sign and size of the second number; wherever you end up, that's the answer!*

Now copy the previous three examples into your book.

You will notice that the answer is written in words before drawing the picture. It's quicker. But always have the picture in your head as the words are written down.

Try doing both at the same time.

$(-5) + (+4)$

Think: 'Five steps to the left, followed by four steps to the right. Where have I got to? One to the left of zero; so the answer is negative one.'

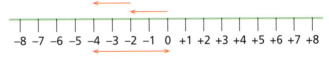

So $(-5) + (+4) = (-1)$.

$(-2) + (-2)$

Think: 'Two steps to the left followed by another two steps to the left; that's four to the left; answer, (-4).'

So $(-2) + (-2) = (-4)$.

Exercise 24.2

Use a number line to help you add the following. Draw separate diagrams for each question if it helps.

1 $(-7) + (+2)$ **4** $(+4) + (-5)$ **7** $(-2) + (+5)$ **9** $(+5) + (0)$
2 $(+3) + (-6)$ **5** $(-5) + (+4)$ **8** $(0) + (-1)$ **10** $(+6) + (-8)$
3 $(-4) + (-1)$ **6** $(-3) + (+3)$

Exercise 24.3

Use a number line to add these integers. You could draw a separate diagram for each question if it helps but see how soon you can do the questions *imagining* a number line in your head.

1 $(-3) + (-2)$ **4** $(+3) + (-7)$ **7** $(-4) + (+3)$ **9** $(+3) + (-4)$
2 $(-2) + (-3)$ **5** $(-3) + (+7)$ **8** $(+3) + (+4)$ **10** $(-3) + (-4)$
3 $(+7) + (-7)$ **6** $(+4) + (-3)$

Subtracting integers

Many shops have electronic cash registers which work out change automatically. But some shopkeepers still *count out* change into your hand.

Just think for a moment how this is actually done.

Say you spent 37p and gave the shopkeeper 40p.

What happens is that the shopkeeper starts with the 37 and counts out the change up to 40 into your hand, saying the numbers '38, 39, 40'.

Spend 22p and offer 30p. How would the numbers go? '23, 24, 25, 26, 27, 28, 29, 30'. The eight pennies would be in your hand.

Buy something for 48p and give £1. '49, 50, and 50p makes a pound', the shopkeeper might say. You end up with 52p.

In each of these examples, nobody actually does a subtraction sum.

You start from the cost and count to the money offered.

Can you see how this could work on a number line?

Let's subtract $(+7)$ from $(+10)$. (This is like offering a shopkeeper a £10 note for a bill of £7.)

Start with the $(+7)$.

Count on to the $(+10)$.

It takes three steps.

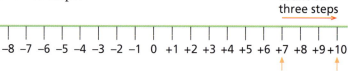

But in which direction did we go? Left or right?
To the right.
Since to the right is positive, the answer is (+3).
Subtract (+2) from (−3).
Start with the (+2).
Count to (−3).
It takes five steps.

But in which direction did we go? Left or right?
To the left.
Since to the left is negative, the answer is (−5).
Many people have a problem with subtraction. (But you needn't have if you take care!)
The problem is usually with the *order* of subtraction.
If you say 'subtract three from four', it's the *three* which is being 'taken away'. But when you write this down using numbers it's written '4 − 3' (read four minus three) where the 'four' is read first. It's possible to get in a muddle about this.

● *So remember, when subtracting, you always start counting from the number being 'taken away'.*

Exercise 24.4

Write down which of the two numbers is being 'taken away'.

1 Eight minus three
2 Take seven from eleven.
3 Buy an article for 34p with a 50p coin.
4 Have a £1 coin and buy something for 57p.
5 38 − 27
6 Subtract 3 from 7.
7 (−4) − (+5)
8 (+5) − (−4)
9 (+4) − (−5)
10 Subtract 7 from 3.

You *can't* take 7 *things* from 3 *things*, but you can certainly *count from* (+7) to (+3) on the number line.

Let's do just that.

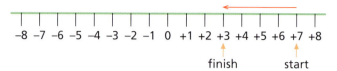

Four steps; but in which direction? Left or right?
To the left of course.
So what is seven from three?
Quite clear: it's **negative** four.
So $(+3) - (+7) = (-4)$.

$(-5) - (-1)$

This is negative five minus negative one. So you start from (-1) and count to (-5).

That's four steps from right to left which is in the negative direction. So the answer is negative four.

So $(-5) - (-1) = (-4)$.

$(+2) - (-7)$

Since we're subtracting (-7) that's where you start. How many steps to get to $(+2)$ and in which direction? This gets you the answer.

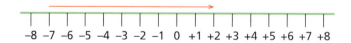

Nine steps to the right, so:

$(+2) - (-7) = (+9)$

● *To subtract integers, start from the number being subtracted, count the steps to get to the other number, and the result is positive or negative depending on the direction in which you have moved.*

Exercise 24.5

Perform these subtractions using the number line. Draw separate diagrams for each question if it helps.

1 $(+6) - (+2)$ **4** $(-6) - (-2)$ **7** $(+4) - (-1)$ **9** $(+5) - (+8)$
2 $(+6) - (-2)$ **5** $(-1) - (+4)$ **8** $(+8) - (+5)$ **10** $(-5) - (-8)$
3 $(-6) - (+2)$ **6** $(+1) - (-4)$

Exercise 24.6

Find the answers to these, drawing each on a number line if necessary. Some people find it helps to point to an imaginary line in the air!

1 $(-3) - (-3)$ **4** $(0) - (-3)$ **7** $(-7) - (+2)$ **9** $(-8) - (+8)$
2 $(-3) - (+3)$ **5** $(+6) - (+6)$ **8** $(+7) - (+2)$ **10** $(+8) - (-8)$
3 $(0) - (+3)$ **6** $(-7) - (-2)$

> **Remember:**
>
> For **addition**, start from zero. Follow one number by the other. How far from zero?
> For **subtraction**, start with the second number. Find direction and distance to the first number.

Exercise 24.7

Do these, noticing that some are addition and some are subtraction.

1 $(-6) + (-4)$ **4** $(-3) - (-1)$ **7** $(-7) - (-1)$ **9** $(+1) + (-10)$
2 $(-6) - (-4)$ **5** $(-3) + (-1)$ **8** $(-1) + (-7)$ **10** $(+1) - (-10)$
3 $(-4) - (-6)$ **6** $(-1) - (-3)$

SUMMARY

- Positive and negative (and zero) numbers together are called **integers**.
- Integers are studied using a number line.
- Moving to the *right* on a number line is in the positive direction.
- Numbers get *bigger* as you move to the *right* along a number line.
- To **add** two integers, the second one *follows on after* the first.
- To **subtract** two integers, count the steps going from *the second* to *the first*.

Exercise 24A

1 a For each question below, draw a number line and put a cross against each of the numbers in the list.
  b Then put the numbers in order, *least first*. This is called an **ascending** list.
     (i) $(+4), (-6), (-1), (+2), (-3), (+5)$
     (ii) $(-4), (+4), (0), (-2), (+3), (-3)$
     (iii) $(+3), (-5), (+5), (-3), (+4), (-2)$
     (iv) $(-6), (+6), (0), (-2), (+2), (-5)$
     (v) $(+8), (-7), (+6), (-5), (+4), (-2), (0), (-1)$
  c Now use the same lists of numbers and put them in new lists, in order, *largest first*. This is called a **descending** list.

Exercise 24B

Do these.

1 $(-1) + (+1)$ 4 $(-1) - (-1)$ 7 $(-2) + (+7)$ 9 $(-10) + (-3)$
2 $(-1) - (+1)$ 5 $(+1) - (+1)$ 8 $(+12) + (-15)$ 10 $(-10) - (-3)$
3 $(+1) - (-1)$ 6 $(-3) + (-6)$

Exercise 24C

Do these.

1 $(-7) + (-5)$ 4 $(+7) - (+5)$ 7 $(+7) - (-5)$ 9 $(-5) - (+7)$
2 $(-7) + (+5)$ 5 $(-7) - (+5)$ 8 $(+7) + (-5)$ 10 $(-5) - (-5)$
3 $(-7) - (-5)$ 6 $(+7) + (+5)$

Exercise 24D

1 I owe £10 and borrow another £3. Write this using integers. Give the answer.
2 I owe £10 and pay back £3. Write using integers. Give the answer.
3 I owe £10 and pay back £13. Write using integers. Give the answer.
4 I save £10 but lose £13. Write using integers. Give the answer.
5 Work out $(-1) + (-2) + (-3)$.
6 Calculate $[(-1) - (-2)] + (-3)$. Do the bit in the square brackets first.
7 Find $[(-1) + (-2)] - (-3)$.
8 Find $(-1) + [(-2) - (-3)]$.
9 Do $[(-1) - (-2)] - (-3)$.
10 Calculate $(-1) - [(-2) - (-3)]$.

25 Coordinates

Here is the plan of the desks in a classroom and the names of some of the children who sit there.

back

	1	2	3	4
5	Joel	Juanita	Jeremy	Joan
4	Sarah	Sam	Sunita	Simon
3	Peter	Pamela	Patrick	Paula
2	Mary	Maurice	Minal	Minesh
1	Jim	Jane	Joe	Jean

door · window

Teacher's desk

front

One day we decided to number the desks in the classroom as shown – from the door to the window and from the front to the back.

For example, Pamela sits two desks to the right and three desks back, which we decided to write as (2, 3) for short.

Who sits three to the right and five back, (3, 5)?

Who sits two to the right and four back, (2, 4)?

Where does Peter sit? He sits at (1, 3) which is one to the right and three back.

The headteacher sent for the girl she thought sat at desk (1, 4). She was very surprised when Jean arrived instead of Sarah!

What mistake had probably been made?

Watch you don't make the same mistake in the next exercise!

Exercise 25.1

Write down the names of the children who sit at the following desks.

1 (3, 4)   **4** (4, 2)   **7** (3, 2)   **9** (1, 2)
2 (4, 3)   **5** (1, 1)   **8** (4, 5)   **10** (2, 1)
3 (2, 5)   **6** (3, 3)

Exercise 25.2

Use the numbers from the above plan to describe the positions of the desks of the following children.

1 Sunita   **4** Jean   **7** Mary   **9** Maurice
2 Minesh   **5** Sarah   **8** Simon   **10** Jim
3 Joel   **6** Pamela

Exercise 25.3

Copy this plan into your exercise book. It has no names on it.

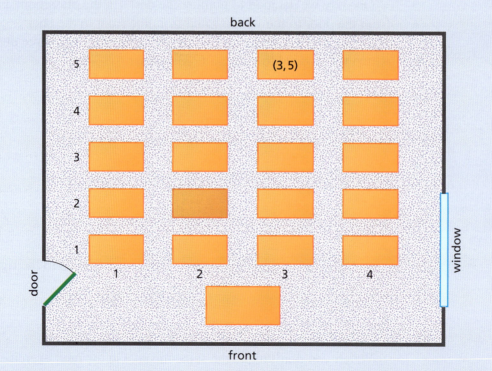

Put the desk numbers in the empty places. One has been done as an example.

The idea of describing position by using numbers in this way is commonly attributed to a Frenchman called René Descartes, probably in the year 1619.

He had been a very frail child and was allowed to stay in bed late every morning. The story is told that this idea occurred to him while staring at a fly wandering across the ceiling of his bedroom!

It is an idea which has turned out to be one of the most important in the whole history of mathematics because of the way it connects algebra to geometry.

Look carefully at the following diagram.

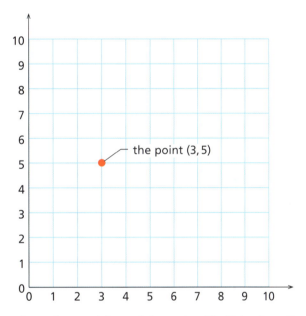

You can see how the position of the point (3, 5) is described just like the position of the desk on the plan of the classroom.

Copy this diagram onto squared paper and below it write these very important details.

- Both sets of numbers *start from zero*.
- The horizontal numbers are written *exactly underneath* the vertical lines and *not in the spaces*.
- The vertical numbers are written *exactly opposite* the horizontal lines and *not in the spaces*.
- *Put arrows* on the ends of the lines to show that the numbers are increasing left-to-right and bottom-to-top.

● *Whenever you draw a diagram like this, always observe these points!*

Look again at a copy of the diagram:

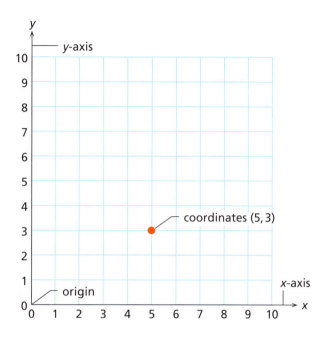

You need to know the following.

- The numbers which give the position of a point are called its **coordinates**.
- The point where you start numbering is called the **origin** (0, 0).
- The horizontal numbered line is called the **x-axis**.
- The vertical numbered line is called the **y-axis**.

Copy the diagram and the notes above into your exercise book.
  Always label the axes with an 'x' and a 'y' as shown in the diagram.
  The x- and y-axes are sometimes called **the coordinate axes**.
  The whole diagram can be called **a coordinate grid**.

● *Coordinates are always described by:*
  going along → before going up ↑

Starting from the origin, move *along* until you get directly underneath the required point, then move *up* to it.
  Move in the *x* direction before the *y*.

x comes before y in the alphabet

Exercise 25.4

Copy this diagram, including the lettered points, and write down their coordinates.

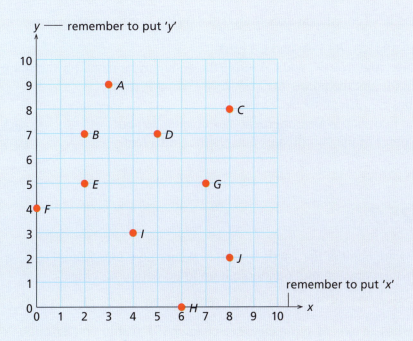

Exercise 25.5

Draw a grid of your own, remembering all the details described previously, and number each axis from 0 to 7.

Plot and label each of these points.

> To **plot** a point means to put it on the grid in the right place according to the coordinates.

1 A (1, 7) **4** D (4, 5) **7** G (3, 7) **9** I (3, 0)

2 B (7, 1) **5** E (0, 0) **8** H (0, 3) **10** J (7, 7)

3 C (3, 6) **6** F (5, 4)

Exercises 25.6 to 25.12 are best drawn on centimetre squared paper using 1 cm squares as the unit.

Exercise 25.6

Draw, number and label coordinate axes from 0 to 8 on the *x*-axis and from 0 to 7 on the *y*-axis.

1 Plot the points *A* (1, 2), *B* (3, 4) and *C* (1, 6).
Using your ruler, join *AB*, *BC* and *CA*. Give the geometrical name for the shape you get.
2 On the same grid, plot the points *D* (2, 1), *E* (4, 3) and *F* (6, 1).
Join up the lines *DE*, *EF* and *FD*.
Notice that the two shapes are congruent (see chapter 19) but reversing the order of the coordinates puts them in different places.

Be careful to get this right!

Exercise 25.7

On a coordinate grid, number the *x*-axis from 0 to 9 and the *y*-axis from 0 to 8.
Plot the following points in order and join it up to go with your chips!

(1, 1), (3, 3), (4, 2), (6, 2), (8, 3), (7, 4), (8, 5), (6, 6), (4, 6), (3, 5), (1, 7), (2, 4), (1, 1)

Notice the shape has an axis of symmetry (see chapter 19). Could you describe, using a number, exactly where this axis of symmetry is?
Spoil the symmetry but bring your shape to life by putting a small circle at (6, 5).

Exercise 25.8

Label an *x*-axis from 0 to 10 and a *y*-axis from 0 to 8. Plot and join the following points in order, but don't let it bite you!

(2, 6), (2, 1), (3, 1), (3, 3), (6, 3), (6, 1), (7, 1), (7, 4), (9, 4), (6, 7), (6, 6), (2, 6)

Join (2, 6) to (1, 5). Put a largish blob at (9, 4) and a dot at (7, 5).
You could add a line joining (8, 4) and (8, 4.5) and even one joining (8, 4) to (7.5, 4.5).

Exercise 25.9

Label an *x*-axis from 0 to 6 and a *y*-axis from 0 to 8. Plot and join the following points in order, but don't let it see exercise 25.8!

(1, 1), (1, 2), (2, 2), (2, 4), (1, 5), (1, 6), (2, 8), (2, 7), (4, 7), (4, 8), (5, 6), (5, 5), (4, 4), (4, 2), (5, 2), (5, 1), (1, 1)

This becomes more life-like if you join (2.5, 5) to (3.5, 5) and (3, 5) to (3, 5.5).
Try dots at (2, 6) and (4, 6).

Exercise 25.10

Label an *x*-axis from 0 to 9 and a *y*-axis from 0 to 9. Plot and join the following points in order to take baby brother for a walk!

(8, 4), (2, 4), (2, 3), (4, 2), (7, 2), (8, 3), (8, 4), (7, 6), (5, 6), (5, 4). Join (2, 4) to (1, 5)

Draw a circle centre (4, 2) radius 1 cm and another circle centre (7, 2) radius 1 cm.

Exercise 25.11

Design some shapes of your own on centimetre squared paper. Write down the coordinates of their corners and give a list of these to a partner.
  See if the right shape is produced!
  Make a class display of these.

Exercise 25.12

On centimetre squared paper, label and number an *x*-axis from 0 to 12 and a *y*-axis from 0 to 9.
  Plot the following sets of points and join them up.

1 (0, 7), (1, 7), (2, 7), (3, 7), (4, 7), (5, 7), (6, 7), (7, 7), (9, 7), (10, 7), (11, 7)
  Put in the missing point in the pattern. Write down its coordinates. Write down something about the *y*-coordinates. Describe what sort of shape you get.
2 (3, 0), (3, 1), (3, 2), (3, 3), (3, 4), (3, 5), (3, 7), (3, 8)
  Put in the missing point in the pattern. Write down its coordinates. Write down something about the *x*-coordinates. Describe what sort of shape you get.
3 (0, 0), (1, 1), (2, 2), (3, 3), (4, 4), (6, 6), (7, 7), (8, 8)
  Put in the missing point in the pattern. Write down its coordinates. Write down something about the coordinates. Describe what sort of shape you get.
4 (2, 1), (5, 2), (11, 4)
  Put in the missing point in the pattern. Write down its coordinates. Describe what sort of shape you get.
5 (1, 6), (3, 5), (7, 3), (9, 2), (11, 1)
  Put in the missing point in the pattern. Write down its coordinates. Describe what sort of shape you get.

SUMMARY

- The position of a point on a flat sheet of paper can be described using a **coordinate grid**.
- A coordinate grid consists of horizontal and vertical lines numbered from left to right and from bottom to top.
- The horizontal line is the **x-axis** and the vertical line is the **y-axis**.
- Always number the *lines* and not the spaces.
- The point from which you start numbering is called the **origin** and has coordinates (0, 0).
- Always put arrows on the axes to show the directions of x and y increasing.
- Always label the x-axis and the y-axis.
- To **plot** a point means to put it on the grid according to its coordinates.
- It is absolutely essential always to put the x-number before the y-number; go *along* before going *up*. Remember that x comes before y in the alphabet.
- The idea for coordinates was due to René Descartes.

Exercise 25A

1 If A is (3, 7), write down the x-coordinate of A.
2 If B is (8, 4), write down the y-coordinate of B.
3 Write the coordinates of a point C whose x-coordinate is 5 and whose y-coordinate is 11.
4 Write the coordinates of a point D whose x-coordinate is 11 and whose y-coordinate is 5.
5 Write down the coordinates of the origin.
6 What is special about the y-coordinates of any point on the x-axis?
7 What is special about points on the y-axis?
8 A point E has coordinates (2, 9). Is 9 the x- or y-coordinate of E?
9 If F is (13, 14), write down the x-coordinate of F.
10 Can you find a reason why these coordinates are sometimes called **Cartesian** coordinates?

Exercise 25B

For this exercise, you are asked to draw various four-sided shapes. Refer back to chapter 6 if you need to remember some of their names.

Draw and label a coordinate grid from 0 to 14 for x-values and from 0 to 12 for y-values.

> **Remember:**
>
> *The diagonal line of a shape is the line joining opposite vertices.*
>
>

1 Plot and label the points A (1, 2), B (3, 0), C (5, 2) and D (3, 5). Draw the shape ABCD. Write down its geometrical name. Draw the diagonals AC and BD. Write down the coordinates of the point where they cross.
2 Plot and label the points E (1, 6), F (4, 7), G (3, 10) and H (0, 9). Draw shape EFGH. Write its geometrical name. Draw the diagonals EG and FH and the coordinates where they cross.
3 Plot and label the points K (6, 3), L (9, 1), M (12, 3) and N (9, 5). Draw the shape KLMN. Write its geometrical name. Draw its diagonals and write down where they cross.

4 Plot and label the points *P* (5, 6), *Q* (6, 5), *R* (9, 8) and *S* (8, 9). Draw and name the shape. Draw its diagonals and write down where they cross.

5 Plot and label the points *T* (11, 6), *U* (12, 6), *V* (14, 12) and *W* (12, 11). Draw and name the shape. Draw its diagonals and write down where they cross.

Exercise 25C

1 Using centimetre squared paper, number an *x*-axis from 0 to 16 and a *y*-axis from 0 to 12. Plot the following sets of points and join each set up (separately) to make a triangle. Put the letter (**a**, **b**, **c**, . . .) for each triangle inside it.

  a (1, 9), (4, 10), (1, 11)
  b (5, 8), (7, 8), (7, 11)
  c (2, 5), (2, 7), (5, 7)
  d (0, 2), (2, 3), (0, 4)
  e (2, 1), (5, 1), (5, 6)
  f (8, 8), (10, 6), (12, 8)
  g (7, 2), (9, 5), (7, 5)
  h (8, 1), (13, 0), (10, 3)
  i (11, 5), (12, 3), (13, 5)
  j (13, 6), (15, 6), (14, 9)

2 List the letters of all the triangles which are isosceles.

3 List the letters of those groups of triangles which are congruent to each other. Shade each group with the same colour.

Exercise 25D

On centimetre squared paper, number an *x*-axis from 0 to 8 and a *y*-axis from 0 to 6. Do the whole exercise on this grid.

1 Plot the points (1, 1), (3, 1), (3, 2), (2, 2), (2, 4), (1, 4) and join them up to make an L-shape. Colour this L-shape.

2 Now plot and join the points (3, 2), (3, 5), (1, 5), (1, 4), (2, 4), (2, 2) and shade this new shape with a different colour.

3 Draw the shape with coordinates (3, 4), (3, 1), (5, 1), (5, 2), (4, 2), (4, 4) and shade with the same colour as used in question 1.

4 Draw the shape with coordinates (4, 2), (5, 2), (5, 5), (3, 5), (3, 4), (4, 4) and shade with the same colour as used in question 2.

5 Continue this pattern to the right with two more L-shapes.

6 List the coordinates of the last L-shape you have drawn.

26 Calculating with fractions

This chapter deals with the addition, subtraction, multiplication and division of fractions.

Adding fractions

The simplest of these processes is the addition of fractions with the same denominators.

Suppose you cut a cake into eight equal pieces.

If you eat one piece and a friend eats two pieces, three have been eaten altogether.

But each piece is one eighth of the cake so in total three eighths have been eaten.

One eighth plus two eighths is three eighths!

Or in symbols:

$$\frac{1}{8} + \frac{2}{8} = \frac{3}{8}$$

Adding fractions with the same denominators is straightforward. Just add the numerators, keeping the denominators the same. For example:

$$\frac{1}{21} + \frac{4}{21} = \frac{5}{21} \qquad \frac{1}{5} + \frac{1}{5} = \frac{2}{5} \qquad \frac{1}{7} + \frac{2}{7} = \frac{3}{7}$$

Exercise 26.1

Add these fractions.

1 $\frac{3}{7} + \frac{2}{7}$

2 $\frac{1}{15} + \frac{7}{15}$

3 $\frac{2}{11} + \frac{5}{11}$

4 $\frac{1}{5} + \frac{3}{5}$

5 $\frac{4}{9} + \frac{1}{9}$

6 $\frac{3}{17} + \frac{9}{17}$

7 $\frac{23}{37} + \frac{12}{37}$

8 $\frac{5}{19} + \frac{4}{19}$

9 $\frac{2}{13} + \frac{7}{13}$

10 $\frac{1}{3} + \frac{1}{3}$

Different denominators

Suppose you had a square cake and you cut a piece which was one quarter of the cake and your friend cut a piece which was half of the same cake.

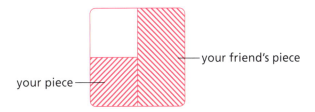

your friend's piece

your piece

You can see from the diagram that three quarters of the cake would be cut altogether.

In symbols, we need to calculate $\frac{1}{4} + \frac{1}{2}$, but since the denominators are different it can't be done quite as easily as in the first exercise.

This is where the work with equivalent fractions from chapter 16 is used, since *we need to arrange that both fractions have the same denominator*.

So write a half with denominator 4, which gets us $\frac{2}{4}$. Now the question can be finished:

$$\frac{1}{4} + \frac{1}{2} = \frac{1}{4} + \frac{2}{4} = \frac{3}{4}$$

as in exercise 26.1. The idea is not hard, but there are many details to sort out.

Equivalent fractions again

Do you remember how to change a fraction into an equivalent fraction?

Write $\frac{3}{10}$ as an equivalent fraction with denominator 20.

20 is the second multiple of 10 and the second multiple of 3 is 6.

So $\frac{3}{10} = \frac{6}{20}$. ← (Since two 10s are 20, and two 3s are 6)

Write $\frac{1}{5}$ as an equivalent fraction with denominator 20.

20 is the fourth multiple of 5 and the fourth multiple of 1 is 4.

So $\frac{1}{5} = \frac{4}{20}$. ← (Four 5s are 20 and four 1s are 4)

Complete $\frac{3}{4} = \frac{}{20}$.

20 is the fifth multiple of 4 and the fifth multiple of 3 is 15.

So $\frac{3}{4} = \frac{15}{20}$. ← ($5 \times 4 = 20$ and $5 \times 3 = 15$)

Use the shortest way as much as you can!!

Complete $\frac{3}{7} = \frac{}{28}$.

So $\frac{3}{7} = \frac{12}{28}$. ⟵ Four 7s are 28 and four 3s are 12

But of course you can't do that if you don't know your multiplication tables well enough!

Exercise 26.2

Work out the required equivalent fraction.

1 $\frac{5}{8} = \frac{}{24}$

2 $\frac{3}{4} = \frac{}{24}$

3 $\frac{5}{6} = \frac{}{24}$

4 $\frac{3}{8} = \frac{}{24}$

5 $\frac{2}{3} = \frac{}{24}$

6 $\frac{1}{2} = \frac{}{24}$

7 $\frac{1}{8} = \frac{}{24}$

8 $\frac{1}{4} = \frac{}{24}$

9 $\frac{7}{8} = \frac{}{24}$

10 $\frac{1}{6} = \frac{}{24}$

It should be clear now why you *need* to be able to change into an equivalent fraction.

Add $\frac{1}{8} + \frac{1}{6}$.

We can only add fractions with the same denominators.
From the last exercise $\frac{1}{8} = \frac{3}{24}$ and $\frac{1}{6} = \frac{4}{24}$.
So $\frac{1}{8} + \frac{1}{6} = \frac{3}{24} + \frac{4}{24} = \frac{7}{24}$
and that's the answer.

Add $\frac{5}{6} + \frac{1}{8}$.

Again, we need to change to equivalent fractions with the same denominators:
$\frac{5}{6} + \frac{1}{8} = \frac{20}{24} + \frac{3}{24} = \frac{23}{24}$

Cover over the next line and try adding $\frac{1}{8} + \frac{2}{3}$ yourself.

Did you get it right?

$$\frac{1}{8} + \frac{2}{3} = \frac{3}{24} + \frac{16}{24} = \frac{19}{24}$$

Exercise 26.3

Use your answers from exercise 26.2 to add the following pairs of fractions:

1 $\frac{1}{6} + \frac{3}{4}$

2 $\frac{1}{4} + \frac{1}{6}$

3 $\frac{1}{8} + \frac{1}{4}$

4 $\frac{7}{8} + \frac{2}{3}$

5 $\frac{3}{8} + \frac{2}{3}$

6 $\frac{1}{6} + \frac{7}{8}$

7 $\frac{3}{4} + \frac{5}{8}$

8 $\frac{2}{3} + \frac{3}{4}$

9 $\frac{1}{2} + \frac{3}{8}$

10 $\frac{1}{4} + \frac{5}{6}$

Subtracting fractions

There isn't really anything new to learn in subtracting fractions.

Just change each to the equivalent fraction with the same denominator and then subtract the new numerators.

$\frac{5}{6} - \frac{2}{3}$

$\frac{5}{6} - \frac{2}{3} = \frac{20}{24} - \frac{16}{24} = \frac{4}{24}$

$\frac{3}{4} - \frac{2}{3}$

$\frac{3}{4} - \frac{2}{3} = \frac{18}{24} - \frac{16}{24} = \frac{2}{24}$

Exercise 26.4

Use the answers from exercise 26.2 to subtract the following pairs of fractions.

1 $\frac{2}{3} - \frac{3}{8}$ **4** $\frac{7}{8} - \frac{5}{6}$ **7** $\frac{1}{6} - \frac{1}{8}$ **9** $\frac{5}{6} - \frac{1}{8}$

2 $\frac{1}{4} - \frac{1}{8}$ **5** $\frac{2}{3} - \frac{5}{8}$ **8** $\frac{1}{2} - \frac{3}{8}$ **10** $\frac{7}{8} - \frac{3}{4}$

3 $\frac{5}{6} - \frac{3}{4}$ **6** $\frac{3}{8} - \frac{1}{6}$

General addition and subtraction of fractions

We used a special set of fractions for the last two exercises so that we could concentrate on the *idea* of addition and subtraction.

Now we must extend the work to *any* fractions.

To add or subtract two fractions we need to find a **common denominator** for the two fractions. This involves sets of multiples again.

Suppose you are adding $\frac{3}{5} + \frac{5}{8}$. How do you find a suitable number for the denominator of the equivalent fractions?

You list the multiples of the larger number until you come to one which is also a multiple of the smaller one.

In this case, the multiples of 8 are 8, 16, 24, 32, 40, ... and we can stop there, because 40 is *also* a multiple of 5 so we can use this as the common denominator.

Yet again, this is only difficult for people who don't know their multiplication tables well.

So change each fraction to its equivalent with 40 in the denominator:

$$\frac{3}{5} = \frac{24}{40} \qquad \frac{5}{8} = \frac{25}{40} \qquad \frac{3}{5} + \frac{5}{8} = \frac{24}{40} + \frac{25}{40} = \frac{49}{40}$$

Try $\frac{2}{3} + \frac{3}{4}$. The denominators are 3 and 4.

Think of the multiples of 4, (4, 8, 12, . . .) but 12 is also a multiple of 3 so change each fraction to its equivalent with 12 in the denominator:

$$\frac{2}{3} + \frac{3}{4} = \frac{8}{12} + \frac{9}{12} = \frac{17}{12} = 1\frac{5}{12}$$

● *The common denominator is also called the **lowest common multiple** – **LCM** for short.*

Find the LCM of 3 and 5.
   Count 5, 10, 15, . . . 15 is the first multiple of 3.
   So the LCM is 15.

Find the LCM of 15 and 12.
   Count 15, 30, 45, 60, . . . 60 is the first multiple of 12.
   So 60 is the LCM of 15 and 12.

Exercise 26.5

Find the lowest common multiple of the following pairs of numbers by counting multiples of the larger until you come to a multiple of the smaller.

1 3 and 2	**4** 3 and 11	**7** 7 and 21	**9** 5 and 16
2 4 and 6	**5** 5 and 10	**8** 3 and 6	**10** 12 and 9
3 3 and 9	**6** 3 and 12		

Exercise 26.6

Use your results from exercise 26.5 to help find the following.
   Notice some are addition and some are subtraction questions.

1 $\frac{2}{3} + \frac{1}{2}$	**4** $\frac{1}{3} - \frac{3}{11}$	**7** $\frac{1}{7} + \frac{1}{21}$	**9** $\frac{2}{5} + \frac{3}{16}$
2 $\frac{5}{6} - \frac{3}{4}$	**5** $\frac{1}{5} + \frac{1}{10}$	**8** $\frac{2}{3} - \frac{1}{6}$	**10** $\frac{7}{12} - \frac{4}{9}$
3 $\frac{4}{9} + \frac{2}{3}$	**6** $\frac{5}{12} - \frac{1}{3}$		

Problems involving addition and subtraction of fractions

In the next exercise, you may have to use addition and subtraction in the same calculation, or deal with more than two fractions. You will first need to think carefully about which sort of calculation to use.

Exercise 26.7

1 A group of friends went to a burger bar after school. One quarter of them just bought a drink, and one third just bought chips. The rest bought a burger and a drink.
   a What fraction of the group just bought one item (drink or chips)?
   b What fraction of the group bought a burger and a drink?

2 Each month, one third of my wages is spent on rent, and one tenth on bills.
   a What fraction of my wages is spent on rent and bills together?
   b What fraction of my wages is left afterwards?

3 At a concert, $\frac{2}{5}$ of the audience were children and $\frac{1}{10}$ of the audience were old-age pensioners. The rest of the audience were adults of working age.
   a What fraction of the audience were children or pensioners?
   b What fraction of the audience were adults of working age?

4 In a class of 16-year-olds, $\frac{1}{2}$ owned a CD system, $\frac{1}{3}$ owned a stereo system without a CD, and $\frac{1}{10}$ owned only a radio.
   a What fraction of the class owned some sort of music-making machine?
   b What fraction of the class either owned a radio or didn't own any sort of music-making machine?

5 At a vet's surgery, $\frac{1}{4}$ of the pets brought in for treatment were dogs, $\frac{1}{3}$ of the pets were cats and $\frac{2}{11}$ were goldfish.
   a What fraction of the pets brought in were dogs or cats?
   b What fraction of the pets brought in were neither dogs, cats nor goldfish?

Multiplication of fractions

Suppose that you originally had a large bar of chocolate, and now you have one quarter left to split equally between you and two friends. How much do you give each person?

In other words, what is one third of one quarter?
Put the situation into a picture to make it easier to see.
The original bar of chocolate has 12 pieces.

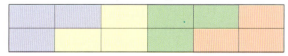

This is one quarter of the bar, which is 3 pieces.

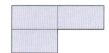

Now you have to split this quarter between 3 people. Each person gets one piece.

So, what *fraction* of the *original* does each person get?

Each person gets *one piece* of the original twelve pieces, or *one twelfth* of the original bar.

'Of' and 'multiply'

The original problem above was one third *of* one quarter.

It's a matter of words again!

People aren't always comfortable with the way that this can be written as $\frac{1}{3} \times \frac{1}{4}$; it does need a little disentangling.

To do this, remember that 3×2 means $2 + 2 + 2$ which is '3 lots of 2'.

So $3 \times \frac{1}{2}$ means $\frac{1}{2} + \frac{1}{2} + \frac{1}{2}$ which is '3 lots of $\frac{1}{2}$'.

So $\frac{1}{3} \times \frac{1}{2}$ means 'a third (of a lot) of a half' or $\frac{1}{3}$ of $\frac{1}{2}$.

In the same way, $\frac{1}{3} \times \frac{1}{4}$ can be written as $\frac{1}{3}$ of $\frac{1}{4}$, which you can see from the above drawings becomes: $\frac{1}{3} \times \frac{1}{4} = \frac{1}{12}$.

Exercise 26.8

Draw diagrams like those above in order to calculate the following.

1 Find $\frac{1}{2} \times \frac{1}{6}$ (start with twelve pieces).
2 Find $\frac{1}{3} \times \frac{1}{2}$ (start with six pieces).
3 Find $\frac{1}{5} \times \frac{1}{2}$ (start with ten pieces).
4 Find $\frac{1}{4} \times \frac{1}{5}$ (start with twenty pieces).
5 Find $\frac{1}{10} \times \frac{1}{2}$ (start with twenty pieces).
6 Find $\frac{1}{4} \times \frac{1}{2}$ (start with eight pieces).
7 Find $\frac{1}{2} \times \frac{1}{3}$ (start with six pieces).

Try to predict the answers to the next three before drawing them.

8 Find $\frac{1}{3} \times \frac{1}{4}$ (start with twelve pieces).
9 Find $\frac{1}{5} \times \frac{1}{3}$ (start with fifteen pieces).
10 Find $\frac{1}{7} \times \frac{1}{3}$ (start with twenty-one pieces).

Try to see a connection between question and answer.

The method extends more generally.

Calculate $\frac{2}{3} \times \frac{4}{7}$.

Start with a diagram of 21 rectangles:

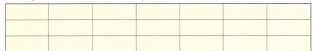

Shade $\frac{4}{7}$ of them:

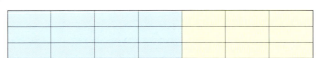

Shade $\frac{2}{3}$ of these:

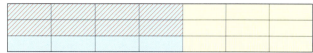

You end up with $\frac{8}{21}$ of the original.
This illustrates that $\frac{2}{3} \times \frac{4}{7} = \frac{8}{21}$.
Try to connect question and answer.

Multiply $\frac{3}{5} \times \frac{1}{2}$.

Start with 10 rectangles:

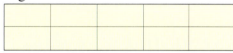

Shade $\frac{1}{2}$ of them:

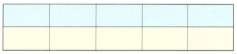

Shade $\frac{3}{5}$ of these:

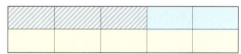

You end up with $\frac{3}{10}$ shaded.
   So $\frac{3}{5} \times \frac{1}{2} = \frac{3}{10}$.

Multiply $\frac{3}{4} \times \frac{2}{5}$.

Start with 20 rectangles:

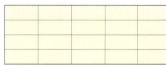

Shade $\frac{2}{5}$ of them:

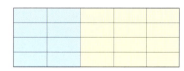

Shade $\frac{3}{4}$ of these:

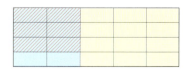

See the connection?!

You end up with $\frac{6}{20}$ shaded.
So $\frac{3}{4} \times \frac{2}{5} = \frac{6}{20}$.

Exercise 26.9

For this exercise, draw diagrams for the first three questions.
   After that, stop drawing diagrams as soon as you are sure of the rule.

1 $\frac{3}{4} \times \frac{1}{2}$ **4** $\frac{3}{5} \times \frac{3}{4}$ **7** $\frac{2}{3} \times \frac{1}{4}$ **9** $\frac{7}{10} \times \frac{2}{3}$

2 $\frac{1}{2} \times \frac{7}{10}$ **5** $\frac{2}{3} \times \frac{3}{4}$ **8** $\frac{3}{8} \times \frac{1}{3}$ **10** $\frac{5}{6} \times \frac{3}{4}$

3 $\frac{5}{6} \times \frac{1}{4}$ **6** $\frac{3}{8} \times \frac{3}{4}$

The diagrams work out most easily if the number of rectangles (or squares) you start with is the product of the original denominators.

Multiplication rule for fractions

Examine your previous results.

● *To multiply fractions, find the product of the numerators and the product of the denominators separately.*

Multiplying mixed numbers

$2\frac{3}{4}$ is two lots of four quarters plus an extra three making eleven quarters altogether.
$2\frac{3}{4} = \frac{8}{4} + \frac{3}{4} = \frac{11}{4}$

$1\frac{2}{3} = \frac{3}{3} + \frac{2}{3} = \frac{5}{3}$

> Remember
> chapter 16: mixed
> numbers and improper
> fractions.

$3\frac{2}{5} = \frac{15}{5} + \frac{2}{5} = \frac{17}{5}$

So, if a question contains mixed numbers, just write these as improper fractions and apply the same methods as before.

Remember:

If an answer is an improper fraction change it to a mixed number.

$2\frac{1}{2} \times \frac{3}{4} = \frac{5}{2} \times \frac{3}{4} = \frac{15}{8} = 1\frac{7}{8}$

$1\frac{3}{5} \times 3\frac{4}{7} = \frac{8}{5} \times \frac{25}{7} = \frac{200}{35} = 5\frac{5}{7}$

$\frac{1}{3} \times 1\frac{1}{5} = \frac{1}{3} \times \frac{6}{5} = \frac{6}{15}$

Exercise 26.10

Work out these multiplications without drawing diagrams.

1 $\frac{11}{8} \times \frac{2}{3}$ **4** $2\frac{1}{3} \times \frac{3}{4}$ **7** $1\frac{7}{10} \times 2\frac{5}{9}$ **9** $5\frac{1}{2} \times \frac{12}{33}$

2 $\frac{7}{4} \times \frac{8}{21}$ **5** $3\frac{5}{6} \times \frac{9}{10}$ **8** $2\frac{1}{3} \times 3\frac{3}{4}$ **10** $2\frac{3}{5} \times 1\frac{6}{13}$

3 $\frac{16}{9} \times \frac{3}{4}$ **6** $\frac{9}{7} \times 1\frac{4}{5}$

Division by a fraction

How many lots of $\frac{1}{3}$ go to make up two units?

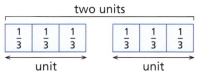

From the diagram you can see that six lots of $\frac{1}{3}$ go to make up two units.
Or $2 \div \frac{1}{3} = 6$.
But $2 = \frac{6}{3}$ so we could write:

$$2 \div \frac{1}{3} = \frac{6}{3} \div \frac{1}{3} = \frac{6}{1} = 6$$

This is no more than saying that six lots of **one third** go to make up **six thirds**.

How many lots of $\frac{1}{3}$ go to make up $\frac{2}{3}$?
So $\frac{2}{3} \div \frac{1}{3} = \frac{2}{1} = 2$.
This is the same as saying there are two lots of **one third** in **two thirds**.

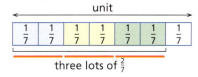

Work out $\frac{6}{7} \div \frac{2}{7}$.
There are three lots of $\frac{2}{7}$ in $\frac{6}{7}$.
Or $\frac{6}{7} \div \frac{2}{7} = \frac{6}{2} = 3$.

● *To divide fractions with the same denominators, divide their numerators.*

Calculate $\frac{2}{5} \div \frac{3}{4}$.

In this example, before we can find how many lots of $\frac{3}{4}$ go to make up $\frac{2}{5}$ we need to change each fraction to its equivalent with the same denominator.

The LCM of 5 and 4 is 20, so write

$$\frac{2}{5} \div \frac{3}{4} = \frac{8}{20} \div \frac{15}{20} = \frac{8}{15}$$

Try $\frac{3}{4} \div \frac{2}{5}$.

$$\frac{3}{4} \div \frac{2}{5} = \frac{15}{20} \div \frac{8}{20} = \frac{15}{8} = 1\frac{7}{8}$$

Notice the difference between the last two examples.

If you have to divide mixed numbers, first change to improper fractions.

$2\frac{2}{9} \div \frac{3}{4}$

$2\frac{2}{9} \div \frac{3}{4} = \frac{20}{9} \div \frac{3}{4} = \frac{80}{36} \div \frac{27}{36} = \frac{80}{27} = 2\frac{26}{27}$

....

$1\frac{3}{4} \div 2\frac{2}{3}$

$1\frac{3}{4} \div 2\frac{2}{3} = \frac{7}{4} \div \frac{8}{3} = \frac{21}{12} \div \frac{32}{12} = \frac{21}{32}$

Exercise 26.11

Do these divisions of fractions.

1 $\frac{4}{5} \div \frac{2}{3}$	**4** $\frac{3}{4} \div \frac{7}{10}$	**7** $\frac{5}{6} \div \frac{7}{4}$	**9** $3\frac{5}{7} \div 1\frac{1}{11}$
2 $\frac{2}{7} \div \frac{1}{2}$	**5** $\frac{1}{4} \div \frac{5}{9}$	**8** $1\frac{1}{2} \div \frac{3}{5}$	**10** $3\frac{1}{5} \div 2\frac{3}{8}$
3 $\frac{4}{9} \div \frac{1}{5}$	**6** $\frac{7}{3} \div \frac{2}{5}$		

Reducing to lowest terms

Remember in chapter 16 we discussed the lowest representative fraction, also called **reducing to lowest terms**.

This involved noticing that numerator and denominator of a fraction were both multiples of the same number (or you could say they have a common factor).

Several answers to questions in the previous exercises would have reduced to their lowest terms but we wanted to concentrate on the operation first.

A complete answer should *always* be reduced where possible.

A reminder:

Reduce $\frac{6}{8}$.

6 and 8 are both multiples of 2; 6 is the third, 8 is the fourth,

so $\frac{6}{8} = \frac{3}{4}$. ◄—— (Or divide both 6 and 8 by their common factor, 2)

Reduce $\frac{8}{12}$.

8 and 12 are multiples of 4; 8 is the second, 12 is the third,

so $\frac{8}{12} = \frac{2}{3}$.

Reduce $\frac{15}{21}$.

15 and 21 are multiples of 3; 15 is the fifth, 21 the seventh,

so $\frac{15}{21} = \frac{5}{7}$. ◄—— (Or in each case divide the numerator and denominator by their highest common factor.)

Read through the next four examples very carefully.
Each one has been reduced to lowest terms to finish it properly.

$$\frac{1}{12} + \frac{1}{6} = \frac{1}{12} + \frac{2}{12} = \frac{3}{12} = \frac{1}{4}$$

$$1\frac{2}{5} - \frac{11}{15} = \frac{7}{5} - \frac{11}{15} = \frac{21}{15} - \frac{11}{15} = \frac{10}{15} = \frac{2}{3}$$

$$\frac{3}{5} \times 4\frac{1}{6} = \frac{3}{5} \times \frac{25}{6} = \frac{75}{30} = \frac{5}{2} = 2\frac{1}{2}$$

$$1\frac{1}{5} \div 2\frac{2}{5} = \frac{6}{5} \div \frac{12}{5} = \frac{6}{12} = \frac{1}{2}$$

Exercise 26.12

Go back over the previous exercises and see if you can spot any answers which could be reduced to their lowest terms.

SUMMARY

■ To add or subtract two fractions, the denominators must be the same.
■ To make two denominators the same, first find their **lowest common multiple**.
■ To multiply fractions, find the product of their numerators and their denominators, separately.
■ To divide a fraction by another, change both to the same denominator and divide the new numerators.
■ With mixed numbers, convert to improper fractions before anything else.
■ Reduce answers to their lowest terms, changing any improper fractions to mixed numbers.

Exercise 26A

1 Find $\frac{4}{5} + \frac{7}{8}$.
2 Calculate $\frac{7}{11} + 3\frac{3}{7}$.
3 Work out $\frac{9}{10} - \frac{8}{11}$.
4 Evaluate $5\frac{1}{7} - 1\frac{6}{7}$.
5 Work out $\frac{4}{5} \times \frac{2}{7}$.
6 Find out $4\frac{1}{2} \times 7\frac{1}{3}$.
7 Find the answer to $\frac{9}{10} \div \frac{5}{6}$.
8 Evaluate $\frac{25}{7} \div \frac{15}{9}$.
9 A chef uses $\frac{2}{5}$ of a packet of flour in a recipe. The next day, he uses another $\frac{1}{2}$ of the packet. What fraction of the packet has he got left?
10 15 books are piled on top of each other. Each book is $3\frac{1}{4}$ cm thick. How tall is the pile?

Exercise 26B

1 Calculate $\frac{3}{7} + \frac{9}{13}$.

2 Work out $4\frac{3}{10} + 7\frac{4}{5}$.

3 Work out $\frac{6}{5} - \frac{11}{10}$.

4 Calculate $5\frac{2}{3} - 3\frac{4}{11}$.

5 Find $\frac{9}{10} \times \frac{16}{7}$.

6 Evaluate $\frac{11}{13} \times 7\frac{4}{5}$.

7 Find the answer to $\frac{8}{3} \div \frac{10}{17}$.

8 Work out $6\frac{1}{8} \div 4\frac{3}{5}$.

9 It takes me half an hour to get to town from my house, and a further $\frac{3}{4}$ hour to go from town to my grandmother's house. How early will I be if I allow two hours for the total journey? Write your answer as a fraction.

10 A mother shares $\frac{9}{10}$ of a kilogram of sweets equally between her five children. What fraction of a kilogram does each child get?

Exercise 26C

1 Calculate $\frac{4}{7} \times \frac{5}{2} \times \frac{8}{13}$.

2 Work out the value of $\frac{7}{8} + \frac{3}{4}$, then divide your answer by $\frac{9}{7}$.

3 Find $4\frac{1}{2} - 3\frac{5}{6}$, then multiply your answer by $2\frac{9}{10}$.

4 Evaluate $4\frac{5}{12} + 5\frac{1}{3} - \frac{66}{31}$.

5 Calculate $\frac{19}{9} \times 4\frac{13}{27} + \frac{2}{3}$.

6 In order to avoid an extremely steep hill, a train travels $3\frac{1}{5}$ miles west, then $2\frac{7}{10}$ miles south and finally $2\frac{5}{9}$ miles east.

  a How many miles does the train travel altogether to avoid the hill?

  b For what fraction of the detour does the train travel east?

7 A tomato plant grows $4\frac{5}{12}$ cm per day.

  a How high will it be when it is 11 days old?

  b The plant will not start to produce tomatoes until it is 50 cm high. How many days old will it be then?

8 A boy is $\frac{4}{9}$ the age of his aunt. The boy is 12 years old. How old is his aunt?

Exercise 26D

The Ancient Egyptians used only fractions with numerator 1, except for two thirds.

All other fractions were expressed as sums of these fractions, with all fractions used in the sum being *different*.

Work out how the Egyptians would have written the following fractions:

1 $\frac{3}{8}$ **2** $\frac{7}{10}$ **3** $\frac{4}{15}$ **4** $\frac{7}{12}$ **5** $\frac{9}{20}$

The earliest Egyptians used a number system with this notation:

1 was written as

10 was written as

100 was written as

To write a fraction with numerator 1, the Egyptians put the symbol above the denominator.

So, one sixth was written as

6 Write these fractions using our notation, and then work out what the last fraction is in our notation (the Egyptians simply put fractions side by side when they added them, without an addition sign).

a   **b**   **c**

d

Try some more of your own.

27 Calculating with decimals

This chapter looks at how to add, subtract, multiply and divide **decimal fractions**.

Adding decimal fractions

Remember:

Decimals are really decimal fractions based on tenths, hundredths, thousandths, etc. (chapter 13).

Since $\frac{3}{10} + \frac{4}{10} = \frac{7}{10}$, then $0.3 + 0.4 = 0.7$.

Since $\frac{3}{100} + \frac{4}{100} = \frac{7}{100}$, then $0.03 + 0.04 = 0.07$.

Since $\frac{3}{100} + \frac{4}{10} = \frac{3}{100} + \frac{40}{100} = \frac{43}{100}$, then $0.03 + 0.4 = 0.43$.

Since $\frac{3}{10} + \frac{4}{100} = \frac{30}{100} + \frac{4}{100} = \frac{34}{100}$, then $0.3 + 0.04 = 0.34$.

You can see that the **addition** of decimal fractions is very easy.
   The above examples are often set out like this:

$$
\begin{array}{r} 0.3 \\ +0.4 \\ \hline 0.7 \\ \hline \end{array}
\qquad
\begin{array}{r} 0.03 \\ +0.04 \\ \hline 0.07 \\ \hline \end{array}
\qquad
\begin{array}{r} 0.03 \\ +0.40 \\ \hline 0.43 \\ \hline \end{array}
\qquad
\begin{array}{r} 0.30 \\ +0.04 \\ \hline 0.34 \\ \hline \end{array}
$$

● *To add decimal fractions, arrange the same place values in their correct columns and add in the ordinary way.*

Make sure the units figures are underneath each other.

$0.7 + 0.08$ [0.7   0.08]

Units

$$
\begin{array}{r} 0.7 \\ +0.08 \\ \hline 0.78 \\ \hline \end{array}
$$

$0.07 + 0.08$ [0.07   0.08]

Units

$$
\begin{array}{r} 0.07 \\ +0.08 \\ \hline 0.15 \\ \hline \end{array}
$$

$1.07 + 0.8$ [1.07   0.8]

Units

$$
\begin{array}{r} 1.07 \\ +0.80 \\ \hline 1.87 \\ \hline \end{array}
$$

$$23.08 + 3.8 + 8 + 13$$

Units

$$
\begin{array}{r}
23.08 \\
3.8 \\
8 \\
+13 \\
\hline
47.88 \\
\hline
\end{array}
$$

We often write zeros in the empty places (but this isn't essential) so that there are the same number of figures to the right of the decimal point in all the numbers; then add.

There is absolutely no reason to use a calculator for these questions!

$$
\begin{array}{r}
23.08 \\
3.80 \\
8.00 \\
13.00 \\
\hline
47.88 \\
\hline
\end{array}
$$

Exercise 27.1

First underline the **units** figure in each number. Arrange in columns so that these units figures line up. Fill any empty places with zeros, then add.

1 $1.07 + 1.7 + 7 + 7.1 + 7.01$

2 $0.6 + 0.8 + 0.9$

3 $0.03 + 0.07 + 0.06$

4 $0.08 + 0.7 + 0.32$

5 $14 + 1.4 + 4.01 + 1.41$

6 $301 + 1.3 + 1.03 + 31 + 0.31$

7 $19.06 + 5 + 0.87 + 3.6 + 7.02$

8 $206 + 9.3 + 16.3 + 72.08$

9 $2032 + 20.32 + 2.032 + 0.2032 + 203.2 + 32$

10 $1.01 + 11 + 1 + 10.1 + 101 + 11.1$

Exercise 27.2

1 Work out 23 + 6.09.
2 Find the sum of 1.06, 14 and 0.7.
3 Add together 43.34, 3.04, 40, 3 and 4.3.
4 Find the value of 26.05 + 8 + 4.7 + 0.06.
5 Evaluate 5.07 + 4 + 6.8.
6 Calculate 8.6 + 0.0006 + 0.086 + 0.75.
7 Find the answer to 7.000006 + 60.007 + 6.
8 Add 5 to 9.5.
9 Sum 51.6, 20.3 and 48.007.
10 Find 19.09 + 90.0007 + 0.0101.

Subtracting decimal fractions

Subtraction is done in a similar way to addition. Arrange the decimals so that the units figures are underneath each other, fill empty places with zeros and subtract in the ordinary way.

Subtract 7.08 from 12.17.

```
  12.17
 −7.08
 _____
  5.09
```

From 0.17 take 0.058.

```
  0.170
 −0.058
 _____
  0.112
```

Exercise 27.3

1 23.58 − 14.37
2 6.08 − 1.8   (write as 6.08 − 1.80)
3 5 − 2.3 (write as 5.0 − 2.3)
4 8 − 0.072   (write as 8.000 − 0.072)
5 6.8 − 2.08
6 15.63 − 12.79
7 1.005 − 0.106
8 203.32 − 40.7
9 14 − 0.537
10 0.068 − 0.0592

Exercise 27.4

When you write these numbers in columns, be very careful which number you put at the top. Read the question slowly.

1 Which is the larger number, 2.03 or 6.3? Subtract 2.03 from 6.3.
2 Which is the larger number, 20.7 or 1.6? From 20.7 take 1.6.
3 Which is the larger number, 19.3 or 20? Take 19.3 from 20.
4 Which is the larger number, 10.6 or 8.9? Calculate 10.6 − 8.9.
5 From 1.05 subtract 0.73.
6 Find the difference between 0.07 and 1.02.
7 From 18.07 take 7.7.
8 Take 5.9 from 10.37.
9 Evaluate the difference between 6.08 and 8.06.
10 Subtract from 31.083, 19.07.

Exercise 27.5

Be careful to notice whether the question is an addition or a subtraction.

1 2.3 + 1.9
2 2.3 − 1.9
3 17.4 − 8.7
4 507 + 50.7
5 9 + 5.6

6 9 − 5.6
7 17.4 + 8.7
8 507 − 50.7
9 0.174 + 0.087
10 57 − 5.07

Exercise 27.6

Notice whether you have to add or subtract and be careful about the order of subtraction.

1 Find the sum of 41.6 and 6.04.
2 Find the difference between 41.6 and 6.04.
3 Add together the numbers 15, 8.07, 16.93 and 0.53.
4 Calculate the total of 16.04 and 14.6.
5 What is 67 minus 43.72?
6 From 19.08 subtract 19.06.
7 Subtract 21.6 from 21.84.
8 Sum the numbers 58.08 and 30.8.
9 Total the numbers 18.0006, 16.08, 10.6, 60.8.
10 How much more than 9.85 is 60.74?

Exercise 27.7

Here are some word problems! First decide whether you should add or subtract, then set the numbers out to find the answer. Give the final answer in the unit of measurement used for the question.

1 I have a rope measuring 3.47 m long. I cut a length of 2.03 m off the rope. What length of rope do I have left?
2 The sides of a triangle which is to be made from thin wood measure 5.7 cm, 4.6 cm and 8.6 cm. Find the total length of wood required.
3 An unwell person has a temperature of 37.3 °C at 4.30 pm. If their temperature rises by 1.2 °C in the next 5 hours find their temperature at 9.30 pm.

4 A tank which is 2.3 m deep contains water to a depth of 1.8 m. How far is the water from the top of the tank?
5 A cake is 3.7 cm thick and is covered in icing which is 0.3 cm thick. Find the total height of the cake.
6 Fortunately, the rather unwell person we met in question 3 recovered over the next few hours and their temperature dropped to normal (37 °C). Calculate their fall in temperature.

7 The rainfall in four weeks of a certain month was 1.1 cm, 2.1 cm, 0.3 cm and 0.8 cm. Work out the total rainfall for that month.
8 A piece of elastic measured 0.15 m long. If I stretched it by 0.06 m, find the new length of the elastic.
9 I bought a calculator costing £8.43, a ruler costing £0.12, a pencil costing £0.23 and an eraser costing £0.05. Calculate the change left from a £10 note.
10 My copy of *Robinson Crusoe* measures 3.1 cm thick. Each of the covers is 2 mm thick. Calculate the thickness of the paper I have to read (in cm).

Multiplication of decimal fractions

Multiplication of a decimal fraction by 10, 100, 1000, etc. is very easy.
We have always emphasised that moving figures one position to the left multiplies by 10 – so that's what you do!

3.26 × 10 = 32.6
41.7 × 10 = 417
0.0067 × 10 = 0.067, etc.

Multiplying by 100 moves the figures *two* places to the left.

5.687 × 100 = 568.7
0.0039 × 100 = 0.39

But, if you have to move beyond the units place, extra zeros are needed!

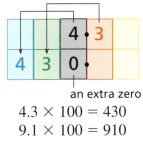

an extra zero

4.3 × 100 = 430
9.1 × 100 = 910

Multiplying by 1000 moves the figures *three* positions to the left.

0.0027 × 1000 = 2.8
16.59 × 1000 = 16 590
572.3 × 1000 = 572 300

Mixed examples:

6.8 × 10 = 68
4.9 × 100 = 490
0.043 × 10 = 0.43
0.016 × 1000 = 16
1.624 × 100 = 162.4

Not too sure?
Try a decimal grid as in
chapter 13.

Exercise 27.8

Write down the answers to these multiplications.

1 2.361 × 10
2 2.361 × 1000
3 2.361 × 100

4 23.61 × 100
5 23.61 × 10
6 236.1 × 1000

7 0.2361 × 10
8 0.2361 × 100

9 0.2361 × 1000
10 23.61 × 10 000

Exercise 27.9

1 5.18×10 **4** 15.6×100 **7** 0.908×10 **9** 6.01×100
2 91.8×100 **5** 0.0104×1000 **8** 4.62×1000 **10** 0.001×10
3 234×10 **6** 161.4×100

More general decimal multiplication

Remember that $\frac{3}{10} \times \frac{7}{10} = \frac{21}{100}$, and translated into 'decimal language' this would be $0.3 \times 0.7 = 0.21$.

And $\frac{7}{10} \times \frac{4}{100} = \frac{28}{1000}$ 'translates' to $0.7 \times 0.04 = 0.028$.

And $1\frac{6}{10} \times 2\frac{1}{10} = \frac{16}{10} \times \frac{21}{10} = \frac{336}{100} = 3\frac{36}{100}$ 'translates' to $1.6 \times 2.1 = 3.36$.

Also $4\frac{5}{10} \times \frac{7}{10} = \frac{45}{10} \times \frac{7}{10} = \frac{315}{100} = 3\frac{15}{100}$ translates to $4.5 \times 0.7 = 3.15$.

And $14\frac{6}{10} \times 2\frac{8}{100} = \frac{146}{10} + \frac{208}{100} = \frac{30368}{1000} = 30\frac{368}{1000}$ means $14.6 \times 2.08 = 30.368$.

Look at these results carefully.

Can you see a rule for multiplying decimal fractions together?

First of all, if you multiply tenths by tenths, since $10 \times 10 = 100$, the answer will be hundredths. ◄── $\frac{1}{10} \times \frac{1}{10} = \frac{1}{100}$

> *Remember chapter 10: the product is the answer to the multiplication.*

The denominator of the answer is the product of the two denominators in the question.

So tenths multiplied by hundredths will be thousandths. ◄── $\frac{1}{10} \times \frac{1}{100} = \frac{1}{1000}$

Can you see why the answer (the 'product') has *three* places filled after the decimal point?

Look at this again:

$$14.6 \times 2.08 = 30.368$$

three places   three places

> Tenths are one place to the right of the decimal point. Hundredths are two places to the right of the decimal point.

Examine 1.6×2.1 again:

$$1.6 \times 2.1$$

two places

So the product (the 'answer') will have two places:

$$3.36$$

two places

● *This connection is true for all the products above.*

Notice also that the numbers in the answers are the products of the numbers in the questions: $16 \times 21 = 336$, $146 \times 208 = 30\ 368$.
So this gives us a routine for multiplication.

- Step 1. Ignore all decimal points for the moment and multiply the numbers together.
- Step 2. Count the number of places to the right of the decimal point which are filled by figures in each number.
- Step 3. Note the total number of these decimal places.
- Step 4. Arrange the decimal point in the product so that there are the correct number of decimal places.

Find 5.8×6.3.

- Step 1. Ignore decimal points and multiply: $58 \times 63 = 3654$.
- Step 2. Count number of decimal places filled.

$$5.8 \times 6.3$$

$$\uparrow \qquad \uparrow$$

- Step 3. Note total: two.
- Step 4. Arrange the decimal point in 3654 so that there are two places filled to the right of this decimal point.

$$36.54$$

So $5.8 \times 6.3 = 36.54$.

Find 5.8×0.63.

- Step 1. Ignore decimal points and multiply: $58 \times 63 = 3654$.
- Step 2. Count number of decimal places filled.

$$5.8 \times 0.63$$

$$\uparrow \qquad \uparrow\uparrow$$

- Step 3. Note total: three.
- Step 4. Arrange the decimal point in 3654 so that there are three places filled to the right of this decimal point.

$$3.654$$

$$\uparrow\uparrow\uparrow$$

So $5.8 \times 0.63 = 3.654$.

Hard to describe but easy to do!

Find 58 × 6.3.

- Step 1. Ignore decimal points and multiply: 58 × 63 = 3654.
- Step 2. Count number of decimal places filled.

$$58 \times 6.3$$

↑

- Step 3. Note total: one.
- Step 4. Arrange the decimal point in 3654 so that there is one place filled to the right of this decimal point.

$$365.4$$

↑

So 58 × 6.3 = 365.4.

Find 0.58 × 0.63.

Following the previous steps, the total number of decimal places is four.
   So 0.58 × 0.63 = 0.3654.

Find 5.8 × 6300.

Great care needed here!

58 × 6300 = 365 400
   Number of decimal places: one.
   So 5.8 × 6300 = 36 540.0 which would be written 36 540.

Find 3.045 × 4.6.

Step 1:   3045   Step 2: four places   Answer: 14.0070 written as 14.007
            46
          ───────
          121800
           18270
          ───────
          140070

The multiplication is done as in chapter 5

because the final zero doesn't affect the number

Exercise 27.10

Check these products. *Do not use a calculator!*

1 7.2 × 1.9 = 13.68   3 0.72 × 0.19 = 0.1368   5 720 × 0.19 = 136.8
2 72 × 1.9 = 136.8   4 0.72 × 1.9 = 1.368

Exercise 27.11

Evaluate these products.

1 8.2×7.6	**4** 0.04×0.3	**7** 18.01×3.6	**9** 14.63×1.01
2 13.1×3.2	**5** 6.1×0.53	**8** 120×6.8	**10** 20.02×132.05
3 4.8×17.1	**6** 7.05×0.62		

Exercise 27.12

Given that $64 \times 93 = 5952$, evaluate these products.

1 6.4×93	**4** 0.64×9.3	**7** 0.0064×0.093	**9** 6.4×930
2 6.4×9.3	**5** 640×930	**8** 0.64×93	**10** 640×0.093
3 0.064×9.3	**6** 9.3×0.0064		

Division of decimals

Division by 10, 100, 1000, . . . is done by moving the figures one, two, three, etc. places to the right.

$$34.67 \div 10 = 3.467$$
$$1.509 \div 10 = 0.1509$$
$$506.3 \div 10 = 50.63$$
$$132.4 \div 100 = 1.324$$
$$7.6 \div 100 = 0.076$$
$$3671 \div 1000 = 3.671$$

Exercise 27.13

Write down the answers to these divisions.

1 $23.4 \div 10$	**4** $14.6 \div 1000$	**7** $6.8 \div 100$	**9** $14.14 \div 1000$
2 $16.83 \div 100$	**5** $0.0134 \div 10$	**8** $9003 \div 1000$	**10** $202.2 \div 100$
3 $301.6 \div 10$	**6** $23\,984 \div 100$		

Exercise 27.14

This exercise mixes multiplication and division.
    Remember that when **multiplying** by 10, 100 etc., the answer gets *bigger*, but when **dividing** by 10 etc., the answer gets *smaller*.

1 4.9×10	**4** $13.7 \div 1000$	**7** 15.63×100	**9** $0.0527 \div 10$
2 $6.8 \div 100$	**5** 19.06×10	**8** $15.63 \div 100$	**10** 0.0527×1000
3 13.7×1000	**6** $237.6 \div 100$		

More general decimal division

In chapter 4 we discussed the division of whole numbers by other whole numbers. This extends easily to the division of decimal fractions by whole numbers. It was also discussed in chapter 13.

You need to know your multiplication tables well!

$$
3\overline{)12.3} = 4.1 \qquad 5\overline{)0.105} = 0.021 \qquad 7\overline{)7.42} = 1.06 \qquad 6\overline{)14.28} = 2.38 \qquad 9\overline{)171.36} = 19.04
$$

Put a decimal point ready in the answer above the one in the question and take extra care where zeros are needed.

Exercise 27.15

1 $158.4 \div 9$	**4** $35.46 \div 6$	**7** $99.63 \div 9$	**9** $0.76 \div 5$
2 $21.56 \div 7$	**5** $65.52 \div 4$	**8** $1208.1 \div 2$	**10** $0.2448 \div 8$
3 $36.96 \div 8$	**6** $156.21 \div 3$		

Look back to chapter 4 if you've forgotten how to divide by numbers greater than 10.

Exercise 27.16

1 $27.2 \div 17$	**4** $2.38 \div 14$	**7** $1.15 \div 23$	**9** $20.52 \div 19$
2 $67.6 \div 13$	**5** $70.15 \div 21$	**8** $108.54 \div 18$	**10** $774.62 \div 22$
3 $92.1 \div 15$	**6** $233.76 \div 16$		

Division by a decimal fraction

Consider the problem of dividing 1.4 by 0.7.

Firstly, it's clear how to do $1.4 \div 7$

$$\begin{array}{r} 0.2 \\ \hline 7)\,1.4 \end{array}$$

But there are going to be *more* lots of 0.7s in 1.4 than there are 7s (since 0.7 is much smaller than 7).

● *The smaller the number you divide by, the larger is the answer.*

So $1.4 \div 0.7 = 2$

This suggests a way to divide by a decimal.

● *To divide by a decimal, change the* **divisor** *(the number you divide by) into a whole number by multiplying by 10, 100, 1000, . . . and change the number you divide into (called the* **dividend***) in the same way. Note that the answer to a division sum is called the* **quotient***.*

> **Quotient**
> (pronounced
> 'kwo-shent'):
> from Latin
> *quotiens*
> meaning 'how
> many'

Then do the division as before.

$0.266 \div 0.07 = 26.6 \div 7$ by multiplying both numbers by 100. Then

$$\begin{array}{r} 3.8 \\ \hline 7)\,26.6 \end{array}$$

$1.41 \div 0.3 = 14.1 \div 3$ by multiplying both numbers by 10. Then

$$\begin{array}{r} 4.7 \\ \hline 3)\,14.1 \end{array}$$

$4.1856 \div 0.32 = 418.56 \div 32$ by multiplying both by 100. Then

$$\begin{array}{r} 13.08 \\ \hline 32)\,418.56 \end{array}$$

The trick is knowing what number to multiply by!

Look for the smallest multiple of 10 which makes the divisor into a whole number.

For example, to change a divisor of 1.7 you say $1.7 \times 10 = 17$.

To change a divisor of 0.06 you say $0.06 \times 100 = 6$.   a whole number
To change a divisor of 0.035 you say $0.035 \times 1000 = 35$.

● *Just look at the value of the last digit in the divisor. If it's tenths, multiply by 10; if it's hundredths, multiply by 100, and so on.*

Exercise 27.17

Write down the power of 10 which would change these numbers into whole numbers.

1	0.8	**4**	0.003	**7**	0.016	**9**	0.0002
2	0.09	**5**	1.5	**8**	0.25	**10**	0.04
3	0.06	**6**	0.1				

Exercise 27.18

This exercise connects with the previous one. Don't forget to change *both* numbers.

1	$2.08 \div 0.8$	**4**	$0.042 \div 0.003$	**7**	$0.0832 \div 0.016$	**9**	$0.0014 \div 0.0002$
2	$0.387 \div 0.09$	**5**	$0.12 \div 1.5$	**8**	$0.0075 \div 0.25$	**10**	$0.488 \div 0.04$
3	$0.03 \div 0.06$	**6**	$0.01 \div 0.1$				

The decimal way of writing numbers was first proposed in 1585 by a Dutchman, Simon Stevin, in a book entitled *The Art of Tenths*. He gave the rules for calculating with decimals as well as suggesting that all weights, measures and coins should use the system. The book was translated into French and English and was very influential throughout Europe despite it taking until 1971 to introduce decimal coinage and until 1995 to introduce metric measurements to Britain.

Simon Stevin also invented many machines, the most famous of which was a steerable, wind-powered 'sailing chariot' capable of carrying 25 people.

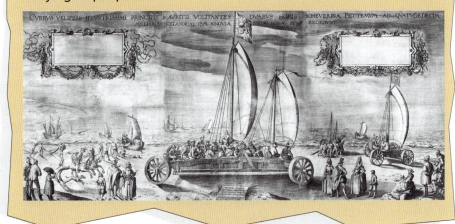

SUMMARY

■ To add decimal fractions, arrange them in columns with the units figures lined up vertically.
■ To subtract decimals, arrange them in the same way, putting the larger number at the top.
■ To multiply by a power of 10, move the figures the appropriate number of places to the left, making the number bigger.
■ To divide by a power of 10, move the figures the appropriate number of places to the right, making the number smaller.
■ In multiplying decimals, the number of figures after the decimal point in the answer has to be the same as the total number of figures after the decimal points in the question.
■ To divide by a decimal, change the divisor into a whole number by multiplying by the appropriate power of 10, multiplying the dividend by the same power of 10.
■ The word 'sum' means 'add'; 'difference' means 'subtract the smaller from the larger'; 'product' is 'the answer to a multiplication calculation' and 'quotient' is 'the answer to a division calculation'.
■ The decimal system was introduced by Simon Stevin in 1585.

 Note. A calculator must not be used for any of the following exercises unless you are told otherwise by your teacher.

Exercise 27A

1 Underline the units figure in each number, arrange in a column and add: 32.54 + 2.3 + 51 + 0.25 + 0.042.
2 Add: 40.04, 4, 0.004, 400, 4.4, 44 and 4.04.
3 Subtract 61.03 from 100.
4 From 80.06 take 7.6.
5 Multiply 91.63 by 0.02.
6 Work out 15.6 × 0.73.
7 Divide 12.222 by 0.63.
8 Calculate 12.81 ÷ 18.3.
9 Find the product of 0.01 and 0.001.
10 From the sum of 14.08 and 18.4 take their difference.

Exercise 27B

1 Underline the units figure in each number, arrange in a column and add: 83 + 0.83 + 8.3 + 0.038 + 0.803 + 80.3 + 8 + 3.
2 Add: 0.09, 18.05, 6, 13.21, 1.4, 23, 60.
3 Evaluate 201.05 − 157.98.
4 Find the difference between 19.19 and 91.091.
5 Multiply 16.03 by 13.6.

6 Find the product of 203.7 and 18.4.
7 Work out 0.896 ÷ 0.32.
8 Divide 7.36 by 3.2.
9 Calculate the quotient 2.3 ÷ 230.
10 Find the product of the sum and difference of 43.8 and 4.5.

Exercise 27C

1 What must be added to 16.03 to make 50.1?
2 What must be subtracted from 27 to make 13.8?
3 Add together 15.5, 5.05, 0.505 and 500.05 without writing these numbers down *anywhere*!
4 By what must 17.6 be multiplied by to get 5.27?
5 Divide 43.19 by 0.001.
6 Multiply 43.19 by 0.001.
7 Does *multiplying* by a number *less than* 1 increase or decrease the original number?
8 Does *dividing* by a number *less than* 1 increase or decrease the original number?
9 Find the quotient of the sum and difference of 44.88 and 31.68.
10 By what must 8.944 be divided by to get 8.6?

Exercise 27D

It might help to draw diagrams for some of these.

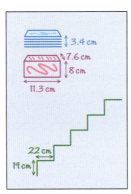

1 A pile of 100 sheets of paper is 3.4 cm high. Find the thickness of one sheet of this paper in millimetres.
2 An open wooden box measures 11.3 cm by 7.6 cm by 8 cm high. The wood is 6 mm thick. Calculate the *internal* measurements of the box.
3 The straight part of the staircase in my house has 12 stairs. The 'tread' of each measures 22 cm and the 'rise' of each measures 19 cm. (You should be able to guess the meanings of these words.)
   a How tall is the straight part of the staircase in metres?
   b How much carpet is needed for the staircase altogether if an extra 2.14 m is needed for the 'turn' at the top?
   c Calculate the cost of this carpet at £7.99 per metre.
4 From a piece of tape 15 m long, 144 pieces each measuring 8.5 cm are cut. What length of tape in metres is left?

5 A hollow metal pipe has internal diameter 9.46 cm. If the pipe is made of metal which is 1.77 cm thick, find the external diameter of the pipe.

6 I needed to make a rhombus-shaped frame recently from thin wood. I used four pieces each 25 cm long, one piece 48 cm long and a sixth piece 14 cm long. Find in metres the total length of wood used.

7 *A*, *B* and *C* are three points in a straight line. If *AB* is 5.67 cm and *AC* is 9.76 cm, find the distance *BC*.

8 In a car park, 37 cars are parked side-by-side 95 cm apart. If each car needs a space 1.83 m wide, find the total breadth of the row from the first car to the last.

9 I can take a stride of 40 cm. If I walk a distance of 10.4 m how many fewer steps would I need in order to cover the same distance if I increased my stride by 12 cm?

10 A farmer needs to enclose a rectangular piece of land measuring 40 m long and 24 m wide. She has sections of moveable fencing which clip together, each of the sections measuring 1.6 m long. Calculate the number of these sections required to make the enclosure.

28 Using data

Frequency tables are a very useful way of organising data.
Look back at chapter 18 to remind yourself.

type of sandwich	tally	frequency
chicken	|||	3
tuna	||	2
egg	|||||	5
	Total:	10 (3 + 2 + 5)

Grouped frequency tables

Sometimes, you will be working with data which covers a wide range of values, but with perhaps only a few occurrences for each value.

When this happens, it can be useful to group your information together, instead of considering every value individually.

You can then produce a **grouped frequency table**.

This grouped frequency table shows the number of miles people in a company travel there each day.

Where would the 5 go?

not here!

You put it into the 5–10 category.

Then 10 goes into the 10–15 category, and so on.

miles travelled	frequency
0–5	47
5–10	134
10–15	98
15–20	54
20–25	27
25 and over	14

From the table you can see that not many of the workers live near the factory.

This could cause problems if travel became difficult, for example due to snow or a train strike.

So a grouped frequency table can provide useful information about a situation.

Exercise 28.1

Work together as a group.

Make the appropriate measurements for the heights of the pupils in your maths group. Then design and draw a grouped frequency table. See if the result tells you anything in particular about the group.

Exercise 28.2

1 As part of a survey of the needs of the residents of a town, the town council recorded the ages of all the people living in various streets.
The council decided to put the people's ages into five categories:

0–20
20–40
40–60
60–80
80 and over

This is the raw data for one small street:

36	35	10	11	9	41	29	86
84	61	26	27	1	4	57	46
19	21	19	20	18	24	76	78
73	13	45	27	42	16	34	39
51	48	6	4	26	24	3	15

a How many people live in the street?
b How old is the oldest person in the street?
c Draw a grouped frequency table of the data, using the council's five categories.
d It is intended to build an old people's home in this street. How will this affect the numbers in the frequency table?

2 100 university students were asked the number of hours of television they watched in a typical week. Here are their answers:

31	15	24	9	0	36	41	23	17	59
11	27	30	42	18	4	34	27	26	51
25	46	37	29	42	19	7	35	26	33
8	26	29	37	21	39	13	29	18	39
53	17	42	25	41	16	32	42	23	3
2	7	36	34	24	38	11	45	23	70
34	8	12	17	54	29	61	56	1	36
29	25	22	19	35	42	16	63	29	54
39	15	24	25	25	10	3	43	13	9
49	42	6	10	61	0	1	13	32	0

a Draw a grouped frequency table for this data, using bands of 10 hours.
b Draw another grouped frequency table using 5-hour bands.
c Which table do you think is the more useful, and why?
d Using only the table in part b, work out how many students watched 40 hours per week.
e Do you think that the general population will have viewing patterns like the university students? What about children? Old people?

Pie charts

As well as bar charts and frequency tables, there are many other ways of displaying information you have collected.

One of these is called a **pie chart**.

Pie charts are useful to compare frequencies of different things with each other. However, they do not immediately tell you the actual frequencies of the categories.

This pie chart shows the hair colours of some people.

> Bar charts and frequency tables tell you immediately the actual frequencies of the categories. Pie charts don't.

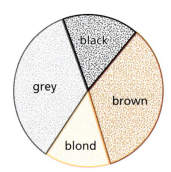

The area of each 'slice' (sector) of the pie chart depends on the size of the category it stands for.

So, in this group of people, you can see immediately that the number of people with black hair is about the same as the number of people with blond hair.

What else can you see?

You can tell that the number of people with grey hair is about twice the number of people with black or blond hair, and a few more than those people with brown hair.

Drawing pie charts

Remember:

The angle at the centre of a circle is 360°. If you stand at the centre, you turn round one complete turn before facing the same way again.

To draw a pie chart (which you must do precisely), you use the frequency table from your original raw data.

This is the frequency table for the pie chart above.

hair colour	black	blond	brown	grey
frequency	20	17	41	42

Altogether, there were $20 + 17 + 41 + 42 = 120$ people.

The sizes of the angles for the 'slices' in the pie chart are calculated by working out the fraction of the whole circle for each category.

People with black hair are $\frac{20}{120}$ of the whole group.

So, the size of the angle of their sector of the circle will be:

$$\frac{20}{120} \times 360° = \frac{1}{6} \times 360° = 60°$$

Don't forget to simplify wherever you can to make your calculations easier.

We work out the sizes of the other angles as follows:

Blond hair:

$$\frac{17}{120} \times 360° = \frac{17}{1} \times 3° = 51°$$

Can you see where this step comes from? It is because you are multiplying by 360 and dividing by 120. (Remember, $120 \times 3 = 360$.)

Brown hair:

$$\frac{41}{120} \times 360° = \frac{41}{1} \times 3° = 123°$$

Grey hair:

$$\frac{42}{120} \times 360° = \frac{42}{1} \times 3° = 126°$$

Check the sum of the angles: $60° + 51° + 123° + 126°$ which is $360°$, as it should be.

Once you have the sizes of the sectors of your pie chart, you can go ahead and draw it!

First, draw a medium-sized circle (about 6 cm should do).

Then draw a horizontal line going from the centre to the edge, like this:

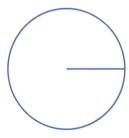

Draw the first of your angles, starting from this horizontal line.

It is a good idea to label your sectors as you go, so that you don't forget which one is which!

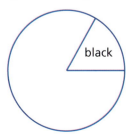

Draw the next angle, starting where the previous one finished.

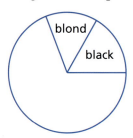

Carry on like this, always starting where the previous angle finished, until you have drawn all of them. You should get back to where you started – if you don't, then you've gone wrong somewhere!

Exercise 28.3

1 Draw a pie chart to show the different hair (or eye) colours in your class.
2 A newspaper has 40 pages. Of these, 22 are news, four entertainment, five health and leisure and nine sport. Show this information in a pie chart.
3 On a cereal packet, the nutritional information showed that a 30 g serving had the following amounts of certain nutrients:

type of nutrient	protein	carbohydrate	fat	fibre	salt
amount in g	2.5	21	0.5	5.5	0.5

A second cereal packet had this information for a 30 g serving:

type of nutrient	protein	carbohydrate	fat	fibre	salt
amount in g	3	25.5	0.5	0.5	0.5

a Show this information in two pie charts. It is easier to compare the information if the circles are drawn the same size.
b Looking at your pie charts, which cereal would be best for someone requiring relatively high fibre in their diet?
c From the pie charts, which cereal contains the most protein?
d *Mini project.* Using pie charts to help you, decide what sort of breakfast gives you a high carbohydrate, low fat, low sugar start to the day. You might want to compare different cereals with different breads. Don't forget to look at margarines and milks as well!

> Sometimes the calculation will not be so easy. You may need to round angles to the nearest degree. Then they may not add up to exactly 360°.

4 During one week, a small leisure centre swimming pool was visited by 578 men, 910 women, 1153 boys and 1076 girls. Show this information in a pie chart.

5 A fashion designer predicts that purple will be 'the' colour one year. She stocks her shop with a mixture of coloured clothes and waits to see what happens. After one month she analyses her sales figures:

colour	black	blue	brown	purple	white	other
frequency	67	45	15	20	36	12

  a Was the designer's prediction correct?
  b Draw a pie chart to show her findings.
  c Would it matter here if you knew what the different clothes were, as well as their colours?

The mean

Get some cubes and arrange them in four piles like this.

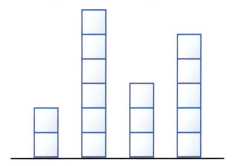

Now move cubes so that all four piles are of equal height.
How many cubes in each pile?
You can see at a glance without counting the number of cubes altogether. (How many?)

Arrange some cubes like this:

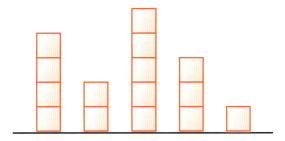

Move cubes so that all five piles are of equal height.
How many in each pile?
How many altogether? (No counting!)

Arrange these piles of cubes:

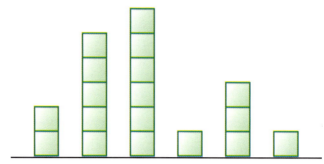

Make the six piles have the same number of cubes in each pile. How many in each pile? How many altogether?

Exercise 28.4

1 Arrange 20 cubes in five unequal piles. Investigate various ways of making the piles equal.
2 Arrange 12 cubes in four unequal piles. Investigate various ways of making the piles equal.
3 Arrange 15 cubes in three unequal piles. Investigate various ways of getting the same number of cubes in each pile.

Fair shares

Exercise 28.5

1 Agnes has two sweets, Alan has six sweets, Arthur has three sweets and Alison has five sweets. Describe the exchanges that could take place so that each child has the same number of sweets. (Compare with the first example on page 283.)
How many sweets does each child end up with?
2 Bethan has four sweets, Ben has two sweets, Barbara has five sweets, Bose has three sweets and Bharat has one sweet. Describe the exchanges that could take place so that each child has the same number of sweets. How many sweets does each child get?
3 Six children have two sweets, five sweets, six sweets, one sweet, three sweets and one sweet respectively. How many sweets should they each have if these sweets are distributed equally among them? (Compare with the third cubes example above.)

Whenever a set of numbers is shared out equally into groups, the number in each equal group is called the **mean** of the original set of numbers.
So the mean of 2, 6, 3 and 5 is 4.
The mean of 4, 2, 5, 3 and 1 is 3.
The mean of 2, 5, 6, 1, 3 and 1 is 3.
The mean of a set of numbers can be used to represent the whole set.

In general:

$$\text{mean} = \frac{\text{sum of all the values}}{\text{number of values}}$$

Exercise 28.6

Find the mean of each of these sets of numbers.

1 7 8 2 9 12 6 3 10 5 7 8
2 67 54 48 37 53 59 41 65
3 103 54 11 76 89 63
4 5 7 6 9 2 2 5 3 7 5 4
5 12 18 14 12 17 14 19 15 14 17 13
6 54 58 53 58 54 52 56 53 57
7 6 9 4 9 11 6 5 9 5 5 8
8 9 20 8 16 7 19 18 10 20 22 16
9 83 58 39 76 79 61
10 A group of fifteen 16-year-olds were asked how many CDs they owned.
Here are their answers:

12 24 8 35 15 6 18 17
14 15 21 27 9 15 19

What is the mean number of CDs owned?

The range

The **range** of a set of values is the difference between the smallest and the greatest in the set.

range = greatest value − smallest value

Find the range of these numbers:

5 8 9 2 4 1 3

greatest value = 9
smallest value = 1
so range = 9 − 1 = 8

The range of a set of data tells you how wide the spread of values is. It is often used together with the mean, as two sets of data may have very different ranges but the same mean. For example, if two athletes had the same mean time over a number of races, their coach might look at who was the most consistent (who had the smaller range of times) to decide which to put in for a competition.

Exercise 28.7

Find the ranges of the sets of values in questions 1–10 of exercise 28.6.

Exercise 28.8

Two athletes kept a record of their discus throws (in metres).

Athlete 1: 20, 22, 19, 18, 24, 21, 23, 21, 19, 24, 20, 22, 18, 23.
Athlete 2: 13, 35, 23, 12, 29, 26, 34, 21, 24, 17, 19, 16, 11, 14.

Calculate the mean and range of each athlete's performance. Who was the more consistent? Which one would you put in the team?

Questionnaire design

In chapter 18 we began to look at some ways of collecting information. You may have created your own class database.

The questionnaire you used for your database was very simple. Questionnaires can be very detailed, and can be used to find all sorts of specific information about people, animals, products: anything!

Exercise 28.9

Design a questionnaire to find out which television programme the pupils in your class prefer to watch.

You could perhaps extend it to cover your whole year? Or even the whole school?
Do you want to look at different age groups, or at boys and girls separately?
How can you make sure that your questions don't influence the answer?
(For example, can you see that 'Do you like _____ or _____ better?' is a poor question?)
How are you going to present your information once you have collected your 'raw' data?

SUMMARY

- **Grouped frequency tables** are used to present information with a large spread of results.
- **Pie charts** are a way of comparing relative frequencies of different quantities.
- The **mean** is the number in each group when sharing into equal groups.
- The **range** is used to look at the spread of a set of results.
- In designing questionnaires, questions have to be written carefully to make sure that they do not influence the answers.

Exercise 28A

1 A factory produces cans of baked beans. One full can should weigh 410 g. To check that the canning machinery is working correctly, a sample of 20 cans is tested every month. Here are the weights of one sample:

410 g	409 g	409 g	410 g	412 g
411 g	410 g	410 g	408 g	407 g
410 g	408 g	409 g	410 g	409 g
410 g	410 g	410 g	409 g	411 g

  a How much does the heaviest can weigh?
  b How much does the lightest can weigh?
  c What is the range of weights in this sample?
  d Draw a frequency table for this data.
  e What is the mean weight of this sample?
  f Do you think that the canning machinery needs to be adjusted? Why?

2 This frequency table shows the number of players in each section of a school orchestra.

type of instrument	strings	woodwind	brass	percussion
number of players	15	8	5	2

  a How many players does the orchestra have altogether?
  b Which section of the orchestra has the fewest players?
  c Show this information in a pie chart.

3 The table below shows the mean weekly earnings for different groups of people in the United Kingdom in January 1995.

type of worker	male manual	female manual	male non-manual	female non-manual
average earnings	£286.20	£186.40	£436.90	£286.90

  a Which of the groups above earns the most? Why do you think that is?
  b Assuming that all four categories are the same size, calculate the overall mean wage for:
    (i) all women
    (ii) all men
    (iii) all workers.
  c Show all these results in a bar chart.
  d Is the assumption made in part (b) accurate? Why?

Exercise 28B

1 A group of 28 primary school children were asked how many pets they had. Here are their answers:

```
3   1   1   2   4   0   6
0   2   1   0   0   4   1
5   2   0   2   1   1   0
3   0   1   1   2   4   12
```

    a Show this information in a frequency table.
    b Calculate the mean number of pets in the class.

2 A student is looking at the lengths of words in books and newspapers. She believes that 'broadsheet' newspapers will contain longer words than in 'tabloid' papers. She first analyses the lengths of words in a paragraph of a 'broadsheet' newspaper.
  Here are her results:

```
7    3    6    11   11   3    4    2    3    6    2
10   2    3    2    3    4    10   3    7    8    7
2    2    5    2    6    7    2    3    4    2    3
6    2    10   6    3    2    3    5    2    3    4
5    2    12   8    2    6    1    9    10   2    11
5    3    8
```

    a Copy and complete the grouped frequency table below for these data.

number of letters	tally	frequency
1–3		
4–6		
7–9		
10–12		

              Total   _____

    b Choose a paragraph, about 60 words long, from a 'tabloid' newspaper. Repeat the student's research for your paragraph and draw a new frequency table.
    c Was the student's idea correct?
    d Do you think that you can give a final answer at this stage? Why?

3 This table shows mean house prices in different parts of the United Kingdom in 1994, to the nearest thousand pounds.

region	price (thousand £s)
Yorks. and Humberside	38
Northern Ireland	38
Wales	41
North	46
East Midlands	48
North West	52
Scotland	53
West Midlands	55
East Anglia	55
South East	60
South West	61
Greater London	64

a In which region are house prices generally cheapest? Can you say why?
b Draw a bar chart to illustrate this information.
c Assuming all the regions are equal, calculate the mean house price for the United Kingdom. What is wrong with this assumption?
d Investigate house prices in your local area. How have prices in your area changed since 1994?

Exercise 28C

Go to your school library or a public library and ask the librarian to help you find a typical household's food shopping bill for one month, so you can fill in this table.

type of food	amount spent (£)
bread and cereals	
meat (raw and cooked)	
fish	
oils and fats	
sugar, jam and sweets	
dairy produce	
fruit	
vegetables	
drinks	
other foods	

1 Show the information in a pie chart.
2 How much is spent overall?
3 Are there any of these figures which surprise you? Which, and why?
4 Roughly what fraction of the typical household's bill was
   a fruit
   b dairy produce.

Exercise 28D

Should pigeon holes (for post) in companies, schools, colleges, etc. give the same space for each letter of the alphabet, or would something else be better? Will the results vary in different parts of the country? If so, why? If not, why not? You may find a telephone directory useful.

29 More on integers

In chapter 4 we said that the multiplication of numbers is repeated addition, and division of numbers is repeated subtraction. This leads to division being the 'inside out' process to multiplication.

These ideas can be applied to negative numbers as well.

Multiplying integers
Positive multiplied by negative

$(+3) \times (-5)$

First of all, $(+3)$ can be thought of as plain 3.
Then $3 \times (-5)$ is 'three lots of (-5)'.
Using the idea of repeated addition, that is the same as calculating:

$$(-5) + (-5) + (-5), \text{ which is } (-15)$$

So $(+3) \times (-5) = (-15)$.

$(+6) \times (-4)$

$$(+6) \times (-4) = 6 \times (-4)$$

'six lots of (-4)' $= (-4) + (-4) + (-4) + (-4) + (-4) + (-4)$
$= (-24)$

So $(+6) \times (-4) = (-24)$.

Can you see the pattern? Here are more examples:
$(+2) \times (-3)$ is 'two lots of -3' or $(-3) + (-3)$, which is -6
$(+5) \times (-2)$ is 'five lots of -2' or $(-2) + (-2) + (-2) + (-2) + (-2)$, which is -10
$(+2) \times (-5)$ is 'two lots of -5' or $(-5) + (-5)$, which is -10
$(+3) \times (-1)$ is 'three lots of -1' or $(-1) + (-1) + (-1) = (-3)$

Exercise 29.1

Write these multiplications as additions and then work out their values.

1 $(+4) \times (-5)$ **2** $(+7) \times (-2)$ **3** $(+6) \times (-7)$ **4** $(+3) \times (-9)$ **5** $(+8) \times (-3)$

If you can work out these multiplications without writing them as additions first, then do so. If not, continue writing them as additions.

6 $(+5) \times (-12)$ **7** $(+4) \times (-7)$ **8** $(+9) \times (-11)$ **9** $(+4) \times (-10)$ **10** $(+6) \times (-6)$

Negative multiplied by positive

> 6 × 7 = 42
> Reverse the order:
> 7 × 6 = 42
> Integers can be
> treated in the
> same way.

So far, the positive number has always been the first one. But what if the first number is negative?

All you need do is to reverse the order.

So:

$$(-6) \times (+5) = (+5) \times (-6)$$

or 'five lots of (-6)', which is (-30).

More examples:

$(-2) \times (+2) = (+2) \times (-2) = 2 \times (-2) = $ '2 lots of (-2)' $= (-4)$
$(-3) \times (+5) = (+5) \times (-3) = 5 \times (-3) = $ 'five lots of (-3)' $= (-15)$
$(-1) \times (+1) = (+1) \times (-1) = 1 \times (-1) = $ 'one lot of (-1)' $= (-1)$
$(-21) \times (+13) = (+13) \times (-21) = 13 \times (-21) = $ 'thirteen lots of (-21)' $= (-273)$

Exercise 29.2

Do these multiplications by swapping the numbers round first, so that the positive number is at the beginning of the calculation.

1 $(-5) \times (+4) = (+4) \times (-5) = 4 \times (-5) =$
2 $(-4) \times (+10)$
3 $(-12) \times (+3)$
4 $(-8) \times (+7)$
5 $(-9) \times (+4)$

With the next questions, see how *little* working you need to write down.

6 $(-6) \times (+8)$
7 $(-8) \times (+3)$
8 $(-4) \times (+4)$
9 $(-2) \times (+15)$
10 $(-5) \times (+7)$

Negative multiplied by negative

> Mathematicians
> often work out new
> results by making
> sure all the rules
> fit together.
> Contradictions are
> not allowed!

So far, you have seen how to multiply a positive number by a negative number, and a negative number by a positive number.

But what about a negative number multiplied by another *negative* number?

A good way to discover the answer is to look at the pattern so far, and try to fit in negative numbers so that they follow the same pattern.

Working out the answer

Look carefully at the following table of multiplications of pairs of integers between (-4) and $(+4)$.

Notice first that we have put '4' where it should be (+4) and −4 where it should be (−4). We drop the brackets whenever possible.

×	−4	−3	−2	−1	0	1	2	3	4
4	−16	−12	−8	−4	0	4	8	12	16
3	−12	−9	−6	−3	0	3	6	9	12

In the table, follow the pattern in the row opposite the '4'.

It's as if you were on the number line going up in fours from left to right.

Examine the row opposite the '3'. Start from the other end this time. The numbers go 12, 9, 6, 3, 0, −3, −6, −9, −12 as if you were on the number line but going *down* in threes.

Copy the table and complete the next row yourself from right to left.

Notice that the same pattern is observed from top to bottom. For instance, the last column goes down in fours, 16, 12, 8, 4, 0, −4, −8, etc.

See how each row and column continues its pattern, left to right, top to bottom and vice versa.

So now complete the whole table:

×	−4	−3	−2	−1	0	1	2	3	4
4	−16	−12	−8	−4	0	4	8	12	16
3	−12	−9	−6	−3	0	3	6	9	12
2								6	8
1	−4	−3	−2	−1	0	1	2	3	4
0	0	0	0	0	0	0	0	0	0
−1					0	−1	−2	−3	−4
−2					0		−4	−6	−8
−3					0		−6	−9	−12
−4					0		−8	−12	−16

Check the final table with other pupils and your teacher.

From your completed table, read off the answers to:

- $(-2) \times (-4)$
- $(-3) \times (-2)$
- $(-1) \times (-1)$

Exercise 29.3

Using your table, write down the answers to these products.

1 $(-4) \times (-1)$
2 $(-3) \times (-3)$
3 $(-2) \times (-1)$
4 $(-4) \times (-3)$
5 $(-2) \times (-2)$
6 $(0) \times (-3)$
7 $(-3) \times (-1)$
8 $(-4) \times (0)$
9 $(-4) \times (-4)$
10 *What do you notice about the signs of all the products of two negative numbers?*

Exercise 29.4

Evaluate these.

1 $(-6) \times (-7)$ **2** $(-5) \times (-8)$ **3** $(-10) \times (-3)$ **4** $(-9) \times (-4)$ **5** $(-11) \times (-10)$

Take care over the following calculations. They include a mixture of positive and negative numbers. Note we are beginning to omit some of the positive signs.

6 $(6) \times (-5)$ **7** $(-6) \times (+5)$ **8** $(-6) \times (-5)$ **9** $(+6) \times (5)$ **10** $(-6) \times (5)$

Dividing integers

Once you know how to multiply negative numbers, it is easy to divide, because of the links between multiplication and division.

Find $(+6) \div (-2)$.

From before, $(-2) \times (-3) = (+6)$.
  So $(+6) \div (-2) = (-3)$.

Evaluate $(-12) \div (+6)$.

Since $(+6) \times (-2) = (-12)$,
  it must be true that $(-12) \div (+6) = (-2)$.

Try to predict the answer to this one before looking at the working!

Calculate the value of $(-21) \div (-7)$.

Since $(-7) \times (+3) = (-21)$, $(-21) \div (-7) = (+3)$.

Exercise 29.5

Write down the multiplication connected with each of the following divisions, and so find the value of the divisions.

1 $(-24) \div (+6)$ **2** $(+30) \div (-10)$ **3** $(-26) \div 2$ **4** $(+36) \div (-6)$ **5** $(-80) \div (-10)$

If you can, evaluate the following divisions without writing down the multiplication connected with them.

6 $(-49) \div (-7)$ **7** $(+30) \div (-6)$ **8** $56 \div (-8)$ **9** $(-100) \div 5$ **10** $(-38) \div (-2)$

Exercise 29.6

1 What do you think the answer to $(+2) \times (+3)$ is?
2 Work out $(+4) \times (+3)$.
3 Find $(+2) \times (+4)$.
4 Evaluate $(+1) \times (+1)$.
5 Calculate $(+3) \times (+3)$.
6 *What is the sign of the product of two positive numbers?*

Look back at the multiplication table.

SUMMARY

- When multiplying a positive number by a negative number, the answer is always negative.
- When multiplying a negative number by a positive number, the answer is always negative.
- When multiplying a negative number by another negative number, the answer is always positive.
- When multiplying a positive number by another positive number, the answer is always positive.
- When dividing a positive number by a negative one, or a negative number by a positive, the answer is always negative.
- When dividing one negative number by another negative number, the answer is always positive.

Exercise 29A

You may use a calculator to work out the larger products.

1 Work out $(-34) \times (+6)$.
2 Calculate $65 \times (-3)$.
3 Evaluate $(-128) \times (-24)$.
4 Find $(+87) \times (+65)$.
5 What is the value of $(-50) \div (-10)$?
6 Find the answer to $(-48) \div (+4)$.
7 Calculate $96 \div (-3)$.
8 Work out $(-254) \div (-2)$.
9 Distances beneath sea level are represented by negative numbers. A diving bell is launched from a ship at sea. It travels down into the sea at a rate of 6 m per minute. What is the diving bell's distance beneath sea level after 15 minutes?
10 In five days one winter, the temperature dropped from 0 °C to -10 °C. What was the mean drop in temperature each day? (Remember chapter 28!)

Exercise 29B

1 Calculate $(-57) \times (+3)$.
2 Work out $345 \times (-8)$.
3 Find $(-200) \times (-4)$.
4 Evaluate $(+654) \times (+9)$.
5 Calculate $(-81) \div (-9)$.
6 What is the value of $(-250) \div (+5)$?
7 Evaluate $770 \div (-11)$.
8 Find the answer to $(-468) \div (-6)$.
9 What is $(-10\,000) \div (-10\,000)$?
10 A man has no money in his bank account, but does not owe the bank any money either. He writes six cheques, each for £25.50. How much is his balance now? (Banks write a negative balance as a negative number.)

Exercise 29C

1 Calculate $(-57) \times (-54)$.
2 Evaluate $(+345) \times (-42)$.
3 Find $(-490) \times (-51)$.
4 What is the value of $47 \times (-32)$?
5 Find $(-70) \div 4$ (write your answer as a decimal).
6 Work out $(+431) \div (-8)$.
7 Evaluate $(-356) \div (-4)$.
8 Calculate $(-357) \div (-5)$.

You'll need to remember work from earlier chapters.

9 Calculate $\frac{25}{7} \times (-\frac{77}{5})$.

10 Evaluate $(-\frac{682}{31}) \div \frac{48}{7}$.

Exercise 29D

In the following, calculate the parts in curly brackets first. Then evaluate the whole expression.

1 $\{(-35) + (-46)\} \times (+21)$

2 $(-512) \times \{(46) + (-87)\}$

3 $\{(+32) - (-45)\} \times \{(-76) - (+43)\}$

4 $\{(+491) - (-465)\} \div (-52)$

5 $3000 \div \{(-456) + (+320)\}$

6 $\{(-451) - (-578)\} \div \{(+34) - (-72)\}$

7 A biologist is studying the link between the growth of a plant above ground (which he describes as positive) and the growth of its roots. He has found that the roots grow an exact multiple of the foliage growth each day.

   a One day, the roots are (-28) cm long and the foliage is $(+7)$ cm. What is the multiple?

   b Some time later, the biologist has transferred the plant to an outside garden where it is difficult to measure the roots. The foliage is now 21.7 cm high.
   What length does the biologist predict that the roots will now be?

8 A surveyor uses positive and negative numbers to indicate distances from a certain point A (usual rules). She puts five posts in a straight line. The furthest post is -30 m away. The posts are evenly spaced. She stretches a rope from A to the nearest post. Describe the position of the nearest post from A.

A note on using calculators with integers

Scientific calculators can operate with positive and negative numbers. However, since there are so many different types now available, precise directions have not been given here for their use.

Find out from your own calculator's instruction booklet how to use integers on your particular machine.

Then you can check your answers to the exercises in this chapter.

30 Volume

Cuboids

Obtain some centimetre cubes and build a cuboid which measures 4 cm long, 3 cm wide and 2 cm high.

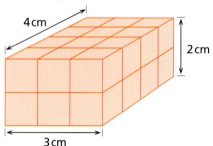

How many centimetre cubes are needed to make this solid shape?

Build a new cuboid with the same number of centimetre cubes but measuring 1 cm high and 4 cm wide. How long is it?

Build a third solid cuboid with the same number of centimetre cubes which is 1 cm high but 3 cm wide. How long is it?

Make a fourth cuboid measuring 2 cm high and 2 cm wide. Write down its length.

Make two more cuboids using the same number of centimetre cubes as before and write down their measurements.

Each of the above cuboids has a different shape but occupies the same amount of space, called its **volume**.

In the same sort of way that **area** is measured in standard tiles of 1 cm^2,

volume is measured in standard cubes of 1 cm^3.

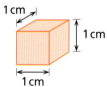

Notice we can only draw a *picture* of a solid object since the solid is 3D but our paper is 2D.

Exercise 30.1

1 Using your centimetre cubes build four different cuboids each with a volume of 12 cm^3.
2 Build the five possible different cuboids of volume 30 cm^3.
3 Build five different cuboids of your own using centimetre cubes, draw pictures of them and write down their volumes.

Exercise 30.2

Write down the volumes of these solids. They are all made from unit cubes.

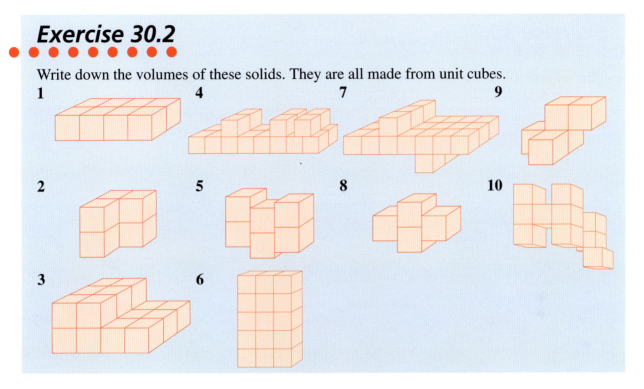

1

4

7

9

2

5

8

10

3

6

Calculating the volumes of cuboids

As with area, volumes are not calculated by counting unit cubes, unless the solid shape is irregular.

Find the volume of this cuboid.

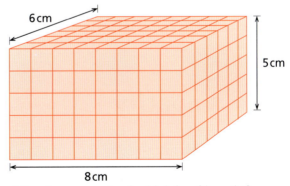

6 cm

5 cm

8 cm

It is made up of five layers, each of which is of length 8 cm and width 6 cm.

Each layer has 8 × 6 = 48 unit cubes,
and there are 5 layers,
making the volume 48 × 5 = 240 cm³.

Remember how important correct units are!

240 is WRONG ✗
240 cm is WRONG ✗
240 cm² is WRONG ✗
240 cm³ is RIGHT! ✔

Exercise 30.3

Find the volumes of the following cuboids or cubes.

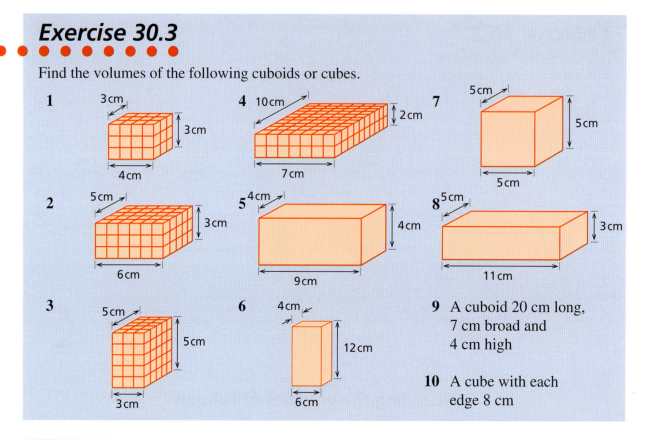

1 3 cm, 3 cm, 4 cm

2 5 cm, 3 cm, 6 cm

3 5 cm, 5 cm, 3 cm

4 10 cm, 2 cm, 7 cm

5 4 cm, 4 cm, 9 cm

6 4 cm, 12 cm, 6 cm

7 5 cm, 5 cm, 5 cm

8 5 cm, 3 cm, 11 cm

9 A cuboid 20 cm long, 7 cm broad and 4 cm high

10 A cube with each edge 8 cm

Exercise 30.4

How many different cuboids can you find which have a volume of 200 cm³?
Can you think of any other solid shapes which could have this volume?

Capacity

Finding the volume of a cuboid is like packing a container with smaller solid shapes.

Another situation which uses the idea of filling space is when you measure the amount of liquid in a can of drink or a carton of milk. This measure is called the container's **capacity**.

The standard metric unit for measuring capacity is the **litre**.
Also, 1 litre is the same as 1000 cm³.
The litre, however, is too large for many purposes, such as measuring out medicines, or chemicals in a science experiment.
So a smaller unit, the **millilitre (ml)** is also used.

- 1 litre is the same as 1000 ml.
- 1 ml is the same as 1 cm³.

Exercise 30.5

1 Write down two examples of liquids measured in litres.
2 How many litres are there in 3000 cm³?
3 How many cubic centimetres is the same as 24 litres?
4 How many cubic centimetres is the same as 65 ml?
5 Work out the sizes in centimetres of three different cuboids which will hold exactly 5 litres of water.

Finding volumes when the units of length are mixed

Find the volume of a cuboid of length 3 m whose end-section measures 6 cm by 4 cm.

3 m is the same as 300 cm so the volume is $300 \times 6 \times 4 = 7200$ cm³.

Find the volume of a cuboid which measures 14 cm by 11 cm by 0.5 m.

0.5 m is the same as 50 cm so this volume is
$14 \times 11 \times 50 = 7700$ cm³.

Exercise 30.6

Calculate the volume of the following cuboids, making sure that all your units are the same in each case.

1 A trunk 40 cm long, 25 cm broad and 1 m high
2 A plank of wood 2.5 m long, with end measuring 3 cm by 4 cm
3 A television set 0.4 m long, 35 cm high and 25 cm deep
4 A wardrobe 0.8 m wide, 1.8 m high and 75 cm deep (work in metres)
5 A mattress 2 m long, 1 m wide and 15 cm thick (work in metres)

SUMMARY

- **Volume** is the measure of the amount of space taken up by an object.
- A good unit for measuring volume is the **cubic centimetre** (cm^3).
- Be careful to measure volume in 'cubic' units.
- Liquid volume is also called **capacity**.
- To find the volume of a cuboid in cm^3, multiply together the number of centimetres in the length, the number of centimetres in the breadth and the number of centimetres in the height.
- You can find the volume of some objects by counting cubes of edge length 1 cm (also called unit cubes).
- Capacity is measured in **litres** or **millilitres**.
- One litre is the same as 1000 cm^3.
- One millilitre is the same as 1 cm^3.

Exercise 30A

Sketch diagrams of the following cuboids and then calculate their volumes. (You do not need to draw them exactly.)

1. Length 8 cm, breadth 5 cm, height 4 cm
2. Length 12 cm, breadth 7 cm, height 3 cm
3. Length 4 cm, breadth 16 cm, height 5 cm
4. 20 cm by 4 cm by 5 cm
5. 6 cm by 18 cm by 13 cm
6. Work out the volume of a cube with edges 7 cm long.
7. A bucket has volume 15 000 cm^3. How many litres of water will it hold?
8. What is the volume of a carton which holds 500 ml of milk?
9. A container on a removal van measures 80 cm by 1.5 m by 3 m. What is its volume in cubic metres (m^3)?
10. A bookcase has shelves 40 cm long and 20 cm deep. It is 1.4 m high. What is its volume? State the units you use clearly.

Exercise 30B

Draw diagrams of the following cuboids and then calculate their volumes. (Don't draw the diagrams exactly.)

1. Width 7 cm, depth 8 cm, height 20 cm
2. Length 3 m, breadth 4 m, height 5 m (be careful!)
3. Length 5 m, breadth 35 cm, height 25 cm (in cm^3)
4. Length 5 m, breadth 35 cm, height 25 cm (in m^3)
5. 53 cm by 67 cm by 12 cm

6 What is the volume of a cube, edges 12 cm?

7 A bath holds 250 litres of water. What is its volume in cm^3?

8 A medicine bottle has volume 75 cm^3. How many 5 ml doses is that?

9 A compact disc case measures 14 cm by 12.5 cm by 8 mm. What is its volume in mm^3? (Remember: 1 cm is the same as 10 mm.)

10 An exercise book is 23 cm long, 17.5 cm wide and 5 mm thick. What is its volume in cm^3?

Exercise 30C

1 There are 100 cm in 1 m. Work out:
  a the number of cubic centimetres there are in 1 m^3,
  b the number of litres there are in 1 m^3.

2 How many cubes of side length 2 cm will fit into a cube of side length 8 cm?

3 A cuboid measures 9 cm by 15 cm by 18 cm. How many cubes of side length 3 cm will it hold?

4 A diving pool at a swimming centre is 6 m deep throughout. It is 3 m long and 4 m wide. How many litres of water does it hold? (Use your answer to question 1 to help you.)

5 Some cereal packets measure 40 cm by 15 cm by 8 cm. Twelve of these packets are to be fitted into a larger container for delivery to supermarkets.
  a What is the volume of the larger container?
  b Find two possible sizes for the larger container.

Exercise 30D

1 Investigate how you could use unit tetrahedrons instead of unit cubes as the standard unit to calculate volume.
(You will need to do plenty of constructions for this! See chapter 3.)
Why is this an impractical way to measure volume?

2 How many cubic millimetres (mm^3) are there in 1 cm^3? How many mm^3 in 1 m^3?

31 Function

You have probably seen one of these big pepper-mills often used in pizza restaurants.

You put peppercorns in, turn a handle or twist the top and ground pepper comes out of the bottom of the mill.

Some people use a coffee-grinder in a similar way to make fresh ground coffee from coffee beans.

Salt mills grind large salt crystals into grains.

In each of these three examples, something is put into a machine, you turn a handle, and something different comes out.

Now think about your calculator.

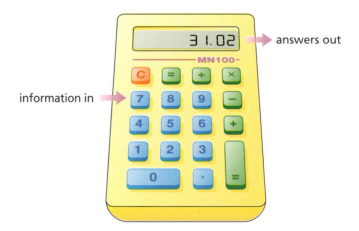

answers out

information in

You put information in using the keys, and out come answers on the display.

A **computer** operates in a similar way. All manner of data go in and all sorts of information comes out.

Exercise 31.1

Think of other examples like these, where a process changes material.

The 'black box' approach

When you put two numbers into your calculator, you certainly don't know exactly how the machine adds them together!

You may know roughly something about silicon chips and electronic gates but only a specialist electronic engineer would need to be aware of *everything* happening inside the case.

But you can still use the calculator to add numbers.

Engineers call this a 'black box' approach.

You don't need to know *how* this 'black box' works – but you do know *what* it does.

For example, imagine we have this (very simple) 'black box' which *adds 1 to every number we put in.*

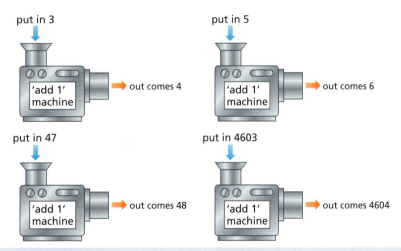

Exercise 31.2

Write down the number which would come *out* of the 'add 1' machine if the following numbers were put *in*.

1 17   **2** 9   **3** 0   **4** −6   **5** 58

Exercise 31.3

This is a 'multiply by 3' machine.

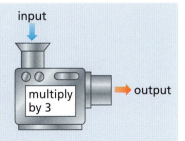

Write down the number which would come *out* of the 'multiply by 3' machine if the following numbers were put *in*.

1 5   **3** 0   **5** 4   **7** 41   **9** −16
2 13   **4** −1   **6** 7   **8** 203   **10** 23

Exercise 31.4

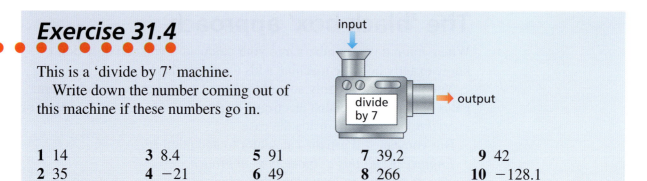

This is a 'divide by 7' machine.
Write down the number coming out of this machine if these numbers go in.

1 14	**3** 8.4	**5** 91	**7** 39.2	**9** 42
2 35	**4** −21	**6** 49	**8** 266	**10** −128.1

What goes in is usually called **input** and what comes out is usually called **output**.

Exercise 31.5

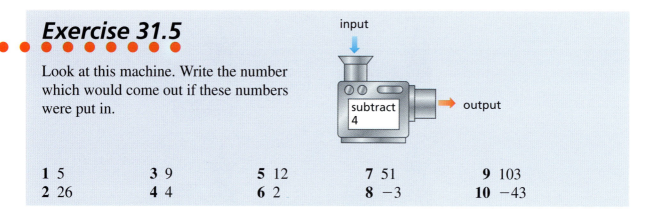

Look at this machine. Write the number which would come out if these numbers were put in.

1 5	**3** 9	**5** 12	**7** 51	**9** 103
2 26	**4** 4	**6** 2	**8** −3	**10** −43

Arrow diagrams

Consider this machine.

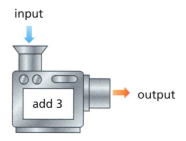

If the input were 1 the output would be 4.
If the input were 2 the output would be 5.
If the input were 3 the output would be 6.
If the input were 4 the output would be 7.   And so on.

We could put this information onto one diagram using arrows:

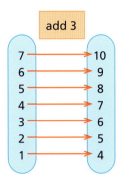

A few more numbers have been put in the diagram. You could use as many as you liked for the left-hand set.

This is a 'multiply by 2' machine.

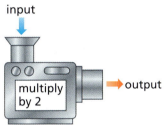

If we choose the numbers 5, 6, 7, 8, 9 for the input set, the **arrow diagram** will be:

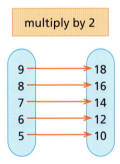

Look at this machine and its arrow diagram:

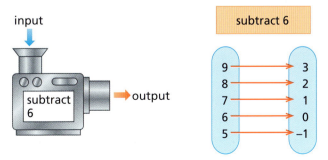

You don't *have to* put the lowest number in the input set at the bottom of the list, but it ties up with later work if you do.

You also don't *have to* use numbers in numerical order for the input set.

Exercise 31.6

Draw arrow diagrams on the set $\{-2, -1, 0, 1, 3, 6\}$ for each of the following machines.

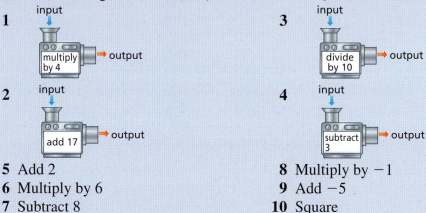

1 multiply by 4

2 add 17

3 divide by 10

4 subtract 3

5 Add 2

6 Multiply by 6

7 Subtract 8

8 Multiply by -1

9 Add -5

10 Square

Function machines

In each of the previous questions, there are three parts:

1 what goes *into* the machine – the input,

2 what happens *inside* the machine,

3 what comes *out of* the machine – the output.

In an arrow diagram, the numbers we list are those which go *in* and those which come *out*. But it's what happens *inside* the machine which *changes* the numbers. It's *turning the handle* of the coffee-grinder which produces the ground coffee!

*What happens **inside** a machine is called its **function**.*

- It is the *function* of a pepper-mill to grind peppercorns.
- It is the *function* of a calculator to do arithmetic.
- It is the *function* of an 'add 1' machine to add 1.

It is the *function* of this machine

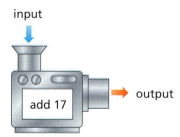

to add 17.

That is why these machines are called **function machines**.

So in this machine

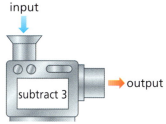

the function is 'subtract 3'.

In this machine

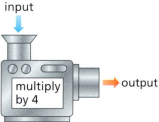

the function is 'multiply by 4'.

In an arrow diagram, the function appears *between* the input and output lists. For instance:

```
multiply by 9 ——— the function

5 ——————→ 45
4 ——————→ 36
3 ——————→ 27
2 ——————→ 18
1 ——————→ 9
```

This is often shortened by writing a letter 'f' for the particular function. So if we write 'f' instead of 'multiply by 9', the arrow diagram becomes:

```
          f
5 ——————→ 45
4 ——————→ 36
3 ——————→ 27
2 ——————→ 18
1 ——————→ 9
```

Finally, you can use any letter instead of the function. So if 'g' stands for 'subtract 7', an arrow diagram could be:

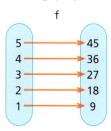

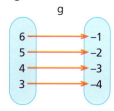

Exercise 31.7

In this exercise,
  f stands for 'add 5',
  g stands for 'multiply by 5',
  h stands for 'subtract 5',
  k stands for 'divide by 5'.
Copy and complete these arrow diagrams:

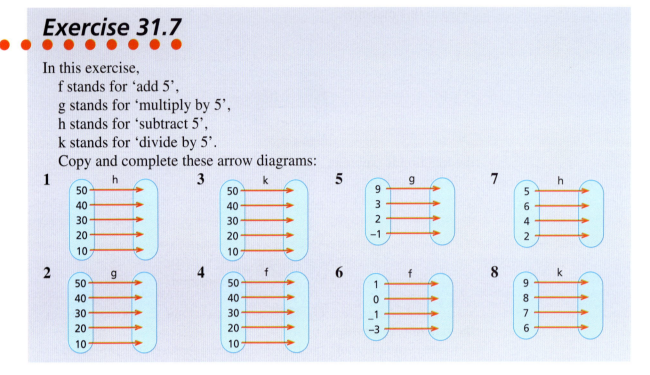

Several functions

The output of one function machine can be used as the input of a second machine.

If f stands for 'multiply by 3' and g stands for 'add 1', you could use the machines separately to give arrow diagrams:

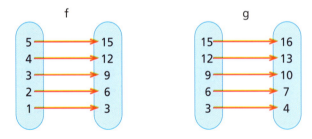

or put the machines together:

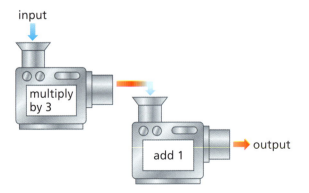

giving arrow diagrams:

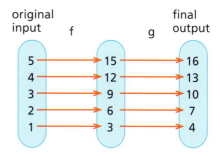

A very neat way of describing this situation is to simplify the diagrams like this:

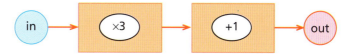

A diagram like this is often called a **flow chart** and can be very useful. For example, if we use {1, 2, 3, 4} as an input list with the flow chart:

the corresponding arrow diagrams would be:

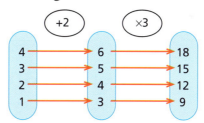

and the output list would be {9, 12, 15, 18}.

If p stands for the function 'subtract 5' and q for the function 'divide by 3' on the set {8, 11, 14, 17, 20} the flow chart would be:

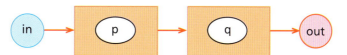

and the output set would be {1, 2, 3, 4, 5}:

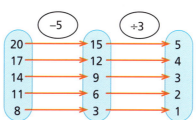

Exercise 31.8

In each of the following, start with the set {1, 2, 3, 4, 5} and the flow chart

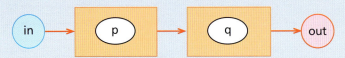

with p and q as described. Write down the final output set as your answer.

1 p is the function 'multiply by 4' and q is the function 'add 1'.
2 p is the function 'multiply by 5' and q is the function 'subtract 3'.
3 p is the function 'multiply by 2' and q is the function 'add 2'.
4 p is the function 'multiply by 1' and q is the function 'add 3'.
5 p is the function 'multiply by 2' and q is the function 'subtract 1'.
6 p is the function 'multiply by 8' and q is the function 'add 3'.
7 p is the function 'multiply by 3' and q is the function 'add 5'.
8 p is the function 'multiply by 6' and q is the function 'subtract 2'.
9 p is the function 'add 4' and q is the function 'subtract 4'.
10 p is the function 'multiply by 5' and q is the function 'divide by 5'.

Exercise 31.9

Ask your teacher for this exercise (Teacher's Resource File 1).

Sequences and number patterns

Consider the 'multiply by 3' function:

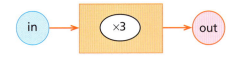

If it were applied to the numbers {1, 2, 3, 4, 5, . . .} as the input set, it produces the list {3, 6, 9, 12, 15, . . .} as the output set.

This could be written as a simple arrow diagram:

$$\times 3$$
$$1 \rightarrow 3$$
$$2 \rightarrow 6$$
$$3 \rightarrow 9$$
$$4 \rightarrow 12$$
$$5 \rightarrow 15$$
$$6 \rightarrow 18$$
$$\vdots \quad \vdots$$

But if we concentrate now only on the output set 3, 6, 9, 12, 15, 18, …
this list of numbers could by itself be described in a different way.

It could be called 'numbers on the three times table' or better still 'a set of multiples of 3'.

We say that the numbers make a **number pattern** or a **sequence**.

For example, it is easy to recognise a pattern in this list of numbers:

2, 4, 6, 8, 10, 12, … ◄── (What is the pattern?)

All that is needed is to spot some way of describing the numbers which works for the whole list.

Try 1, 3, 5, 7, 9, 11, …

Exercise 31.10

Play this game in pairs. Take it in turns with your partner to start, then go back to the beginning so that each of you has done all five.

1 Start with the number 3 and keep on adding 2s until you reach the number 15.
2 Start with 2 and keep on adding 3 until you get to 17.
3 Start with 53 and subtract 10 until you get to 3.
4 Start with 2 and multiply by 2 until you get to 128.
5 Start with 81 and divide by 3 until you get to 3.

Exercise 31.11

Go back to exercise 31.10 and write down the list of answers to each of the five questions.

Exercise 31.12

Write a short sentence describing the following number patterns. Use mathematical words if you can, but anything which works will do! For example, you could say that the numbers in question 1 are all 'multiples of 4'.

Then write down the next three numbers in the sequence.

1 4, 8, 12, 16, 20, 24, 28, 32, …
2 100, 200, 300, 400, 500, …
3 4, 3, 2, 1, 0, −1, −2, −3, …
4 5, 8, 11, 14, 17, 20, 23, …
5 1, 2, 4, 8, 16, 32, 64, …
6 3, 6, 12, 24, 48, 96, …
7 1, 2, 3, 4, 5, 6, 7, 8, …
8 1, −1, 1, −1, 1, −1, 1, −1, …
9 10, 0.9, 0.8, 0.7, 0.6, …
10 10, 1, 0.1, 0.01, 0.001, 0.0001, 0.00001, …

Exercise 31.13

Make up five sequences of your own and see if a partner can guess the next three numbers in each one.

Exercise 31.14

Triangle numbers

Look at these patterns of dots:

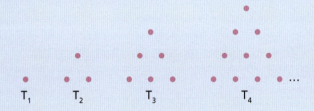

You might find it clearer to make these triangles right-angled.

T_1 T_2 T_3 T_4

a Draw the next three patterns in the sequence.

b Write down the number of dots in each 'triangle'.

c Can you see why the sequence 1, 3, 6, 10, 15, 21, ... is called the **set of triangle numbers**?

d Can you see why they are labelled T_1, T_2, T_3, T_4, ... ?
Write down the next two lines in this sequence:

$$T_1 = 1$$
$$T_2 = 3$$
$$T_3 = 6$$
$$T_4 = 10$$
$$T_5 = 15$$
$$\vdots$$

e Write down the set of *differences* between triangle numbers like this:

$$T_2 - T_1 = 3 - 1 = 2$$
$$T_3 - T_2 = 6 - 3 = 3$$
$$T_4 - T_3 = 10 - 6 = 4$$
$$\vdots$$

f Make a list of the first *ten* triangle numbers.

Exercise 31.15

Square numbers

Look at these patterns of dots:

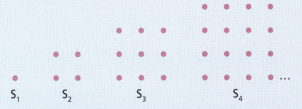

a Draw the next three patterns in the sequence.

b Write down the number of dots in each 'square'.

c You should be able to see why the sequence 1, 4, 9, 16, 25, … is called the **square numbers**.

d Can you see why they are labelled S_1, S_2, S_3, S_4, … ?

Write down the next two lines in this sequence:

$$S_1 = 1$$
$$S_2 = 4$$
$$S_3 = 9$$
$$S_4 = 16$$
$$S_5 = 25$$
$$\vdots$$

e Write down the set of *differences* between successive square numbers.

f Make a list of the first *ten* square numbers.

Exercise 31.16

Pentagonal numbers

Look at these patterns of dots:

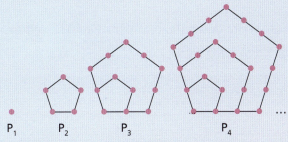

a Draw the next pattern in the sequence.

b These diagrams represent the **pentagonal numbers**.

c Write down the number of dots in each of the first five pentagonal numbers.

Exercise 31.17

Continue these patterns for another three lines. Do you recognise the sequence?

$$
\begin{aligned}
1 &= \tfrac{1}{2} \times 1 \times 2 = 1 \\
1 + 2 &= \tfrac{1}{2} \times 2 \times 3 = 3 \\
1 + 2 + 3 &= \tfrac{1}{2} \times 3 \times 4 = 6 \\
1 + 2 + 3 + 4 &= \tfrac{1}{2} \times 4 \times 5 = 10 \\
1 + 2 + 3 + 4 + 5 &= \tfrac{1}{2} \times 5 \times 6 = 15
\end{aligned}
$$

Exercise 31.18

Continue these patterns for another three lines. Do you recognise the sequence?

$$
\begin{aligned}
1 &= 1 \times 1 = 1 \\
1 + 3 &= 2 \times 2 = 4 \\
1 + 3 + 5 &= 3 \times 3 = 9 \\
1 + 3 + 5 + 7 &= 4 \times 4 = 16 \\
1 + 3 + 5 + 7 + 9 &= 5 \times 5 = 25
\end{aligned}
$$

Exercise 31.19

Continue these patterns for another three lines. Do you recognise the sequence?

$$
\begin{aligned}
1 &= \tfrac{1}{2} \times 1 \times 2 = 1 \\
1 + 4 &= \tfrac{1}{2} \times 2 \times 5 = 5 \\
1 + 4 + 7 &= \tfrac{1}{2} \times 3 \times 8 = \\
1 + 4 + 7 + 10 &= \tfrac{1}{2} \times 4 \times 11 = \\
1 + 4 + 7 + 10 + 13 &= \tfrac{1}{2} \times 5 \times 14 =
\end{aligned}
$$

Exercise 31.20

Examine these diagrams made from equal sticks. Write down the number of sticks used to make each diagram in the sequence. Can you see any patterns?

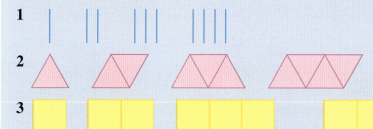

Exercise 31.21

1 Continue and complete this pattern.

$37 \times 3 =$
$37 \times 6 =$
$37 \times 9 =$
$\vdots$

2 $12\,345\,679 \times 9 =$
$12\,345\,679 \times 18 =$
$12\,345\,679 \times 27 =$
$\vdots$

The Fibonacci sequence

Examine this diagram carefully. It represents the way the stalks grow on several common plants.

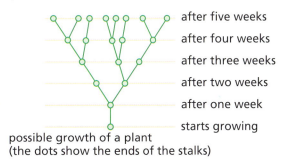

after five weeks
after four weeks
after three weeks
after two weeks
after one week
starts growing

possible growth of a plant
(the dots show the ends of the stalks)

Count the number of stalks which grow at each new stage (including the very first one). You get the sequence:

$$1, 1, 2, 3, 5, 8, \ldots$$

Can you see that each new number in the sequence is the sum of the previous two?

Continue the sequence for another five numbers.

This simple-looking sequence turns up within mathematics, in biology, in physics, in computing and elsewhere. It was discovered by an Italian mathematician called Leonardo of Pisa who later become known as Fibonacci [pronounced Fib-on-achi] (which means 'son of Bonaccio') and first published in a book called *Liber Abaci* in 1202.

Fibonacci himself did not investigate the sequence – this was done by a nineteenth-century Frenchman named Edouard Lucas who was the first to call it the **Fibonacci sequence**.

Exercise 31.22

1 If you start the Fibonacci sequence with the numbers 1 and 3 the pattern is sometimes called the Lucas sequence.
Continue the following for five more numbers

1, 3, 4, 7, 11, 18, . . .

2 Start with any two numbers and invent a Fibonacci-type sequence of your own.
3 Look at these sequences

1, 6, 7, 13, 20, 33, 53, . . .
4, 5, 9, 14, 23, 37, 60, . . .
↓ ↓ ↓ ↓ ↓ ↓   ↓
5, 11, 16, 27, 43, 70, 113, . . .

Notice that the third sequence, which is the sum of the other two, is again a Fibonacci type. Continue the pattern for three more columns.
4 Repeat question 3 with two sequences of your own.
5 Why do you think this sequence

1, 2, 4, 7, 13, 24, 44, 81, . . .

is called a **TRIbonacci sequence**?

Pascal's triangle

If you spin a (fair) coin it can only fall as a head (H) or a tail (T).
This could be described as:

T
(no heads)
1

H
(one head)
1

Now consider two coins which are spun together and the results recorded. There are four possibilities:

TT
(no heads)
1

TH   HT
(only one head)
2

HH
(two heads)
1

Consider three coins. There are eight possibilities:

TTT
(no heads)
1

TTH THT HTT
(only one head)
3

THH HTH HHT
(only two heads)
3

HHH
(three heads)
1

With four coins there are sixteen possibilities. See if you can find them all yourself.

The numbers record the ways of getting no heads, two heads, three heads, etc. If these numbers are assembled into a triangular formation they form a very important array known as **Pascal's triangle**.

One way of setting this out is

$$\begin{array}{ccccccc} & & 1 & & 1 & & \\ & 1 & & 2 & & 1 & \\ 1 & & 3 & & 3 & & 1 \\ . & . & . & . & . & . \end{array}$$

The triangle is usually completed with a figure one at its apex:

$$\begin{array}{ccccccc} & & & 1 & & & \\ & & 1 & & 1 & & \\ & 1 & & 2 & & 1 & \\ 1 & & 3 & & 3 & & 1 \\ . & . & . & . & . & . \end{array}$$

Pascal's triangle is named after a French mathematician Blaise Pascal (1623–1662) who used it in research about the subject of probability. Although Pascal was not the first to use these numbers (it was known to the Chinese possibly as early as 1100) he wrote the best book on the topic.

He was a brilliant scholar when very young, writing an important maths book at the age of sixteen. He also made the first mechanical calculating machine (in 1642)!

Notice the way in which the numbers are linked:

$$\begin{array}{ccccccc} & & & 1 & & & \\ & & 1 & & 1 & & \\ & 1 & & 2 & & 1 & \\ 1 & & 3 & & 3 & & 1 \end{array}$$

Write the next row.

Check your answers by looking back at the sixteen possible results from spinning four coins.

TTTT
TTTH, TTHT, THTT, HTTT
TTHH, THHT, HHTT, THTH, HTHT, HTTH
THHH, HTHH, HHTH, HHHT
HHHH.

Exercise 31.23

Make a copy of Pascal's triangle. Find the sum of the numbers in each of the rows and predict the sum of row eight. Work out row eight and see if you were right.

```
                    1
                1       1
            1       2       1
        1       3       3       1
    1       4       6       4       1
  1     5      10      10      5       1
1     6     15      20      15      6       1
1   7    21      35      35      21      7       1
```

Exercise 31.24

Describe the sequence outlined in this copy of Pascal's triangle.
   Predict the next number and write down the eighth row to see if you were right.

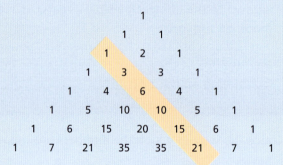

Exercise 31.25

Add together the numbers in each of the sequences indicated and make a list of the answers. You should recognise the new sequence. Write down the next number in this new sequence. Check by writing the next line in Pascal's triangle.

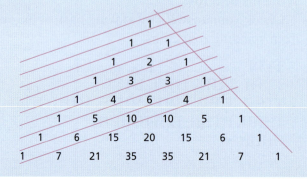

Index